BAD MOTHERS

REGULATIONS, REPRESENTATIONS, AND RESISTANCE

Funded by the Government of Canada
Financé par la gouvernement du Canada | Canada

Demeter Press
140 Holland Street West
P. O. Box 13022
Bradford, ON L3Z 2Y5
Tel: (905) 775-9089
Email: info@demeterpress.org
Website: www.demeterpress.org

Demeter Press logo based on the sculpture "Demeter" by Maria-Luise Bodirsky <www.keramik-atelier.bodirsky.de>

Printed and Bound in Canada

Front cover artwork: Freddie Robins, "Bad Mother," 2013, machine knitted wool, machine knitted lurex, expanding foam, broken knitting needles, glass beads, sequins, dress pins, crystal beads on an oak and maple wood shelf, 780 x 160 x 160 mm. In Private Collection. Photograph: Douglas Atfield.

Library and Archives Canada Cataloguing in Publication

Bad mothers (2017)
Bad mothers : regulations, representations, and resistance / edited by Michelle Hughes Miller, Tamar Hager, and Rebecca Jaremko Bromwich.

Includes bibliographical references.
ISBN 978-1-77258-103-4 (softcover)

1. Motherhood—Moral and ethical aspects. 2. Mothers—Conduct of life. 3. Mothers—Social conditions. I. Miller, Michelle Hughes, 1963-, author, editor II. Hager, Tamar, 1960–, author, editor III. Bromwich, Rebecca, author, editor IV. Title.

HQ759.B185 2017 306.874'3 C2017-901047-6

BAD MOTHERS
REGULATIONS, REPRESENTATIONS, AND RESISTANCE

EDITED BY
Michelle Hughes Miller, Tamar Hager, and Rebecca Jaremko Bromwich

DEMETER
DEMETER PRESS

To mothers whose identities have been harmed and judged harshly, whose mothering has been devalued, and whose motherhood has been colonized, questioned, or negated. You've had a daunting responsibility, and our social world should have done better by you.

From Michelle
To Kiri and Finley: thank you for holding me accountable to authenticity. Being your mother has been the greatest joy of my life.

From Tamar
To my daughters Naomi and Shira, with the hope that they will not have to be subject to such maternal surveillance.

From Rebecca
For my mother, and my daughters Helaina, Andromeda, and Myrina, and my son Desmond, and for Matt: may they know they are enough and are good enough.

Table of Contents

Acknowledgements

As with any edited volume, nothing can be accomplished without the dedication of the authors and the support and guidance of the publishers—in this case the indomitable Andrea O'Reilly and her staff at Demeter Press, especially Angie Deveau. To our authors, we extend gratitude for your thoughtful, creative, and critical analyses of bad mothers that appear in this volume, along with your patience and commitment throughout the long editorial process. To the artists who shared their work with us, thank you. We knew early on we wanted visual representations of mothering and the "bad mother" in our volume, and your complex, emotive work allowed us to realize this vision. We would also be remiss if we didn't acknowledge each other. As co-editors of this volume, we started out as strangers living in three separate countries with significant time differences, yet along the way, we found a way to work together collaboratively and openly—talking through our disagreements over skype and email, acknowledging each others' time and personal commitments and challenges as they came along, and growing into both colleagues and friends who accomplished this task, and every aspect of this task, together. The outcome is a volume that merges our scholarly and creative vision for work on bad mothers that makes us all proud.

Any scholarly work needs time to come to completion and supportive care for the scholar. For Michelle, the time was made possible by the constant loving efforts of her husband, Rob Benford, while her emotional care was provided by a host of individuals who celebrated each accomplishment along the way, including Rob, her children, Kiri and Finn, and her colleague, Diane.

Tamar would like to thank her partner Yaron and her daughters, Naomi and Shira, for tolerating the fact that she was more busy than usual. She was wondering—usually with a smile—during the period of preparing the manuscript how odd it was that editing a book about bad mothering forced her to turn her back to her daughters, apparently becoming a bad mother.

Rebecca also acknowledges a debt of gratitude for the steady and unwavering support of her husband Matthew Bromwich, and the strong mentorship of her mother Beverley Smith, without whose feminist collaboration and creative vision, her politics and writing would not have been possible.

The Bad Mother, in Relief

MICHELLE HUGHES MILLER, TAMAR HAGER,
AND REBECCA JAREMKO BROMWICH

And why is it in the case of women that we always blame the individual and not the social structure. That we see failure in discrete lives and do not question "the way things are."
—Susan Griffin (37)

Yes, Mother. I can see you are flawed. You have not hidden it. That is your greatest gift to me.
—Alice Walker (270)

Bad mothering is something that most of us assume we can recognize in all of its manifestations. It is abuse and neglect. It is failure to feed your child, and it is failure to care that your child is not thriving. It is abandonment. It is immoral conduct that contaminates the worldview of the vulnerable child. It is emotional and psychological violence. In is most extreme form, it is infanticide. These are not flaws, to use Alice Walker's word. These are behaviours that we believe harm children, so of course mothers who engage in them are bad mothers. Good mothers are not violent or neglectful. Good mothers nurture and care for their children. Most importantly, good mothers and bad mothers are perceived to do different types of mothering and be different kinds of mothers. Thus, the failures of bad mothers are perceived to be in their maternal actions (or inactions) and in their identities, for which they alone are responsible. As Susan Griffin notes, we rarely pay attention to the context within which women mother or the structures that constrain their mothering choices. Instead, we focus our collective efforts on finding (and punishing) the bad mothers, so easily identified, we think, by the harm they do to their children.

If only it were that simple. In each of our home countries, as is the case elsewhere in the world, structures, systems, assumptions, and discourses continue to marginalize, punish, and define bad mothers in ways that go well beyond the naïve assumptions about what constitutes a bad mother. As these 2016 examples illustrate, mothering is rarely contextualized and the challenges that mothers face are rarely acknowledged when the trope of the Bad Mother[1] is applied:

a) As part of the fight against childhood obesity in Israel, health authorities displayed huge advertisements in bus stations depicting body parts and faces of obese children. One of the ads showed the stomach of a child with the caption in Hebrew: "Mother, this is your child." The ads were removed a few weeks later after public outcry.

b) Sophie Gregoire-Trudeau, wife of Canadian Prime Minister Justin Trudeau, was widely ridiculed with the hashtag #prayforsophie, after she had the audacity to suggest that with three small children and a large number of charitable and governmental duties to perform, she would need more help. She was widely disparaged in particular because the family already employs two nannies.

c) H.B. 6064, a bill submitted by two white male representatives in the Illinois legislature, would require an unmarried mother to name a father on her newborn's birth certificate. Failure to do so—or to designate "another family member who will financially provide for the child" in the event that the father is not identified through DNA evidence—would require the state to refuse to issue a birth certificate for the child and would make the mother ineligible for state financial aid to help care for the child (Cynic). The bill is currently tabled in committee.

What these examples illustrate is the diversity of ways that bad mothers are constructed. Single mothers, working mothers, wealthy mothers, mothers who do not work outside the home, poor mothers, and mothers of obese children are only a few of the mothers so labelled in our social worlds. Mothers who drink, smoke, eat cold cuts, take cold medicine, exercise too much, exercise too little, eat the wrong fish, drink caffeine, paint the nursery, do not get prenatal care, use a midwife, or ignore the doctor's "recommendations" during pregnancy are bad mothers. Mothers who are unemployed, on welfare, poor, or homeless are bad mothers. Mothers who work too much, travel too much, or stress too much are bad mothers. Mothers who have too many children are bad mothers, especially if they are women of colour or poor or on welfare. Mothers who give their children up for adoption are bad mothers. Mothers who do not want the children they have but raise them anyway are bad mothers. Mothers with diagnosed mental health issues are bad mothers. Mothers who self-medicate to avoid mental health diagnoses are bad mothers. Mothers who self-medicate to deal with their mental illnesses are bad mothers. Mothers with disabilities are bad mothers. Mothers of children with disabilities are bad mothers. Mothers of colour or Aboriginal mothers—especially if they are poor or unmarried—should not be mothers; thus, they are bad mothers. Single mothers. Non-heterosexual mothers. Too young mothers. Too old mothers. Too anxious mothers, worried about the welfare or achievements of their children. Too distant mothers, too selfish to concern herself with her children's needs. Too busy. Too connected to social media. Too tired....

Need we go on?

If the violently abusive mother who kills her child, the woman who had an abortion, and the mother working out of state whose boyfriend kills her child while a thousand miles away, are *all* presented by the media and treated in the courts as murderers, our cultural and punitive use of the Bad Mother trope has moved into a complex political, social, and ideological label. The Bad Mother is not just the mother who is perceived to harm her child in some unambiguously wrong way. Other mothers, whose inferior identities in the social structure make them suspect, are struggling to fulfill their own motherhood obligations and proscriptions, and in the process doing or saying things that may be perceived as harmful to their children. Such mothers also find themselves sucked into the maelstrom of the Bad Mother label. It is the stories of these mothers that our authors analyze in this volume, as they strive to broaden our understanding of the institutionalized intrusiveness of the Bad Mother trope in mothers' lives.

As we are writing this chapter the film, *Bad Moms* is in theatres across North America and around the world. The film focuses on three mothers who decide they have had enough of the demands of perfect motherhood. Amy, the protagonist, (played by Mila Kunis) articulates this frustration when she states: "I'm so tired of trying to be this perfect mom. I'm done." The mothers form an alliance and resist cultural expectations to be a perfect mother, pledging instead to be bad moms. For Amy, trapped in a never-ending pattern of caring for others, this pledge has major consequences. After she stops making her middle-school children breakfast, she identifies other ways to be bad. Following a typical Hollywood trajectory, her bad mom identity and increasingly bad behaviours—such as bringing store-bought food to the school bake sale, missing work, or throwing a drunken party—initially empower her and, in some ways, strengthen her relationships with both children. But this temporary reprieve eventually results in social punishment for both her and her children as various social forces rein her in. After her daughter is benched on her soccer team, as punishment to her mother, Amy finds herself alone and bereft. She has lost her job, her children (who decide to stay with their father for a while), and her understanding of herself as a mother. The movie culminates in redemption: Amy publicly asserts her bad mom identity and urges other moms to admit that they are not perfect either, which results in her support and acceptance by her fellow bad moms in the parent-teacher association.

The movie oozes white, Western, upper-middle-class privilege, which gives Amy the opportunity to claim her maternal "failures" as gifts, as the above-quoted Walker quote asserts. The middle-class privilege, in particular, allows all of the changes that Amy makes in her life to assume her bad mom identity. But beyond the racial and economic privilege the mothers have that allow them to be bad, what is fascinating about the movie in the context of this edited volume is the way being bad is defined and resisted in this film. Amy and her friends do not critique the systems within which mothers struggle to survive—such as the American corporate world, which is unconcerned about their multiple responsibilities, or the cultural and marketing images that reinforce their self-blame and frustration. Nor do they critique their children's other parents who might share some of the burdens leading to the mothers' crises. As Griffin's quote from the beginning of this chapter articulates, the film does not "question how things are." Rather than identifying those aspects of Western contemporary culture that are complicit with societal institutions (particularly medical, legal, economic ones), which seemingly are designed to control and denigrate mothers' lives through inadequate and/or punitive policies and practices, the film tells mothers that the goal should be to work harder to be good but to accept that they are bad. Not only does this message narrow the Good Mother trope to include only perfection, it constructs bad mothering as relatively innocuous behaviours for which middle-class mothers are judged and punished. Such a construction is insufficient as a cultural critique of motherhood because in this model, all mothers are presumed to be good, which is rare, or are trying to be good, which is more likely. Such differentiation erases the possibility of bad mothering as discussed in this volume (and which many mothers find their behaviours labelled). In this strange dichotomy, the film does not contrast the Good Mother with the Bad Mother; instead, it contrasts the Good Mother with a lesser version of itself. Our volume rejects this restricted view of bad mothering. Instead, our authors show how the Bad Mother trope is not invisible but rather is a distinguishable cultural image that is used to control and manipulate mothers. Nor is the Bad Mother simply an aspiring Good Mother, although its origin is derived from research on the good mother.

THE BAD MOTHER AND THE GOOD MOTHER

The definition of a bad mother is determined and culturally structured in light of the definition of the Good Mother, a relatively new concept. The term good motherhood—instinctive maternal love—did not exist in Western culture prior to the eighteenth century, and it is the result of complex economic and political processes (Chase and Rogers; Forna; Gillis; Hufton; Rich; Smart). The historians John Gillis and Laurence Stone assert that until the eighteen century women gave birth but did not necessarily raise their children because of status and economic reasons. Yet in the wake of massive social changes and demographic fears of widespread death of their children in the eighteenth century, a need arose to create a specific social agent who would care for children, which resulted in the creation of the mother role as it is known today (Forna; Ladd Taylor and Imansky). This role determines that women are supposed to not only give birth to children but also to raise them and take care of their education. The mothers' social value and psychological welfare hinge on performing their roles in the socially and institutionally proscribed manner.

One of the strongest social mechanisms for establishing the mother role was the figure of the Good Mother, which is a formula of the norms and the social and psychological demands of motherhood at any given time. In her classic book on mothering, *Of Woman Born: Motherhood as Experience and Institution*, Adrienne Rich describes the Good Mother as a person with no identity other than her motherhood, who finds deep gratification in spending a whole day in the company of small children; she is attuned to the needs of others. Motherly love is unconditional love, devoid of egoism.

Rich was not the only person who identified this ideal of motherhood and criticized it as a mechanism of oppression. Early feminist writing on motherhood critiques the cultural image of the Good Mother (Badinter; Bernard; Chase and Rogers; Dalley; Douglas and Michaels; Griffin; Lazarre; Rubin Sulieman; Ruddick). At the base of these studies lies the concept of the institution of motherhood. The term was first posited by the sociologist Jesse Bernard, who argues that motherhood is not an inborn biological process but a changing social role composed of norms and a tradition of concern for raising their children. Rich claims that motherhood is a patriarchal institution managed and controlled by men, who have legal, technical, and ideological control over all aspects of childbirth and motherhood. The Good Mother ideal and its incumbent expectations thus imprison women within patriarchal motherhood. Today, good motherhood is a mechanism of surveillance and regulation to which all mothers are held accountable (Douglas and Michaels). We assert that it is the Good Mother's elusiveness (as a goal) and her reification (under patriarchy) that mark her prominence in our cultural motif.

Ultimately, the Bad Mother trope arises from the cultural inculcation of the Good Mother and its successful institutionalization. The Good Mother shapes the Bad Mother through its mechanisms of accountability to the expectations that it holds. Consequently, the Bad Mother becomes an additional effective social and cultural mechanism of surveillance and control. Furthermore, the Bad Mother helps to understand and analyze the Good Mother through the processes by which bad mothers and bad mothering are defined and, more importantly, regulated. Both labels are bound to patriarchal motherhood and women's oppression as mothers within patriarchy. Although our collection refers to the norms at the foundation of the Good Mother, our authors energize scholarship on the Bad Mother to better understand this less researched cultural and social trope and its explicit power in the lives of mothers.

The Bad Mother has been discussed in books before this one, which has provided a wealth of theoretical and empirical scholarship to learn from and build on in this book. From Ladd-Taylor and Umansky's edited volume *"Bad" Mothers: The Politics of Blame in Twentieth Century America* to Thurer's *The Myths of Motherhood: How Culture Reinvents the Good Mother* and Caplan's *The New Don't Blame Mother: Mending the Mother-Daughter Relationship*, scholars have embraced the need to critically analyze the construction and the effect of the Bad Mother. In considering the Bad Mother image, however, most feminist research on motherhood presents specific cases of mothers who abused, abandoned, neglected, and even murdered their children (Douglas and Michaels; Forna; Rich) but avoids generalized description of the figure, which continues to be largely defined as the "Other" in comparison to the Good Mother.

Demeter Press has greatly contributed to our understanding of the Bad Mother label by publishing several volumes in recent years dealing specifically with aspects of this social and cultural construction. In *The Mother-Blame Game*, Vanessa Reimer and Sarah Sahagian consider how the narrowing of standards of good mothering broadens the construction of the Bad Mother when we assess the effects our parenting has on our children. Whenever we question the source of our children's mishaps or misbehaviours, mother blame is there as a ready explanation. Joanne Minaker and Bryan Hogeveen in *Criminalized Mothers, Criminalizing Mothering* take a different approach: they highlight the systems of control that surround and (sometimes) literally imprison mothers for situations often beyond their control. Yet the criminalized mothers are not powerless, as they sometimes envision themselves as good or "good enough" mothers and reject the Bad Mother label for their mothering practices. Demeter Press has also published volumes in which the Bad Mother appears, such as in *Disabled Mothers: Stories and Scholarship By and About Mothers with Disabilities*. Several chapters discuss the labelling and stigmatization of mothers with disabilities (Motopanyane; McDonald-Harker).

From these sources, it is clear that bad mothering is ubiquitous, as mother blame permeates our social worlds. Bad mothering has been defined and punished around the world, yet the Bad Mother is not constructed the same in all social contexts or in all locations. So the discursive presence of widely held assumptions about bad mothers, while expected, may mean different demands and accountabilities for mothers with different positionalities (e.g. race, ethnicity, sexuality, bodies, etc.) in different locales.

Mother blame is frequently the mechanism by which the Bad Mother trope is applied. It arises from an assessment of harm or risk, which requires a surveillance culture within which such assessments can arise along with individual "experts" willing to designate such behaviours as risky or harmful. Thus, mother blame necessitates a standard by which mothers can be compared—contained in the Bad Mother trope—and individuals invested in enforcing it. Conversely, mother blame may also arise from identity claims that have little to do with harm or risk but much to do with a gross discomfort with difference. Mothers of colour, mothers with disabilities, queer mothers, impoverished mothers, Aboriginal mothers—all these groups and many others have faced disapprobation not because of their actions as mothers but because of their identity and social status as mothers who do not fit the narrow racist, classist, gendered, ableist and heterosexist standards of idealized motherhood in Western culture. Such mothers' burden to mother, to be valued in their mothering, and to resist the Bad Mother label is then more difficult (at times, impossible) because their identities and their failures intersect to mark them within the surveillance culture.

What do we not know about bad mothering and the Bad Mother image? Although some research has discussed bad mothers, the characteristics of this label elude us, possibly because it is so context specific. Scholars have also not yet fully explored how institutions such as the law, medicine, or the media transform the Bad Mother trope into social control over mothers, often with disastrous consequences. In other words, we are still working to identify the processes by which the Bad Mother is used by state actors, cultural channels, and other officials to designate and punish bad mothers. How and why are identities and ideologies woven into policy and by whom? We need to investigate the surveillance culture within which mothers live, including how we maintain it within an evolving social context and ongoing resistance to the Bad Mother label. Unpacking the gendered and intersectional aspects of surveillance is key to assessing the social psychology and the sociology of these interactional, power-driven dynamics. Most importantly, we do not yet know how and under what conditions resistance to Bad Mother mechanisms of control and regulation is effective and transformative. Given the damage this label has done to mothers over the past few centuries, understanding more about resistance—including its forms, its strategies and its targets—would help us to envision a world where mothers are not unjustly prosecuted and judged and where the patriarchal demands of the Good Mother are themselves regulated by a collective awareness of context and a rejection of standardization. To do this, we need to work toward an understanding of the intersections of patriarchal motherhood with other global constructs—such as capitalism, neoliberalism, and nationalism—topics our authors briefly examine in this volume but are natural foci in future examinations of the Bad Mother.

ORGANIZATION OF THE VOLUME

Our collection considers the Bad Mother from different angles and different cultures to create a mosaic of the insidious ways that the Bad Mother label defines mothers and is used to evaluate them, regulate them, and punish them within their social worlds. In each section of this volume, our authors work to unveil the image of the Bad Mother—its representations in culture, its construction and management within policy, and its reification in social interactions. In describing the Bad Mother, some of our authors labour to reveal the ideologies and discourses that create this image and its control over mothers' lives. Others describe the context of the existence of this trope, debating when, for whom, and against whom it is used. Several of our authors detail various forms of resistance against the Bad Mother label. Collectively, our authors address issues of mother blame, maternal practice, surveillance, stigmatization, and vilification. Along the way, they confront racism, classism, nationalism, and sexism as interlocking tools wielded by other mothers, by popular culture, by various authorities, and by the state in constructing, manipulating, and applying the Bad Mother label. In academic writing and creative writing our authors speak about and to the elusive image of the Bad Mother. Our authors bring various types of academic discourses into this discussion—including gender studies, sociology, history, cultural studies, legal studies, social work, media studies, and literary analysis—and frequently apply them through a feminist lens. Some of our authors use fiction and visual art as their medium for understanding this cultural, social, and political phenomenon; the reader will find such writings and artistic images scattered throughout the volume. The collection begins with our cover art by Freddie Robins (more on Robins's art is in Section IV). In the artistic pieces that are integrated into our volume, visual depictions of (bad) mothers and mothering are shown in glorious diversity, reminding us of the various manifestations of this cultural and social trope in mothers' lives and its interconnections with the powerful myth of the Good Mother. We are excited about these contributions to our volume, as our artistic pieces often provide a subtle consideration of the Bad Mother in ways that our scholarly pieces do not.

There is also much overlap between our sections, although we have thematically grouped the chapters to address issues of regulation, representation, and resistance, per the subtitle of our volume. Resistance to the Bad Mother trope, for instance, runs throughout our volume, along with an acknowledgment of the synergy between cultural and institutional processes of social control. In Section I, we present four chapters that consider the legal and regulatory landscape of bad mothers. We begin with the legal world because when state power employs the Bad Mother trope, the effects are punitive, as any and every policy becomes a potential opportunity to control the lives of mothers and of women. Criminalized, marginalized, incarcerated, or regulated, the mothers in these chapters face the cruelty and arbitrariness of state policy targeting their ways of mothering or their identities, even as it is disguised as bureaucratic management. The outcome is a narrowing of maternal possibilities and practices as the mothers—who are *a priori* marginalized through their social class, indigeneity, or social location—are permanently stamped with the Bad Mother label.

In her chapter titled "Arctic Motherwork," Rebecca Jaremko Bromwich begins the collection with a visual depiction of the paradoxical and fraught social position of Inuit mothers in contemporary Canada through their artistic surrogates, polar bear mothers. In describing her painting, Bromwich notes the intimate historical connection between the Inuit and polar bears and the similar constructions of these mothers as dangerous and bad by Canadian authorities. Yet the reality—that their vulnerability is because of the regulations that have violated their cultures and their homes—is overshadowed by their official denigration under the law. This powerful image is followed by two chapters that further discuss the indictment of Aboriginal mothers as bad. In "Still Wearing Scarlet? Discursive Figures of the Unfit Mother as Pervasive Phantoms Active in Governing Mothers through Ontario's Child Protection Regime," Bromwich asks how mothers' fitness is assessed within Canadian child protection discourse, specifically that of the country's largest province. Her critical discourse analysis details how the stripping of stereotypes from official policy discourse did little to eradicate the power of the "unfit mother" stereotype to label racially marginalized mothers. By assuming the stereotype is true but removing it from official discourse, protective service workers' decision making becomes the key to the continuation of the disproportionate labelling of Aboriginal and racially marginalized mothers as unfit.

To add to this conversation, Mandi Veenstra and Marlee Keenan trace current ideologies of bad mothering for Aboriginal mothers to their history of colonization. In "Manufacturing Ideologies of the 'Bad' Mother: Aboriginal Mothering, 'Neglectful' Caregiving, and Symbolic Violence in the Ontario Child Welfare System," the authors describe the ways that Aboriginal mothers have experienced symbolic violence, such as through the historical forced removal of their children and through the contemporary criminalization of their poverty. The authors' description of the latter is particularly poignant, as the mothers' cultural and survival strategies become reconstructed as neglect rather than being seen as powerful indicators of successful maternal practice. They conclude by warning that social change cannot occur without Aboriginal communities gaining authority over child welfare practices within their own communities.

In "Mothering in Prison: The Case of Spain's New External Mother Units," Sophie Feintuch approaches the legal landscape of motherhood differently by looking inside a women's prison at the mothers who reside there. Examining Spain's new external mother units, Feintuch demonstrates how such units, designed to empower and educate the mothers so as to reduce recidivism among them, in fact reify a white, Western, and middle-class vision of motherhood that few of the mothers embraced. Incorporating the perspectives of prison personnel and the mothers themselves, Feintuch explores such issues as maternalism and identity, as she describes the mothers' efforts to manage their own and others' expectations within the metaphorical Panopticon that is their prison home.

Section II considers the complicity of the medical establishment in the regulation of mothers. In this section, the Bad Mother can be detected within the duplicity of medicalization that purports to improve mothers' lives just as it dictates their behaviours. Mothers, in these chapters, make bad choices from the perspectives of health authorities who are actively surveilling the minute details of their mothering, which results in the perceived need to moderate and manage the mothers that they watch in increasingly intrusive ways.

In "Mea Culpa," Noa Arad Yairi visually depicts her struggle with mother blame following her son's ADD diagnosis, despite the fact she sees herself as a good mother. Her failures become his burden to bear. In "'Bad Mothers' and the HIV/AIDS Epidemic in Saskatchewan, Canada," Pamela J. Downe maps the incursion of the Bad Mother rhetoric into the lives of women living with HIV/AIDS or injection drug use. Because of the high rates of HIV in Aboriginal communities, the target of public interventions has frequently been Aboriginal mothers, who are depicted as central to the epidemic. This intense gaze has not gone unnoticed by Downe's Aboriginal mother participants, who share their frustrations with being seen as "poison" or a risk to their children. In response, the mothers talked of rejecting these imposed images by asserting their connections to kin and historical Aboriginal caregiving practices.

Risk is also a theme in "The Risky Mother: The Medicalization of Mothering," by Alexandra Campbell. Campbell takes on fetal origins research and attachment theory to argue that "scientific" mothering focuses on marginalized mothers, even as it ignores inequalities within the science itself. And using Michel Foucault's conceptualization of power, she illustrates the discursive shift from regulation to self-regulation, with pregnant women particularly subject to coercive medicalization. Rela Mazali 's short story "Hospital Archive" follows, in which the reader is taken to an abortion committee in Israel, where her protagonist has requested to receive a state-funded abortion. Painting the restrictive approval process as filled with pronatalist policies and conservative family values, Mazali shows us the path chosen by the protagonist to achieve her goal—a lie—and its consequences.

Kelsey Ioannoni's chapter, "Fat Blame and Fat Shame: A Failure of Maternal Responsibility," finishes this section. Ioannoni discusses the growing literature that merges fat studies with motherhood studies. As nurturers, role models and disciplinarians, mothers have the burden of ensuring the health of their children, which today is defined, in part, by their weight. Taking authors' writings in both fat studies and motherhood studies to task, she demonstrates the contradictions embedded in mothering expectations that shame mothers for surveilling children's weight while they blame mothers for their children's obesity. Ioannoni argues that both fat- and mother-shaming discourses hold mothers accountable for the complex conditions that lead to childhood obesity, which are beyond their control, and reifies the culture of thinness that shames their children.

Section III considers media and cultural representations of the Bad Mother and cultural stories about bad motherhood. In these chapters, bad mothers are not dictated through force of policy or public health mandate; rather, more insidiously, they are shown in artistic, literary, and cinematic displays that highlight their failure, assess them through their children's perceived outcomes, and contrast them with the Good Mother. Authors in this section begin to parse the elements of the Bad Mother in our cultural narratives as they show how images such as *La Malinche* can be invoked to understand bad mothering, or how the defiant bad mother is blamed because of how her defiance affects her children. In these international analyses, the Bad Mother takes different but always politicized forms. By considering the cultural politics of the Bad Mother trope, our authors argue for a closer acknowledgement of the power of such representations to sustain mother blame and to also spark resistance.

Nonavee Dale begins this section by sharing "Protection," a complex image that shows both the idealized Good Mother holding the child and the dark, restless context within which this protection occurs. The demands of mothering are evident in the painting, as are the mothers' strengths and challenges in fulfilling them. Her art is followed by María Alonso Alonso's "Malas Madres in Contemporary Latin American Literature: Representing Ill-Fated Motherhood in Myriam Laurini's *Qué Raro Que Me Llame Guadalupe*." Alonso's chapter is disturbing. It traces the development of a *mala madre* in the character of Bere, a girl raised as a sex worker by her own mother, who gives birth to a child whom she later kills. Alonso argues the novel is a form of feminist analysis of oppression within Latin American society. The text challenges both patriarchy and burgeoning neoliberal societies, in which citizens are exploited. By representing prostitution and motherhood in a hyper-realist and violent context, Alonso criticizes the effects of misogynistic and vicious cultures on women's and girl's lives.

Michelle Hughes Miller, Geraldine M. Hendrix-Sloan, and M. Joan McDermott focus on crime and film in their chapter "Celluloid Marys: Discovering and Listening to the Bad Mothers behind the Criminals in Popular Crime Films." Directly taking on the topic of mother blame within crime films, they use critical feminist film analysis to argue that such films sometimes explain criminals' behaviours in terms of the alleged bad mothering that they endured, although mothers are rarely afforded the opportunity to respond to the bad mother claims made against them. Analyzing three films across two decades, the authors conclude that it is the reification of maternal practice that forms mother blame, which links the Good Mother to the Bad Mother in media images.

In the final chapter in this section, "Bad Motherhood in Contemporary Argentine Cinema: Illustrating the New Political Agenda," Fernando Gabriel Pagnoni Berns, Patricia Vazquez, and Juan Juvé show that the effects of film are both cultural and political. Through political analysis and a careful reading of several films, they argue that the movement away from the self-sacrificing mother from earlier Argentine cinema reflects the political split within that society, resulting in a resurgence of bad mothers—often defined by their failure to sacrifice—in film. However, these bad mothers are actually portrayed as complex characters, emblematic of the progressive politics of the Argentine ruling party.

Although resistance to the Bad Mother trope is important in the chapters in Section IV, each author approaches this resistance in different ways. Nevertheless, it is clear in their fictionalized and scholarly work that some mothers, across time and across domain, have stood up to cultural shaming, often earning the Bad Mother label for their impudence. And other mothers, in telling their stories, have poignantly articulated the processes by which the Bad Mother label was applied to them so that others may be empowered to reject its cultural dominance. In making these arguments, these authors not only analyze the Bad Mother image in various social and cultural contexts, but they explicitly challenge its effects on the lived experiences of mothers. In highlighting the surveillance culture within which mothers are defined and also self-define, these authors outline the conditions under which the Bad Mother is invoked, by whom and against whom, and which mothers within which contexts have the authority to effectively respond.

Section IV begins with Freddie Robins's artwork "Bad Mother" which depicts her struggles to be an artist and a mother. Her pieces speak about adaptation and integration, as her images show how she knits her own tapestries of motherhood. Following Robins's work are two chapters about infanticide, although they approach the volatile topic in starkly different ways. In Tamar Hager's creative contribution to our volume, "Underneath Broadmoor," the narrator goes on an ambitious self-reflective research journey as she struggles to understand the motives for maternal abandonment and infanticide, and the role of mental illness, poverty, and patriarchy in the lives of her historical figures. "Underneath Broadmoor" introduces several mothers whose behaviours are perceived as bad. There is a mother who has committed infanticide, a mother who has placed most of her children into care, and a mother (the narrator) who, in order to advance her academic career, has left her child behind under the care of a hostile stepmother. By locating these stories in their social and historical contexts, the author challenges the Bad Mother label and exposes its rigid and unjust nature. Yet empathy and awareness intertwine in this chapter, as the contexts of mothering are made visible.

In "Feminism, Infanticide, and Intersectionality in Victorian America," Keira V. Williams writes about early feminists' rhetoric regarding infanticide. Focusing on two cases from the nineteenth century, Williams describes how feminists of the era used their white, elite privilege to challenge the punishment of two mothers who killed their children. But Williams points out that this resistance had a goal beyond justice: with the cases, feminists found platforms upon which to call attention to the political, social, and economic needs of women and mothers of the day.

In "Fixed or Shifting Notions of 'Bad Mother'? Considering Past and Future Australian Adoption Practice," Susan Gair argues that the public making of good mothers from bad mothers through adoption masks a much deeper tragedy. She notes that the bad mothers, those who were single and pregnant or those who were married and childless, were discursively turned into good mothers through the adoptive act, although frequently birth mothers and adoptive mothers were dichotomized into bad and good to simplify the story. But the apparent success of this model was called into question when birth mothers' narratives of coerced adoption, missing children, and closed adoption practices challenged the public record. Gair ends by urging transparency, instead of blame, in adoption practices.

Section IV concludes with "Refusing to Obey: Bad Mothers in the Israeli Culture," a chapter by Omri Herzog and Tamar Hager, in which they discuss motherhood in a militaristic society—where becoming a bad mother may be as easy as refusing to accept the circumstances of your child's death or capture. Herzog and Hager share news accounts of two mothers who faced public condemnation for failing to fulfill their designated roles as patriotic mothers. Instead, each mother used her mother identity as a forum to seek answers and social change, rejecting in the process the narrow box within which mothers of soldiers often find themselves. The mothers' risks and losses became compounded by a public unwilling to accept the women's private motherhood entering the political arena.

The volume ends with three pieces that challenge us to rethink the possibilities of the Bad Mother concept. Section V begins with Heather Munro's "Wings and Roots," a joyful offering to a new mother. The mother character in the image has both roots and wings. Seeing the tenderness in the piece, we also marvel at how it demonstrates the impossibilities of motherwork: how, practically speaking, is she to be both the roots that ground her children while flying away into her own goals and dreams? What is the price she pays for such a demanding position?

In "FurryLove," Liat Elkayam considers mother-child interactions through the artificial eyes of a robot, separating mothers, even bad mothers, from the intimate connections that frame the understanding of what it means to mother. Her story recreates mothering artificially in a not-so-subtle critique of technology and consumer culture. When mothering is commerce, who are the bad mothers?

The final piece, a theoretical one, by Miri Rozmarin, "Medea Chic: On the Necessity of Ethics as Part of the Critique of Motherhood," posits that bad mothers are romanticized in feminist critiques of motherhood because they do not embrace patriarchal motherhood as good mothers do. Thus, those who enact patriarchal motherhood face feminist derision, even as they (sometimes) receive social rewards. Because of this, she urges a closer consideration of the ethics of bad mothering, calling for a feminist morality that can associate but also differentiate the context of mothering and the choices of mothers.

FINAL THOUGHTS

While editing this volume, we were constantly aware of the insurmountable nature of our aspirational task. Our anthology surveys diversity, but it is not comprehensive of all possible circumstances and does not articulate all voices. Despite our efforts, many mothers labelled as bad by various societies and cultures are still missing from the text—because of space and time constraints and the reality that even a book that intends to be comprehensive cannot be—although they definitely deserve attention. Mothers with disabilities, mothers of children with disabilities, queer mothers, religious mothers, older mothers, mothers from the Global South (with the exception of Latin America), and many more are left out. Such a short volume cannot analyze the diverse use of the Bad Mother label across all social contexts or all intersectional identities. We regret these absences and hope that our work will encourage other scholars to continue to share voices of, and bring recognition to, the multitude of ways the Bad Mother image defines mothers across time, geography, culture, and society. We hope that more anthologies will follow ours, contributing further to knowledge of the Bad Mother.

In the context of this broad yet narrow volume, the quotes at the beginning of this chapter relate two perspectives of bad mothers that seem to us complimentary. Griffin protests against mother blame. For her, mothers are in many cases falsely accused because the label is applied singularly onto women with little regard for the structural context of their mothering. Walker's focus, on the other hand, is on the individual mother asserting that flaws are integral to mothering itself. This is the gift we give to our children: a celebration of imperfection through a rejection of mother blame. Unfortunately, claiming our flaws is a matter of privilege, as there can be significant risks for marginalized mothers in this hyper-punitive society to assert their flaws as valuable to their children and to the social world, and to protest the structural and ideological foundations of their bad mothering.

These two authors show what we must do to seek social change. We must name our context, as Griffin reminds us. We must question "the way things are." Describing the interconnections between our oppressions and our mothering, we lessen the power of the pointed finger to individually blame mothers. We must assert our mothering, as Walker confirms, reject the burgeoning lists of bad mother dictates and reconceptualize, whenever we can, the standards by which we evaluate ourselves. Combined, we must detail the structures that surround us, the cultural ideologies that fail to nurture us, and we must speak our own truths.

If through academic critique or collective action the Bad Mother label eventually loses its social, political, cultural, and psychological power, we might find ourselves seeing that new vision, where neither the Bad Mother nor the Good Mother trope structures the experiences of mothers and their lives. Instead, we might find humane recognition of the challenges of motherhood, the need for social, political, and economic support of mothers, and a rejection of oppressive efforts to marginalize those mothers whose identities already are suspect in this often unkind and unequal world. We might find, in other words, a mother existing without oppressive and judgemental modifiers or an iconic status. It is for all the flawed mothers, like ourselves, who struggle for respect and support in the midst of our punitive and surveilled mothering world, that we edited this volume.

ENDNOTE

[1]A note about language. When we are referring to the tropes of the Bad Mother or the Good Mother we will capitalize the phrase, otherwise the terms reflect the lived experiences of mothers so defined.

WORKS CITED

Caplan, Paula J. *The New Don't Blame Mother: Mending the Mother-Daughter Relationship*. Routledge, 2000.

Cynic, Arron. "Illinois Bill Would Make Life Even More Difficult for Single Moms." *Chicagoist*, 20 Feb. 2016, chicagoist.com/2016/02/20/lawmakers_file_legislation_that_wou.php. Accessed, 1 Jan. 2017.

Douglas, Susan J., and Meredith W. Michaels. *The Mommy Myth: The Idealization of Motherhood and How It Has Undermined All Women*. The Free Press, 2004.

Filax, Gloria and Dena Taylor, editors. *Disabled Mothers: Stories and Scholarship By and About Mothers with Disabilities*. Demeter Press, 2014.

Gillis J. R. *A World of Their Own Making: Myth, Ritual and the Quest for Family Values*. Harvard University Press, 1996.

Griffin, S. "Feminism and Motherhood." *Mother Reader: Essential Writings on Motherhood*. 1974. Edited by M. Davey, Seven Stories Press, 2001, pp. 33-46.

Hufton, O. *The Prospect Before Her: A History of Women in Western Europe 1500-1800*: *Vol.1*. Fontana, 1997.

Ladd-Taylor, Molly. "Mother-Worship/Mother-Blame: Politics and Welfare in an Uncertain Age." *Maternal Theory: Essential Readings*, edited by Andrea O'Reilly, Demeter Press, 2007, pp. 660-667.

Ladd-Taylor, Molly and Lauri Umansky, editors. *"Bad" Mothers: The Politics of Blame in Twentieth Century America*. New York University Press, 1998.

McDonald-Harker, Caroline, editor. *Mothering in Marginalized Contexts: Narratives of Women Who Mother in and through Domestic Violence*. Demeter Press, 2016.

Minaker, Joanne and Bryan Hogeveen, editors. *Criminalized Mothers, Criminalizing Mothering*. Demeter Press, 2015.

Motopanyane, Maki, editor. *Motherhood and Lone-Single Parenting: A Twenty-First Century Perspective*. Demeter Press, 2016.

Reimer, Vanessa and Sarah Sahagain, editors. *The Mother-Blame Game*. Demeter Press, 2015.

Rich, Adrienne. *Of Woman Born: Motherhood as Experience and Institution*. Norton, 1976.

Smart, Carol. "Disruptive Bodies and Unruly Sex: The Regulation of Reproduction and Sexuality in the Nineteenth Century." *Regulating Womanhood: Historical Essays on Marriage, Motherhood and Sexuality*, edited by Carol Smart, Routledge, 1992, pp. 7-32.

Stone, Laurence. *The Family, Sex and Marriage in England 1500-1800*. Penguin Books, 1990.

Thurer, Shari L. *The Myths of Motherhood: How Culture Reinvents the Good Mother*. Houghton Mifflin Co, 1994.

Walker, Alice. *Possessing the Secret of Joy*. Harcourt Brace Jovanovich, 1992.

1.
THE LEGAL AND REGULATORY LANDSCAPE

Rebecca Bromwich, "Arctic Motherwork," 2015, Acrylic on canvass, 11 x 14 inches.

Arctic Motherwork

Troubling the Figure of the Bad Mother

REBECCA JAREMKO BROMWICH

THIS PAINTING, done in acrylic on canvass, is a representation of a polar bear mother and her cubs. It was done in contemplation of the Report of the Truth and Reconciliation Commission of Canada (TRC), released in 2015. Already well known, but made clearer in the findings of that report, is the fact that in the context of assimilative regimes imposed against Aboriginal people, mothering by First Nations mothers, and Inuit mothers, was considered "bad" by definition for more than a century, to a point that it was seen as useful to sterilize them. Their motherwork, as culture bearers of traditional, indigenous lifeways, was seen as an evil to be eradicated. From the 1860s until late in the twentieth century, Inuit children, as with the children of other First Nations groups, were forcibly removed from their mothers and housed in residential schools where they were assimilated into European lifeways, lost their ancestral languages, were often abused, and died from neglect, malnutrition, disease, and violence in appallingly high numbers. Although the residential schools are now closed, there a significant number of First Nations children remain in the care of the state in group homes and foster families, a fact which is of great concern to Aboriginal people in Canada and should be of great concern to all Canadians.

Like First Nations mothers, polar bears have often been stereotyped as "bad." They are seen as vicious and dangerous hunters. It is true that polar bear attacks on humans are not uncommon and that they are highly carnivorous. Yet despite the stereotypes, polar bears are not territorial and will prefer retreat to attack.

Their primary diet is seals, so they are accustomed to hunting large animals and are adapted to surviving the harsh temperatures and swimming in the frigid waters of the Arctic Ocean. They are also nurturing mothers. Polar bears are exceptional in the natural world for their unusually high parental investment. They spend more of their lifespans mothering their young than virtually any animal other than humans; they nurse their young for an average of two and half years. Polar bears spend three to four years of their average fifteen-year lifespan with a single litter of cubs, which they will nurture from a size of less than two pounds to their adult size of around five hundred pounds for females and up to fifteen hundred pounds for males (Wilson and Reeder).

There is a special relationship between the Aboriginal peoples of the Arctic and polar bears. In Inuit traditional folklore, polar bears are known as *Nanuq*, which means "almost a man." Legend runs that polar bears take off their furs in the privacy of their homes. Subsistence hunting of polar bears by Aboriginal peoples continues and is permitted. A 1973 International Agreement on the Conservation of Polar Bears ensures that the subsistence harvest of polar bears is an exclusive right of Aboriginal peoples. Canada's Federal government regulates this hunt within the nation's borders ("The Inuit and Polar Bears").

This painting was intended to evoke a sense of the connectedness between all those who mother and their young, and specifically of the connectedness of Inuit people with their cultural lifeways and traditions, as well as the special relationship of Aboriginal people with the polar bear—all in order to trouble the categories of what has been constructed as a "bad" mother in Canada.

WORKS CITED

Wilson, Don, and DeeAnn Reeder, editors. *Mammal Species of the World*. Johns Hopkins University Press, 2005.

"The Inuit and Polar Bears." *Polar Bears International*, 10 Aug. 2015, www.polarbearsinternational.org/about-polar-bears/essentials/indigenous-and-polar-bears. Accessed 10 Jan. 2017.

Truth and Reconciliation Commission of Canada. *Honouring the Truth, Reconciling for the Future*: *Summary of the Final Report of the Truth and Reconciliation Commission of Canada*. CreateSpace Independent Publishing Platform, 2015.

Still Wearing Scarlet?

Discursive Figures of the Unfit Mother as Pervasive Phantoms Active in Governing Mothers through Ontario's Child Protection Regime

REBECCA JAREMKO BROMWICH

IN NATHANIEL HAWTHORNE'S *The Scarlet Letter* (1850), the fitness of Hester Prynne to care for her child is called into question because of her past infidelity and her general identity as a sinner. In a public child protection hearing, at which Hester is stigmatized with a scarlet letter "A," Governor Bellingham tries to take Prynne's illegitimate daughter, Pearl, away from her. Her Puritan neighbours, with the exception of the child's secret father, Reverend Dimmesdale, urge the governor to take Pearl away, as they claim that the sin of her adultery makes Hester an unfit mother.

Determination of a mother's "fitness" remains a legal determination in child welfare regimes and a deciding factor about whether a mother will lose her child. As discussed below, across Canada, child welfare decisions are made on the basis of whether a child is in need of protection, and if there is such a need, a determination of what to do next is arrived at on the basis of the so-called best interests of the child. Historically, juridical determinations that women were not fit to care for their children were made on the basis of a wide range of characteristics not related, or only indirectly related, to their parenting conduct or skills and were closely linked to such things as irreverence, infidelity, poverty, marital status, interracial relationships, political views, and profanity. Thus, such examples do not solely exist in historical fiction. The use of criteria relating to the character or conduct of the mother quite apart from her parenting role as making her "fit" or "unfit" for the sacred mother role have been legitimized in law for centuries. Women routinely lost custody of their children if they committed adultery, or even to have acted questionably in the eyes of a court.

The prevalent cultural grand narrative in Canada runs that legal determinations of child custody and child protection are no longer made with reference to stereotypical assumptions about who is a good or bad mother. The formal law has been reformed. Determinations about children's placements, child protection, and child custody are made not with mothers in mind but with reference to the "best interests of the child." The purposes set out in s. 1 of Ontario's Child and Family Services Act enjoin system actors to make decisions on the basis of the best interests of the child, and to prioritize placement of "Indian" children and members of racialized minorities with caregivers from their own communities where possible.

In this chapter, I explore the discursive construct of the unfit mother in legal documents and cases, administrative decisions, news media, and online texts. I argue that legal reforms have done less than is assumed to erode or eradicate the prevalence of stereotypes about class, race, and socioeconomic status as defining the so-called bad or unfit mother in legal decision making. Law reform has not overwhelmed the power of the discursive figure of the unfit mother in contributing to inequality and marginalization for racialized minority mothers, including Aboriginal women, mothers of lower socioeconomic status, and mothers with disabilities. A variety of representative figures in discourse of the unfit mother continue to contribute in complex ways to the disempowerment of mothers across a variety of contexts in their involvements with child protection systems. More than law reform, (re)education of actors and officials in the child protection system—including lawyers, police, social workers, health care providers, and even the public at large—towards the deliberate construction of counter-discourses of empowered mothering would aid in ameliorating the conditions in which marginalized mothers work.

Figures of the unfit mother are given shape by dimensions of the social location of "ideal" mothers. In mainstream discourses found in contemporary Western societies, the "good mother" as a representative figure is defined in ways that support patriarchal systems of power with reference to her (white) race, (married) marital status, (heterosexual) sexual orientation, and (middle-class) socioeconomic status (O'Reilly; Goodwin and Huppatz; Arendell). As discussed in the introduction to this anthology, figures of the good and bad mother are shifting, complex, and often contradictory. What constitutes good or bad motherhood is a contested discursive terrain in which mothers often occupy a double-bind position. They are expected to do impossible and incompatible things—such as have perfect (white, youthful) bodies, ensure their children go to a wide range of extracurricular activities, bake organic, locally-sourced foods, exclusively breastfeed for an appropriately long (but not *too long*) period of time, work outside the home full time, and be at home full time. Feminists have challenged the definition of who constitutes a good mother in patriarchal Western ideologies.

Although the good mother as a representative figure is a social construct, the unfit mother as a subgenre of this construct is *inherently legal*. Unfitness is the legal category into which the social notion of bad mothering is placed. As a discursive category, the unfit mother overlaps significantly with the bad mother, although it is an extreme variant of the broader notion of badness. There would be mothers who are socially rendered bad whose so-called badness would not suffice to make them unfit to continue to have access to their children. Interestingly, being a feminist and an activist, has, at times, been understood to be a basis for a mother to be found unfit. Alice Rossi, co-founder of NOW, a U.S. feminist organization, was widely reviled and accused of being an unfit mother in the 1970s because of her writings about women's life courses, the need for gender equality, and birth control.

METHODOLOGY

This chapter presents a social constructivist study that deploys the tool of critical discourse analysis (CDA) to make visible the implicit ideological content of the mother as represented in child protection law as lived or operationalized. I conduct a CDA with qualitative and quantitative dimensions of the ways in which unfit or otherwise bad mothers are represented in texts widely available in Ontario that engage the legal concept of child protection. I analyze the figurations of the "mother" that emerge in three discursive sites: two of these are genres of formal legal texts—legislation and caselaw—and the third one is in the popular realm of internet postings and mainstream media reports.

I reviewed legislative provisions, regulations, and caselaw dealing with Ontario's child protection regime and the basis for which a child can be found to be "in need of protection." I looked for themes in the texts, specifically for express or implicit definitions of "mother" and "fitness" and especially "unfit mother." I also looked at historical legislative provisions from previous versions of Ontario's child welfare laws. I also looked at studies of the impacts of Ontario's child protection regime on different socioeconomic, racial, ethnic and otherwise differently situated groups. To obtain popular texts, I searched media articles on the Factiva database. Then, to study online popular texts, I did web searches for the phrases "unfit mother," "child welfare" "child protection," and "Ontario" using the Google search engine, thus replicating what an average Ontarian would access when searching contemporary web-based documents.

Critical discourse analysis is employed to unpack the implicit ideological content of representative figures of the mother that are present in talk about child welfare.[1] The constructed nature of discourse and the fact that it mediates our understandings of the real can make it hard to distinguish what is inevitable or unchangeable from what is contingent or possible to change. Having these ideas in mind, I examine how legal, expert, and educational definitions of the "parent" in Ontario's child protection law—and of what is "normal" for a parent—confine some mothers while completely excluding others. What identities and options are available to women with children are, to a large extent, defined by various discourses or constructs of the unfit mother. These discourses are always being generated in social interaction, and each interaction has potential to shape and reshape how phenomena (such as mothers) are defined. Discourse is what configures the dimensions of the stamp of "mother" that is impressed upon women. In describing and defining phenomena in the real, discourses contain constructed representations of those phenomena. Representations are powerful socially constructed images formed using implicit preexisting, widely accepted cultural "truths." I use the constructionist theory of representation set forth by Stuart Hall, which employs Foucault's study of discourse—not primarily as language but as a system of representations. I accept Hall's formulation that the process of representation itself constitutes the world it represents. The dominant discourses in a culture provide a map that signals meanings of the real, yet these representations do not simply reflect the real. They constitute a fiction that can affect facts. Representations not only are not the real, but they do not even derive their value or power—as Edward Said argues from analyzing textual representations of the Orient—from being realistic. Representations are powerful for their ability to define phenomena and to have those definitions accepted, not for being verifiable in some objectively empirical sense. When discourses define the real, they make certain things unsayable and constitute subjects' identities.

CDA is the methodological framework used in conducting research into how discourses function as instruments of power and control. CDA looks at social structures and processes involved in text production. It is an analytical way to make visible relationships of causality that are otherwise opaque and to see links between texts and broader social and cultural power relations and discursive processes. CDA makes visible interlocking webs of domination, power, discrimination, and control that exist in language. It is a framework for looking at discourse as tool in the social construction of reality. CDA relies on a basic assumption that there is a dialectical or mutually constitutive relationship between events and the discursive context in which they are embedded. CDA looks at the production of reality performed by discourses and at how ideologies and existing relations of power are presented in and maintained by discursive sites studied. I draw on major contributions to the development of CDA by Norman Fairclough, who developed methodological tools for looking at discourse as a social practice that contributes to the maintenance and reproduction of existing social practices.

LEGISLATION: FORMAL DISCOURSES OF CHILD PROTECTION LAW

Child protection law is in provincial and territorial jurisdiction under the Canadian constitution. The chapter's focus is on the provincial regime in Ontario, but it is important to note that similar regimes are in place across other Canadian jurisdictions, all of which rely on the best interests test for child placement.[2] In Ontario, as in other Canadian provincial and territorial jurisdictions, child protection law is not criminal but quasi-criminal legislation. It is not understood as a source of punishment and stigma for parents, because it does not result in dispositions that interfere with their personal liberty. Consequently, mothers before the court in child welfare proceedings are afforded far fewer evidentiary protections than are people accused of crimes,, and the threshold for a finding of fact is the "balance of probabilities" standard. Nonetheless, determinations made in the child protection context have profound consequences for the lives of mothers and their children. Child protection involves the deployment of the state as a complex and opaque bureaucratic web constructed with the benevolent intention of advancing and protecting the best interests of children.

The figure of the unfit mother has no place in the official story of contemporary child protection as legally formalized in Ontario (Bala). This does not mean that the unfit mother as a figure is specifically precluded from being deployed, assumed, or otherwise relied on but rather that it is not explicitly present. The formal discourse of child welfare legislation in this province hardly mentions mothers, let alone the fitness of mothers.

In the terms of the formal discourse of law as written on the books, determination of whether the state should intervene to protect children is officially a two-step question in Ontario. Since 1984, the preliminary test of whether a child is thought to be "in need of protection" has been that set out under s. 37(2) of Ontario's Child and *Family Services Act* (CFSA). Under that provision, the state has authority to apprehend when a child is in need of protection based on a list of possible harms. If protection is found by a court to be warranted, only then will a second question be asked: what placement will be in the child's best interests. Determination as to placement of the child is to be made based on the child's best interests pursuant to s. 37(3) of the CFSA once the threshold question has been addressed by a finding that protection is necessary. Both tests are ostensibly referential to particular conditions faced by the child. Neither test is officially a question of who the parents, and in particular the mother, are, and the determinations are not, officially, questions of their identity. However, the best interests test is notoriously indeterminate, and is called in the official narrative of the law "fact specific." It is discretionary and depends on the exercise of judgment and agency by socially situated judges. In December 2016, Ontario's governing Liberals introduced a bill that would replace the CFSA with what will be called the *Child, Youth, and Family Services Act*. The proposed new law would seek to provide more culturally appropriate child welfare solutions to address the circumstances of racialized and Aboriginal children and would ensure the provision of services to youth aged sixteen to eighteen. At the time of writing, this bill has not yet passed, and it is not clear if it will pass or in what form. Furthermore, the bill does not change the fundamental gender neutrality of the existing legislation, nor does it change the administrative scheme through which child protection is administered through scores of not for profit societies. This chapter considers the law and administrative mechanisms in place at the time of writing. Although the formal discourse of Ontario's child protection statute may change in the near future, those changes will not materially alter the way in which the law and the regime of legality through which it is implemented interact with the cultural figure of the unfit mother.

On the face of the legislation, then, the fitness of the mother is not an official question to be adjudicated in the formal discourse of child protection legislation in Ontario. The CFSA is technically gender blind. In section three, which sets out definitions, "mother" is *not* a defined term. Under universally accepted principles of statutory interpretation, therefore, the term has its ordinary meaning (Craies). For the purposes of the legislation, "parent" is described but not defined for the purposes of the entire Act at s. 3(2).[3] In section thirty-seven of the Act, "parent" is defined for the purposes of the protection provisions, which focuses on who may constitute the father of the child. This is a unique provision in the Act because the term "mother" actually appears:

> "parent," when used in reference to a child, means each of,
> (a) the child's mother,
> (b) an individual described in one of paragraphs 1 to 6 of

> subsection 8 (1) of the Children's Law Reform Act, unless it is proved on a balance of probabilities that he is not the child's natural father,
> (c) the individual having lawful custody of the child,
> (d) an individual who, during the twelve months before intervention under this Part, has demonstrated a settled intention to treat the child as a child of his or her family, or has acknowledged parentage of the child and provided for the child's support,
> (e) an individual who, under a written agreement or a court order, is required to provide for the child, has custody of the child or has a right of access to the child, and
> (f) an individual who has acknowledged parentage of the child in writing under section 12 of the Children's Law Reform Act, but does not include a foster parent.

CASELAW

A recent Supreme Court of Canada case originating in Ontario has reaffirmed the best interests test for child welfare decisions. In *Syl Apps Secure Treatment Centre v. B.D.*, the court found that the Children Aid's Society had no "duty of care" to the parents of children in its care or any proximate relationship with them. With this 2007 decision, the Supreme Court of Canada reaffirmed the jurisdiction and role of Children's Aid Societies under Ontario's CFSA to act in the best interests of the child by protecting children and youth, ensuring their wellbeing, and preventing their exposure to abuse and neglect. *In Syl Apps* decision, Justice Abella writes the following:

> When a child is placed in the care of the Children's Aid Society, or if Crown wardship is ordered, the Act gives the Children's Aid Society or Crown "the rights and responsibilities of a parent for the purpose of the child's care, custody and control" (s. 63(1)). This creates an inherently adversarial relationship between parents and the state.
> ....
> The primacy of the best interests of the child over paren-

> tal rights in the child protection context is an axiomatic proposition in the jurisprudence. (pars. 42-44)

Although caselaw confirms the overall language of the legislation, it also expands on it; while the gendere figure of the unfit mother is not referenced in the legislation, it does appear in caselaw. Searches of the CanLii (Canadian Legal Information Institute) database reveal occasional, and even recent, references, to a mother's unfitness in judgments concerning child protection in Ontario. Notably, maternal unfitness is deployed as an assumed concept and is not defined with reference to any criteria. Although it is unsurprising, in light of the historical configuration of the good mother in mainstream Canadian discourse as middle class, white, self-sacrificing, and religious to find this concept in earlier cases,[4] it is perhaps more surprising to find express references to maternal unfitness in more contemporary cases. A recent example of casual reference to undefined maternal (un)fitness is found in the 2015 case *Valoris v. Jina Ramlall and Christopher Lanston*, 2015 ONSC 207. In that decision, the court holds the following: "The evidence establishing that *the mother is an unfit mother* is substantial. It is not refuted in any way. She left the Hawkesbury hospital wearing her hospital gown. She has admitted using heroin. The father is also a heroin user. When apprehended, her 4 other children showed signs of having been physically and sexually abused (my emphasis; para. 5)." Significantly, not only is the fitness of the mother being explicitly adjudicated in this case, but also the abuse that the condition of the children is understood to evidence is connected in the language to the mother's fitness, although there is no suggestion that it was her who did the abusing. Failure to protect the children from abuse is seen as component to her unfitness.

THE REGIME

The formal discourses of Ontario's child welfare regime are applied in a regime that is diffuse and opaque (Hughes and Chau), and involves a myriad of actors at a variety of levels. Child protection law in Ontario is not solely, or even primarily, administered by judges in an open courtroom. Rather, child welfare governance operates in an opaque web, in which there is interplay between the micro-level decisions of public officials, legal actors, social workers, educators, neighbours, lawyers, and judges, most of which are never made transparent to later scrutiny. Section seventy-two of the CFSA places declares that all members of the public have a positive duty to report concerns they have about children being in need of protection. Child protection law in Ontario is administered indirectly by the province's Ministry of Child and Youth Services. Child protection services, in turn, are provided by fifty-three separate Children's Aid Societies, which are publicly funded but are not-for-profit nongovernmental organizations (NGO). These NGOs are tasked with facilitating administration of the same legislative regime, but they each have their own mandates, visions, and values, many of which are rooted in particular religious and cultural heritages. Children Aid's Society interventions involve the discretionary decisions of social workers, who in turn rely on reports made by individuals. Thus, the vast preponderance of decisions made in relation to how the child protection system intervenes in the lives of families resemble what Foucault has called "microprocesses" (Calavita). They are small, administrative decisions made at the everyday level of discretionary action taken by low-level bureaucratic actors and private citizens who "report."

When the formal legal discourses of the "best interests of the child" and the determination of who is in need of protection are performed and enacted and deployed in a myriad of situations, what constitute a child's best interests is not chiefly litigated in court but rather determined in an opaque space in which it is predictable that they intersect with problematic, socially located figures of the good and bad mother. It is in these opaque, bureaucratic, administrative and community-based space where the child welfare regime intersects with social meanings of mother and juridical meanings of the discourse of the unfit mother.

Low-level decision-makers, front-line social workers, teachers, recreational staff, childcare workers, and others who make discretionary decisions under Ontario's child protection regime hold various credentials. They have attended of a variety of training and educational programs, and are licensed in a variety of ways. They are not generally lawyers, and they operate in a cultural and social context enmeshed in powerful preexisting discursive formulations of good and bad parenting, especially the figure of the unfit mother. To act justly, they have to be conscious of the problematic presence of this figuration, which may affect what protection concerns get reported, how, and why. Education for these positions does already exist, and this chapter provides evidence for the continuing necessity of it.

The impact of child welfare legislation is felt unevenly across socioeconomic and racial groups in Ontario and Canada, as well as in the United States (Smith). In a recent qualitative study of mothers' experiences of their interactions with child protection authorities in Canada, all the women interviewed said that their social location influenced the way in which they were received by officials within the child welfare system. More affluent, middle-class mothers reported more power in being able to make child welfare complaints "go away" while poorer, and racialized mothers reported "not feeling heard" (Hughes and Chau 688). The disparity is not an imagined one. Mothers living in poverty, mothers associated with substance abuse, racialized mothers, and especially Aboriginal mothers are much more likely, statistically speaking, to have child protection findings made that result in their children being removed from their homes. Most Children's Aid Societies in Ontario do not release demographic data, but the Toronto office started doing so in July 2015. It reveals that 31 percent of children in the society's care are black and, in addition, a further 11 percent have one parent who is black. Put in the demographic context of Toronto, where 8.2 per cent of people under eighteen are black, this is a gross overrepresentation. The report also acknowledges a "disproportionality, disparity and discrimination in services provided to Black families by child welfare agencies across North America" ("Addressing Disproportionality"). And the Toronto study does not even mention Aboriginal children.

Many researchers have documented troubling circumstances around disproportionate representation of Aboriginal children in care (Johnston). However, significantly, although public acknowledgement is now being made of the genocidal impact of the historical oppressive deployment of child protection regimes on

Aboriginal people, little of this acknowledgement currently includes critical reflexivity about the continuity of this cultural eradication through contemporary regimes and their effect on Aboriginal people today. Much has been made in popular media, and in expressions of support by governments and churches, about the 2015 release of the final report of the Truth and Reconciliation Commission into the residential schools that First Nations children in Canada were forced to attend. However, much less is being said about the fact that a comparable—perhaps even higher—number of First Nations children have been apprehended by the government under child protection regimes across Canada and are in state care or have been adopted into non-Aboriginal families. First Nations heritage, in the wake of Canada's history of colonialism and the ongoing legacy of the residential schools is too often statistically linked to substance abuse and domestic violence, is a key factor that disproportionately correlates with interventions by Children's Aid Societies in Ontario in First Nations children's lives (Canadian Council of Child and Youth Advocate 34). The impact of child welfare law on First Nations communities continues to be tragic and, arguably, is nothing short of "a new modality of colonialist regulation of First Nations in the post-Second World War period" (Kline 381).

UNFIT MOTHERS IN POPULAR AND LEGAL TEXTS

The development of child protection law in Ontario, as in other jurisdictions, has been informed by these shifting prevalent understandings of maternal fitness found in the mainstream culture. Understandings of who could be a fit mother that connect to the perceived virtue, class, race, and other dimensions of the social location of the mother have been cherished assumptions of the founders of Ontario's child protection system from its inception. Crusading journalist and reformer J.J. Kelso, who was central figure in the 1891-93 founding of Ontario's Children's Aid Societies, once argued that "the experience of ages has proved conclusively that no unmarried mother can successfully bring up her child and save it from disgrace and obloquy. [However] the child, if adopted young by respectable, childless people, will grow up creditably, and without any painful reminders of its origins" (qtd. in Chambers 29).

Culturally, the good or fit mother, although it is shifted as a discursive category, is no less narrow, exclusionary, raced, and classed in the twenty-first century than it was in the past. Arguably, it is growing more confining and exclusionary with the proliferation of more powerful "intensive mothering" discourses (O'Reilly). An array of unfit mother figures are prevalent as part of mother blame in psychological and scientific discourses. Maternal unfitness has been and is still blamed for various mental health disorders and other perceived social problems on the part of children including autism, schizophrenia, promiscuity, homosexuality, and obesity. In mainstream discourse, and in the narratives provided by social workers and educators, mothers are blamed for social ills, including for their children's exposure to domestic violence (Strega; Johnson).

Current approaches to child protection have been critiqued as patriarchal not just because they are grounded in a racist and classist past but also because they place all responsibility for children's protection on mothers (Strega et al.). Mothers, in child protection discourse, are even found responsible for violence in their homes when they themselves are also the victim of it (Strega et al.).

Contemporary News Media

The unfit mother appears frequently in popular texts, which, in turn, need to be taken seriously as sources of governmentality and law (Sarat) in the diffuse web that is Ontario's child protection regime. For this section, the critical discourse analysis involved searches of the Factiva media source database for the phrase "unfit mother" limited to Canadian news publications from the year 2010 to 2015; I identified eighty-nine news articles. A search of the database for the same time period but not limited to Canada (i.e., not constrained by region) returned 783 news articles. A review of these articles shows that the figure of the unfit mother is implicitly referential to law, although its meaning is rarely expressly defined; the meanings of "unfitness" and "fitness" are assumed. These popular references to the unfit mother are complicated, sometimes contradictory, and certainly not unitary. Discourses of the unfit mother are contested, messy, and in perpetual flux.

These articles address a wide range of (often salacious) situations: there are stories about the "Ikea Monkey," and about surprise births at Walmart, when the women did not know they were pregnant. There are patterns in these representations. The term "unfit mother" is associated in recurring and predictable ways with crime, infanticide, domestic violence by men, religious prohibitions or restrictions on maternal behaviour, promiscuity, and obesity. This search confirms that popular news media is a site of textual production in which feminists are actively engaged in creating texts. Mainstream news journalists, in 2017, are neither overwhelmingly male nor generally unaware of feminist critiques. This is evident in contemporary articles. Although there are articles that invoke or deploy conventional notions about the unfit mother, there are other articles that refer to the figure of the unfit mother to refute it. Feminist media portrayals of the unfit mother, for example, include critical pieces on mother blame and obesity. Examples include reviews of the Disney film "Maleficent" (Rosenberg). Notably, the term "unfit mother" is frequently used in the period between 2010 and 2015 in media articles. Yet it is rarely defined and only sometimes questioned. Its presence is ubiquitous, and it shows no pattern of decline.

Online Texts

The figure of the unfit mother is a discursive construct that relies for its definition on popular understandings of legality, and has a vibrant and continuing existence in popular culture. It is found in a variety of easily accessible texts in Ontario. Typing the term "unfit mother" into Google yields over one million documents. Searching "unfit mother Ontario" produces over thirty thousand results and "child protection Ontario" produces over six million. From an analysis of the most relevant documents, it is evident that the discursive figure of the unfit mother is circulating in mainstream popular discourse alongside the formal discourses of child welfare law.

Although it has no official or explicit presence in Ontario's child welfare laws, the fitness of parents and the figure of the unfit mother are present discursive figures in online documents produced in Ontario that purport to address and explain child protection law.

For example, in an article written by a Canadian lawyer for *The Ontario Family Law Blog*, the author casually refers to what may "make a parent unfit" (Nieuwhof). Furthermore, the unfit mother is part of the formal discourse of U.S. laws in several states. The pervasive influence of the legal regimes of other jurisdictions in Ontario is compounded by the Internet, which makes statements of law from elsewhere not only accessible to average Ontarians but also not necessarily distinguishable by their point of origin. These online statements of law often do not reference their jurisdiction of origin. The physical jurisdiction in which the statements of law were produced is often not easily determined. Sites such as *legal-dictionary.com* and *yourdictionary.com* provide definitions for "unfit parent" and "unfit mother." Other sites, such as *Wisegeek*, provide explanations about the legal consequences of such unfitness: "If both parents are found to be unfit, the child may be put in foster care or in the care of another relative."

Notably, there is little interplay between online erroneous or extra-jurisdictional understandings of the unfit mother and the official discourses of child welfare law in Ontario. Official websites do not engage with, but rather ignore, the proliferation of online explanations of child welfare law that reference maternal unfitness and talk about parental rights. A search of the wrong terms does not lead back to the formally correct ones. By being silent on what is a good or bad mother, and not mentioning the irrelevance or limited and tangential relevance of maternal vice or virtue to child welfare law, official government sites and the formal discourses of the law are not connected to or appear on websites that offer alternative interpretations, which are wrong according to the doctrinal law of Ontario under the CFSA. It may be useful for government to develop online content expressly refuting understandings about the unfit mother and to link that back to the official sites.

Research on the Internet transcends jurisdictional boundaries: understandings of child welfare law from jurisdictions outside Ontario confuse public awareness of the legal regime here, but this is not simply a mistake: it forms part of the plurality of normative orders interacting. In online or popular culture sources, I did searches that included "Ontario" in the query and also ones that did not. Both sets of queries led me to the same U.S.-based documents when the phrase "unfit mother" was included. It is important to recognize that laypeople may not appreciate jurisdictional distinctions. Marginalized people in particular are not necessarily going to perform nuanced searches of Ontario sites only. Thus, information posted on websites from other provinces and even U.S. states is likely to form and confirm public understandings of the law as it relates to child protection. Online legal (mis)information from places other than Ontario is likely to have unintended, unmanageable, and unruly roles in shaping governmentality in this province.

Interestingly, modifying the query to "unfit mother Canada" produces search results that include web question and answer forums where questions entered from Canadian IP addresses include "how do I prove my child's mother unfit?" Online texts, in large number, engage the agencies of readers who are understood by the narratives contained in the documents to be seeking to deploy the figure of the unfit mother to gain advantage in custody and related family law disputes. There are many sites where readers can find tips about how to prove a mother unfit.

INTERSECTING ORDERS AND NORMS: CRITICAL DISCOURSE ANALYSIS

Lawyers often contend that there are many popular misconceptions about child welfare law. However, the theoretical framework on which this research is based problematizes the claim that laypeople and the media get the law wrong. Rather this study makes evident that a diversity of normative orders interact to govern mothers in the child protection context. This critical discourse analysis reveals a plurality of normative orders, interacting and interacting with one another. As Kitty Calavita has stated, government in the Foucauldian sense exists in "a multiplicity of normative orders, and a diversity of legal systems" (91). This is the case with Ontario's child protection regime, through which the problematic dimensions of the unfit mother as a cultural construct are deployed in a range of troubling ways. Although discursive figures of unfit mother are not officially present in Ontario's formal discourses of child protection legislation, they are also not excluded by them. This study has shown unfit mothers to be present as discursive figures in court judgments in relation to child welfare, and to not just be present but to be ubiquitous in popular texts about child protection readily available in contemporary Ontario.

The construct of the bad mother or unfit mother is a persistent and pervasive discursive figure that remains present in conducting the conduct of, or governing, mothers and motherhood in Canada. Conventional and widely assumed attributes of the unfit mother figure, thus, inform the "ordinary" meaning of mother deployed in processes of sense making undertaken by actors in the child protection system. A myriad of points of contact and connection between popular understandings of maternal fitness and the formal legal regime for child protection exist in Ontario.

Critical discourse analysis reveals that micro-level decisions about whether to report protection concerns, and how to respond to reported concerns, are taken by scores of socially situated actors who act in a cultural context in which raced, classed, heteronormative, and other biased notions of the unfit mother are deeply ingrained. In a context where discretionary microprocesses by agentic individual actors situated as educational and governmental agents take place before any child protection matter is formally adjudicated by the courts, the argument that child protection decisions are adjudications of mothers' moral and cultural fitness are not incorrect. Rather, the construct of the unfit or bad mother continues to be at work in governing the lives of women and children, and, by extension, fathers when child welfare law is considered. The usual absence of the construct of the unfit mother from the formal language of the law represents a superficial divergence, which obscures the reality that government of mothers on the basis of the spectre of bad or unfit motherhood is still prevalent in the child protection legal context.

CONCLUSION

This chapter has tried to move toward theorizing how governmentality operates in the complex and murky interactions between law, society, and culture that together constitute the contemporary child protection system of Ontario. It has specifically provided a critical reading of how preexisting, widely assumed figures of the unfit mother are involved in how governmentality operates. Although the scarlet letter worn by Hester Prynne in the seventeenth-century century child protection hearing in the book of the same name is no longer an official tool sanctioned by the state, stigma associated with unfitness remains a sign that mothers wear, and are disempowered by, when child protection decisions are taken in Ontario.

This analysis cannot fully confirm that discriminatory decision making based on figures of the unfit mother is active in shaping particular decisions by individual actors in specific cases. Widely assumed understandings of the fit or unfit mother are naturalized. It would be difficult to ever know what biases people act from because they are not often conscious acts of discrimination. Equally, alternative explanations can be postulated for demographic distortions in child protection, as it could be argued that it is the social marginalization of Aboriginal and black families alone, and not bias or discrimination, that has led to the apprehension of disproportionately more of their children. However, what this study can and does show is that Ontario's child protection decisions are manifold microprocesses taken in an opaque web in which child protection law is neither separate from social structures, conflict, and inequalities, nor purified from the ordinary meaning of its terms. Furthermore, the study has shown that circulating within that context are problematic discourses of what constitutes maternal fitness.

Reasoning from a critical discourse analysis of formal and informal sources of governmentality—including formal legislative provisions, caselaw, regulatory provisions of a variety of kinds, and popular texts on the Internet—I contend in this chapter that the construct of the unfit mother as a subgenre of the broader social construct of the bad mother is a persistent discursive figure that remains present in the government of mothers and motherhood in Canada. I argue that the silence of the formal discourse of legislation on the construct of the unfit mother represents only a superficial divergence that masks and helps perpetuate the power of the spectre of the figure of the unfit mother as a discursive technology active in the government of mothers. Perhaps excluding the unfit mother from Ontario's child protection regime by explicitly refuting or rejecting the notion that the virtue of a mother is adjudicated in child protection proceedings in the preamble to the CFSA may have some efficacy. However, law reform alone will not address important dimensions of the situation. Concerted efforts are necessary to reeducate officials in a wide variety of capacities as well as the general public. Efforts to deliberately reconfigure of mothers and mothering in popular discourses may be at least as important as formal law reform in creating change.

The significance of child protection decisions is underscored by the match between demographic disproportions in child protective care and incarceration rates of the same demographic groups. Black and Aboriginal children compose more than their share of children in state care, whereas black and Aboriginal adults make up a disproportionately large number of incarcerated adults. Research has shown a conduit from state care as a child welfare ward to criminalization and incarceration—the "cradle to prison pipeline" (Jones). Addressing the social construct of the unfit mother may help combat over-incarceration.

ENDNOTES

[1]As explained by Claudia Castaneda, figuration is the process by which a representation is given a particular form: "a figure is the simultaneously material and semiotic product of certain [discursive] processes." A figuration is "a specific configuration of knowledges, practices and power" (47). Accordingly, I qualitatively studied texts from media sources and official legal texts addressing child protection in Ontario to determine what figurations of the "mother" emerge in these cultural domains.

[2]The child welfare laws, and grounds for apprehension, of other Canadian jurisdictions operate similarly to those of Ontario but their specifics are beyond the scope of this research.

[3]As follows: In this Act, a reference to a child's parent shall be deemed to be a reference to,

(a) both parents, where both have custody of the child;

(b) one parent, where that parent has lawful custody of the child

or the other parent is unavailable or unable to act as the context requires; or
(c) another individual, where that individual has lawful custody of the child.

WORKS CITED

Legislation

Ontario's Child and Family Services Act RSO 1990 c. 1

Caselaw

(C.A.) v. Children's Aid Society of Hamilton-Wentworth, 1980 CanLII 236 (ON SC) [1980] OJ No 1901 (QL); 2 ACWS (2d) 363.
Syl Apps Secure Treatment Centre v. B.D., 2007 SCC 38
Valoris v. Jina Ramlall and Christopher Lanston, 2015 ON SC 207

Other Sources

Anderssen, Erin. "Let's Stop Pointing the Finger at Mothers and Address the Real Issues around Children's Health." *The Globe and Mail*, 1 Dec. 2014, www.theglobeandmail.com/life/parenting/flipping-a-non-motherly-gesture-at-sexist-science/article21833778/. Accessed 11 Jan. 2017.
Arendell T. "Hegemonic Motherhood: Deviancy Discourses and Employed Mothers' Accounts of Out-of-School Time Issues." Working Paper no. 9. *Centre for Working Families*. University of California, 1999.
Bala et al. *Canadian Child Welfare Law: Children, Families and the State*, edited by Nicholas Bala et al., Thompson Educational Publishing, 1991.
Calavita, Kitty. *Invitation to Law & Society: An Introduction to the Study of Real Law*. University of Chicago Press, 2010.
Castaneda, Claudia. *Figurations: Child, Bodies, Worlds*. Duke University Press, 2002.
Chambers, Lori. *Misconceptions: Unmarried Motherhood and the Ontario Children of Unmarried Parents Act, 1921-1969.*

Osgoode Society for Canadian Legal History, 2007.

Canadian Council of Child and Youth Advocates. "Aboriginal Children Canada Must Do Better: Today and Tomorrow." *Canadian Council Of Child And Youth Advocates*, 2011, www.cccya.ca. Accessed 11 Jan. 2017.

S. G. G. Edgar. *Craies on Statute Law*, 7th ed. Sweet & Maxwell, 1971.

Fairclough, Norman. *Critical Discourse Analysis: The Critical Study of Language*. Harlow, UK: Longman, 1995.

Goodwin, Susan, and Kate Huppatz. *The Good Mother: Contemporary Motherhoods in Australia* Australia: Sydney University Press, 2010.

Hall, Stuart. *Representation: Cultural Representations and Signifying Practices*. London: Sage, 1997.

Hughes, Judy, and Shirley Chau. "Children's Best Interests and Intimate Partner Violence in the Canadian Family Law and Child Protection Systems." *Critical Social Policy*, vol. 32 no. 4, 2012, pp. 677-695.

Johnson, S. P. "How Child Protection Workers Support or Further Victimize Battered Mothers." *Affilia*, vol. 23, no. 3, 2008, pp. 242-258.

Johnston, Patrick. *Native Children and the Child Welfare System*. Toronto: Lorimer, 1983.

Alexander, Michelle, *The New Jim Crow: Mass Incarceration in the Age of Colourblindness*. The New Press, 2012.

Kline, Marlee. "Child Welfare Law, "Best Interests of the Child" Ideology, and First Nations." *Osgoode Hall Law Journal*, vol. 30, no. 2, 1992, pp. 375-425.

"Locate a Children's Aid Society." *Ontario Association of Children's Aid Society*, 2015, http://www.oacas.org/childwelfare/locate.htm. Accessed 11 Jan. 2017.

O'Reilly, Andrea. *From Motherhood to Mothering: The Legacy of Adrienne Rich's* Of Woman Born. SUNY Press, 2004.

Nieuwhof, Toni "Kids and Divorce" *Ontario Family Law Blog*, 13 Apr. 2015, www.ontariofamilylawblog.com/2015/04/articles/divorce/kids-and-divorce/. Accessed 11 Jan. 2017.

Said, Edward. *Orientalism*. Vintage, 1984.

Sarat, Austin. "The Law Is All Over": Power, Resistance, and the

Legal Consciousness of the Welfare Poor." *Yale Journal of Law and the Humanities* 2 (1990) 343–79.

Smith, Nora A. "Empowering the 'Unfit' Mother: Increasing Empathy, Redefining the Label," *Affilia,* vol. 21, no. 4, 2006, pp. 448-457

Strega, Susan et al., editors. *Failure to Protect: Moving Beyond Gendered Responses.* Fernwood, 2013.

Toronto Children Aid Society. "Addressing Disproportionality, Disparity and Discrimination in Child Welfare: Data on Services Provided to Black African Caribbean Canadian Families and Children" *Children's Aid Society of Toronto*, 2001, www.torontocas.ca/app/Uploads/documents/baccc-final-website-posting.pdf. Accessed 11 Jan. 2017.

"What Is an Unfit Parent." *Wisegeek*, www.wisegeek.com/what-is-an-unfit-parent.htm. Accessed 11 Jan. 2017.

Manufacturing Ideologies of the "Bad" Mother

Aboriginal Mothering, "Neglectful" Caregiving, and Symbolic Violence in the Ontario Child Welfare System

MANDI VEENSTRA AND MARLEE KEENAN

THIS CHAPTER dives into the social and political entanglement of the label "bad" mother as it relates to ideologies of Aboriginal[1] mothering within the province of Ontario. It is difficult to ignore the extent to which Aboriginal mothering is problematized within the Ontario child welfare system. As a constitutionally mandated protective service, the Ontario child welfare system plays an instrumental role in manufacturing and sustaining ideologies of Aboriginal mothering as "unfit," with agents of the state surveilling and policing caregiving practices that fail to demonstrate prescriptive ideologies of intensive mothering.[2]

As authors of this chapter, we come to this research as white settlers and are, therefore, inherently implicated in the project of settler colonialism in Canada. As we theorize and place into context Aboriginal mothering, we recognize that we do not have the "authority of knowledge" to carefully depict particular lived experiences (Lugones and Spelman 24). Although we do have experiences in the fields of mothering and child welfare, our positionality cannot claim understanding Aboriginal experiences past our immersion of academic texts and research into social and political policies. Ultimately, this chapter seeks to critique one of the most significant state structures that maintain the marginalization of Aboriginal peoples— namely the child welfare system—to shed light on the ways in which the system continues to reinforce the earlier violence of the white settler state. In this respect, this research strives to contribute to (if even just in small part) the broader goal of decolonizing Canada.

Today, Aboriginal children—referring to children of Inuit, Métis, and First Nations descent across Canada—continue to be removed en masse from their communities and are exceedingly overrepresented at all phases in child welfare decision making (Chabot et al. 98). Provincially and territorially, Aboriginal children involved in substantiated child maltreatment investigations and out-of-home care placements represent anywhere from 9 percent involvement, in Ontario for example (Fallon et al. 66), to findings of 90 percent evidenced in regions of Manitoba (Baum).

With the application of a Bourdieusian framework, this chapter argues that the state's ongoing erasure of colonial violence is evidenced through Ontario child welfare practices and policy, including the normalization of Aboriginal child apprehensions. This chapter will demonstrate that white settler practices in Canada created conditions of material and social marginalization and inequality, which, over time, became naturalized as part of Aboriginal heritage. This naturalized image of "neglectful"[3] existence, including the subjective determination of neglectful mothering practices, continues to be sustained by the child welfare practices of removing children from their families rather than addressing the real causes that create the deplorable conditions under which some Aboriginal families live. In this way, the experiences of Aboriginal mothering, and the state's manufactured ideologies of the "bad" Aboriginal mother, cannot be understood outside of the legacy of colonization (Cull 153; Reich 42; Waterfall 60). We focus on what Bourdieu refers to as symbolic violence, evident in the state's construction of child neglect and the normalization of generative schemes in the reproduction and manufactured stereotype of the unfit Aboriginal mother. It is important to convey that although the focus of this chapter is on Aboriginal caregiving within the context of Ontario child welfare, we recognize that there exists further social identities and racialized bodies involved with the child welfare system today. For example, in 2014 the Toronto Children's Aid Society highlighted the overrepresentation of black families of Caribbean descent in the Toronto district (Contenta et al.). The issue remains that in the intersecting literature on mothering and child welfare, there exists a disparity and disconnect of a representative landscape (Swift and Callahan). Although the

Commission on Sustainable Child Welfare, a provincial mandate from 2009 to 2012, recommends that racial and ethnic data be collected by all agencies, Contenta and colleagues note that the Ontario government refuses to mandate such a collection and the few agencies that do collect this data are reluctant to speak to it. Respectively, this chapter seeks to highlight the ways in which contemporary child welfare in Ontario acts as another colonial strategy that specifically targets Aboriginal communities through the forceful removal of these children from their families.

A BOURDIEUSIAN FRAMEWORK

This chapter theoretically draws on the analytic concepts of Pierre Bourdieu, including his discussion of field, capital, habitus, and particularly processes of symbolic violence. The application of a Bourdieusian framework provides insight and explanation into how and why the bad mother label becomes synonymous with marginalized women and, more specifically, with Aboriginal mothers.

Employing the concept of "field," the field of mothering can be seen as the social arena in which the struggles of mothering take place over specific resources or stakes and access to them. Each field, including the field of mothering, has a different logic and hegemonic structure of necessity and relevance (Jenkins 84). Within the field of mothering, it is argued that the social institution of child welfare—governed and funded by the state—serves as a regulating mechanism of control over what constitutes adequate and inadequate caregiving practices. This control subsequently includes the authority to subjectively interpret child welfare policy, including the introduction of "neglect" in reforms to The Child and Family Services Act in 2000 as a classification of child maltreatment. Together with governing policy, agents of the state and gatekeepers of the field—including social workers, supervisors, police officers, lawyers, and judges—possess the necessary capital, class, and attributed power to persecute and label.

For Bourdieu, "habitus" is central to participation within a field. Although all mothers are considered players within the field, their habitus, positioning, and access to capital vary. To participate within the field of mothering and to successfully play the game, or arguably try to avoid state gaze and surveillance, one must, according to Bourdieu, "possess at least the minimum amount of knowledge, or skill or talent to be accepted as a legitimate player" (Bourdieu, *Cultural Production* 8). Applied to the field of mothering and its intersection with the field of child welfare, upholding and performing ideologies of intensive mothering arguably project a position of good standing and legitimacy within the field. Although the interests and boundaries of the field are "imprecise and shifting," players are generally "concerned with the preservation or improvement of their positions," including the acquisition of relevant capital required to do so (Jenkins 85). Although it is evident that all mothers are subjected to the state's regulatory control of caregiving practices, not all mothers are equally positioned or surveilled.

Within a Bourdieusian framework, the notion of habitus is fundamental in bridging individual experiences and the broader social structure. Habitus serves as the "mediating link" between individuals' subjective experiences and the ever-changing social world shared with others (Jenkins 75). Developed throughout socialization, the habitus includes cognitive and affective factors, which become embedded in both conscious and unconscious interpretations (Jenkins 76-77). The embodiment of habitus, then, understands that the individual dispositions of a mother, which contribute to the formation of the habitus, are primarily the regeneration (or lack thereof) of generative schemes of the dominant-held ideologies and institutions within society (Swartz 104-106).

Practices of mothering are produced in and by the encounter between habitus and its dispositions as well as the constraints, demands, and opportunities of the social field to which the player is participating (Jenkins 78). Furthermore, institutions—such as the media, politics, and medical and psychological experts—are successful in manufacturing and manipulating images of mothering ideals, which generates schemes that become embedded in dispositions, which in turn, affect practice. This being said, the construction and label of the bad mother serves in opposition to dominant cultural ideals; the label itself represents defiance in relation to the existing norms of the field. Additionally, it is critical to convey the important role mothering dichotomies and stereotypes play in constructing labels of both good and bad mothering. Practices associated with each dichotomy are socially defined in part by the practices of players who are differently positioned within the field; culturally defined practices of bad mothering are shaped by culturally defined practices of good mothering and vice versa.

As a social theorist, Bourdieu believes that we live in a world where perceived reality is taken for granted by members of society (Bourdieu, *Cultural Production* 2). He theorizes how "doxa" (taken-for-granted elements) and marginalization are the paramount inequalities that play out in social life. He unveils how power associated with symbolic capital generates a *symbolic violence* that legitimates institutions and individuals within a given field. As such, those that hold the greatest symbolic capital (consisting of prestige and honour) exercise power over those who hold less. This act of violence is often concealed in broadly acceptable and unquestioned processes (Bourdieu, *Cultural Production* 2). Symbolic violence is then, the subtle impositions of systems of meaning that legitimize and solidify systems of inequality (Bourdieu, *The Logic of Practice* 133; Bourdieu, *Pascalian Meditations* 172,188). As a result, experienced inequality and marginalization within the field is often naturalized and perceived as inevitable. While we recognize the various acts of resistance that take place within specific fields and the elasticity of the field to permit such practices—including a mother's rejection of such labels (or refusal to comply to the demands of a social worker for example) —we primarily explore the durability of generative schemes involved in processes of symbolic violence, and acknowledge the potential impact this may have on the intergenerational transmission of dispositions.

Julian Go, a sociology professor at Boston University, argues that Bourdieu's conceptualization of colonization is imperative to understanding processes of symbolic violence (50). Bourdieu theorizes colonialism primarily as a "relationship of domination" (qtd. in Go 55). In Bourdieu's fieldwork on Algerian society, he places coercion and racial privilege at the centre of his analysis to illustrate the "colonial state's monopoly on violence" (Go 56). Go comments the following: "Bourdieu argues that the colonial system entails distinct and logically necessary roles for colonizer and colonized: For the former, colonialism necessitates racism and paternalism, and for the latter, subservience and the adoption of related stereotypical behaviours" (58). Although these distinct roles Go references are stretched and challenged by acts of resistance, such resistance is often constrained by access to capital. In today's society the reproduction of the colonial order is masked by perceptions of the power of individual choice, with an emphasis on micro-level explanations rather than dissecting and understanding the intersection of both macro and micro processes—or structure and agency. Indeed, Aboriginal mothers, often constructed as bad mothers, experience symbolic violence as they are individually blamed for the difficulties they face as mothers. Child welfare authorities are often unable to recognize "the roots of those difficulties in the history and current structures of colonialism and racial oppression" (Kline, "Contemplating the Ideology" 318).

THE ONTARIO CHILD WELFARE SYSTEM

Today, the Ontario Ministry of Children and Youth Services is responsible for governing forty-seven independent Children's Aid Societies in Ontario (nine are controlled by Aboriginal groups and three are faith based). Agencies throughout the province use *The Child and Family Services Act* as governing legislation in compilation with risk assessment tools and standards of practice that are intended to promote consistency in processes of decision making, and address past scrutiny over subjective determination (Swift and Callahan 148).

Although this chapter does not dive into the evolution of Ontario child welfare policy over the last century, it is important to note for further context the substantial shift in categorizations of child maltreatment implemented within *The Child and Family Services Act* in 2000. Such a shift continues to significantly affect marginalized populations and negatively impact state-family relations by increasing the surveillance and scope of policing caregiving practices. Arguably a response to state scrutiny over the high-profile deaths of children while in state care in the 1990s

(Cameron et al. 4; Swift and Parada 3; Vandenbeld Giles 120-122), substantial policy changes undertaken in 2000 include the following: the introduction of neglect as child maltreatment; the classification of emotional abuse—with specific reference to exposure to domestic violence—as child maltreatment; the expansion of mandated duty-to-report obligations to include the public; and the inclusion of any perceived risk of maltreatment to constitute grounds for investigation and potential apprehension. Social work scholars argue that categorizations of what constitutes emotional abuse and neglect remain ill-defined within policy, and instead rely heavily on gatekeeper subjectivity (Swift and Callahan 11; Swift and Parada 3).

The most recent Ontario Incidence Study of Reported Child Abuse and Neglect (OIS-2013) provides a snapshot of the landscape of clientele involved in substantiated child welfare investigations across Ontario. Statistics from this study reveal that biological mothers represent 86 percent of involved primary caregivers, reinforcing gender stereotypes surrounding caregiving and associated maternal blame (Fallon et al. 68). The study confirms the marginalized social contexts in which many involved mothers navigate life for both themselves and their children: 49 percent of involved primary caregivers are victims of intimate partner violence, 34 percent are classified as having few social supports, and 27 percent experience mental health issues (Fallon et al. 70). The OIS-2013 reports 24 percent of substantiated child maltreatment investigations to be a result of neglect (Fallon et al. 55).

GENERATIVE SCHEMES AND THE REPRODUCTION OF BAD MOTHERS

The demands within the field of mothering are characterized by intensive mothering (Hays, *Cultural Contradictions* 122; Hays, *Why Can't a Mother* 412-414). Ideologies of intensive mothering require access to capital that is beyond, in most cases, what the habitus of the individual bad mother involved with child welfare is able to generate (McRobbie 136). By establishing the norms of the field as intensive mothering, it is argued that gatekeepers knowingly understand that some "players" will not be able to meet such standards. Furthermore, the dispositions and constraints of the individual mother's habitus are then determined to be in need of change or adjustment (McRobbie 136). This is evident in mandated parenting classes premised on the basis of the acquisition of knowledge deemed adequate by the state. The gendered habitus of the lower-class, and often racialized, mother becomes the site for understanding how "social inequalities are perpetuated as power relations [are] directed directly at bodies and the 'dispositions of individuals'" (McRobbie 140).

Symbolic violence is evident in the expectation that women are to fulfill tenets of white, Eurocentric, and middle-class versions of mothering, which is obvious in the state's past and current treatment of Aboriginal mothers and their children in Canada. The residential school system and the Sixties Scoop alone highlight the authority of the "field of power" in constructing classifications of adequate and inadequate mothering. By trying to reform subjects, the state was instrumental in manufacturing ideologies that the Aboriginal mother, and Aboriginal way of life, was unfit, constructing their children as in need of saving (Cull 141; Swift and Callahan 139; Waterfall 59). Since we argue that the state's manufactured stereotype of the bad Aboriginal mother still persists today, recognizing symbolic violence toward Aboriginal populations is critical in analyzing ideologies of the bad mother.

MANUFACTURING IDEOLOGIES OF THE UNFIT ABORIGINAL MOTHER

It is important to understand the category and label of the bad mother in its historical and cultural context. Bourdieu understands habitus to be "a product of history that produces individual and collective practices—more history—in accordance with the schemes generated by history" (Jenkins 80). History is continuously carried forward in a process of production and reproduction in the practices of everyday life (Swartz 115). This section provides a brief historical overview of the state's relations with Aboriginal mothers and their children across Canada over the last century, which acknowledges the importance of the history of colonization in current constructions.

Residential Schools and the Sixties Scoop: A Historical Overview

Since European contact, Aboriginal peoples in Canada have been subject to overtly racist and assimilationist policies, which have subjugated, segregated, and, in some cases, completely annihilated Aboriginal populations. These policies were designed to eliminate what Deputy Superintendent General of Indian Affairs Duncan Campbell Scott referred to as the "Indian question" (Royal Commission on Aboriginal Peoples 235). Marlyn Bennett and her colleagues argue that it is primarily through Aboriginal children, and the construction of Aboriginal caregiving as "inadequate," (9) that the Canadian government sought to achieve its objective of doing away with the "Indian problem" (Royal Commission on Aboriginal Peoples 240). Bennett and her colleagues remind us of the following: "the subjugation of our nations has always been through those whom we cherish the most, through those whom we hold out the most promise for our future and the next generation of parents. The tactics used to suppress Aboriginal nations has constantly been aimed at those who are considered our nations' most prized gifts—our children" (9). These tactics began primarily with the residential school system. Sonia Harris-Short has maintained that understanding the continued trauma caused to Aboriginal families and communities by child removal policies of the past is imperative to understanding the complex difficulties experienced by many Aboriginal families and children today (37). The purpose of this section is to outline the development of the various state policies sanctioning Aboriginal child apprehensions and to highlight settlers' constructions of Aboriginal mothering throughout these periods.

Lina Sunseri argues that colonization has fundamentally altered and dismissed sociocultural structures, including Aboriginal gender relations and families (147). Prior to colonization, women in most Aboriginal societies enjoyed a large amount of status and power. They were leaders in political, spiritual and military spheres (Smith 18). Cheryl Gosselin argues that prior to colonization, Aboriginal motherhood was highly respected among families, communities, and nations (198-199). The implementation of the education policy of the residential school system in Canada had a primary goal of achieving total assimilation of Aboriginal people into the body politic of Canadian society by systemically removing children from their families and communities (Lawrence 106). The schools were in operation from the 1890s until the late 1990s (Truth and Reconciliation Commission 3). They were administered by a church-state partnership, in which the federal government provided the funding and oversaw the administration of the schools, and the church was responsible for their day-to-day operation. There were eighteen residential schools in operation between 1838 and 1974 in the province of Ontario alone (Kozlowski et al.).

Suzanne Fournier and Ernie Crey argue that the mandate of the government-funded schools was to "eradicate all that was Indian in the children" and replace it with Euro-Western culture, knowledge, and spirituality (54). It was believed that Aboriginal children needed to be released from the shackles of their "savage" culture in order to "live the life of White children" (Milloy 36). As such, it was imperative that the children be separated from their parents, communities, and cultures, and be placed in the schools under the "care of a mother" in the form of "circles of civilized care" (Greenwood and De Leeuw 175; Milloy 38). Not only was the separation between mothers and children imperative to the socialization process, but it was also an attack on Aboriginal ontology—"on the basic cultural patterning of the children and on their worldview" (RCAP 431). More specifically, the residential school system worked to indoctrinate patriarchal norms into the social fabric of Aboriginal familial and community structures in order for women to lose their place of leadership within them (Gosselin 198-199). Through the separation of these children from their maternal knowledge and cultures as well as through the teaching of traditional gender relations and gender roles to reflect Euro-Canadian ideologies, which are clearly antithetical to Aboriginal ways of knowing gender and gender roles, admiration for and the leadership of Aboriginal motherhood was destroyed (Gosselin 199; Greenwood and De Leeuw 175). This transformation ultimately led to abuse, poverty, family breakdown, and internalized and negative understandings of female identities (Gosselin 199). Indeed, Gosselin argues that "the Residential School System can be viewed as the policing of Aboriginal mothers as it dislodged the centrality of women from the family and labeled their parenting skills as abnormal" (199).

In addition to the systemic attempt to erase Aboriginal language, culture, and spirituality, Aboriginal children attending residential schools were also forced to endure horrific levels of abuse and mistreatment in the name of discipline, which according to government officials was a virtue of civilization (Milloy 43). Aboriginal parenting was perceived as inherently flawed, lenient and permissible when positioned alongside European practices and norms because it was thought that these children could not become productive members of society without strict rules and harsh physical discipline (Radmore 31). Institutional intervention was thus required.

Aboriginal children were not only deprived of the opportunity to learn the traditions of their people, but also trained to be ashamed of Aboriginal practices, disrupting the passing of traditional practices from one generation to the next (Bennett et al. 16). The Truth and Reconciliation Commission of Canada (TRC) has recently stated that residential schooling was far more than an educational program; rather, the Canadian government used the schools as its main weapon in committing cultural genocide against Aboriginal peoples and in manufacturing Aboriginal caregiving as inadequate and unfit (57). Today, the trauma caused by the residential school system continues to affect generations of Aboriginal mothers and their abilities to love and nurture their own children. To apply Bourdieu's terminology, the intergenerational transmission of dispositions has been interrupted and affected by the experiences of the residential school system. Generative schemes that construct Aboriginal mothering as neglectful and unfit continue to affect the habitus of the Aboriginal mother. Rather than understand perceived neglect or carelessness in caregiving practices as a symptom of the intergenerational wounds caused by failed government policy, the habitus of the individual Aboriginal mother becomes the site for scrutiny and attributing blame.

THE "SIXTIES SCOOP"

During the second half of the twentieth century, the residential school system slowly began to phase out. However, as the schools began to shut down, the number of Aboriginal children admitted to provincial-territorial child welfare systems increased dramatically, as child welfare agencies replaced residential schools as the preferred system of care for Aboriginal children. The increase of Aboriginal children in care occurred as a result of an amendment to the Indian Act in 1951, implementing section eighty-eight, which extended provincial legislation to include the provision of child welfare services to all Aboriginal children and families living in Canada, including to those living on reserves (Walmsley 20). With the enforcement of this new legislation, provincial child welfare authorities had the power to apprehend Aboriginal children living on reserves for the first time. As a result, the number of Aboriginal children made legal wards of the state quickly escalated as Aboriginal children were removed en masse from their families and communities. Prior to this legislation, less than 1 percent of the children in care in Ontario were Aboriginal (Kozlowski et al.). However, by 1977, it is estimated that nearly 8.7 percent of children living in out-of-home care in the province were Aboriginal (Kozlowski et al.). Patrick Johnston, a researcher for the Canadian Council on Social Development, coined the term "Sixties Scoop" to name this segment in Aboriginal child welfare history (Fournier and Crey 88; Sinclair 66).

Despite the fact that this phenomenon was labelled the Sixties Scoop, the apprehension of Aboriginal children persisted long past this decade. By 1977, close to 20 percent of the total number of children in care across Canada were Aboriginal (Kline, "Child Welfare Law" 387). At this time, one in four status Indians had been separated from his or her family (Fournier and Crey 88). Fournier and Crey argue that if non-status and Métis children were included in the count, statistics would show that one in three children, and in some provinces every other Aboriginal child, had been seized from their families and made wards of the state (88). Once removed, it was highly unlikely for an Aboriginal child to be placed in an Aboriginal foster or adoptive home (Monture-Angus 192). Instead, thousands were adopted by or were fostered by white, middle-class families across Canada, in the United States, and overseas (Fournier and Crey 89; Sinclair 66).

Social workers arguably did not have the skillset, knowledge, or resources to address the poverty, disempowerment, and multigenerational grief that came as a result of colonization and the assimilationist policies of the residential school system (Blackstock et al., "Child Maltreatment" 903). At this time, reserves in Canada were approaching a state of emergency. They urgently required housing, safe drinking water, sanitation, hospitals, and clinics (Fournier and Crey 84). As a result, social workers justified their actions by arguing that the apprehension of these children was "in the best interest of the children," a rhetoric that continues to some extent today. There existed a prevailing view among social workers and policymakers that Aboriginal children would be more adequately cared for if they lived off reserve and in the care of non-Aboriginal families in order to "save them from the effects of crushing poverty, unsanitary health conditions, poor housing and malnutrition, which were facts of life on many reserves" (Blackstock et al., "Reconciliation" 61; Johnston 23). Rather than the establishment of programs and infrastructure to address such problems, social workers were mandated by the state to remove children (Blackstock et al., "Child Maltreatment" 904). Aboriginal mothers were blamed for these conditions and were portrayed as ignorant and unable to properly care for their children (Cull 143). These constructions were present in governmental reports dating back to the early twentieth century, which document the belief that high infant mortality in Aboriginal communities as well as the prevalence of tuberculosis was because of inadequate mothering practices (Cull 143). As such, Aboriginal mothers were constructed as inferior, inadequate, and unfit parents, which ultimately enabled the continued state intervention into their lives in order to "save" Aboriginal children from conditions deemed the result of individual difficulties rather than the byproduct of settler colonialism.

Child Welfare Today: Ongoing Symbolic Violence

The structure of Aboriginal child welfare services in Canada is rapidly changing. Concerns over the number of Aboriginal children entering the system as well as their treatment in the hands of provincial and territorial child welfare authorities, coupled with increased activism by Aboriginal peoples, set the stage for Aboriginal groups to pioneer federally funded child welfare agencies to provide services both on and off reserve. In Ontario, these efforts have resulted in the development of five delegated Aboriginal child welfare agencies, which are granted the authority to enforce *The Child and Family Services Act*, one urban Aboriginal agency serving Aboriginal families living in Toronto and six premandated Aboriginal child and family services offering a limited range of services (Kozlowski et al.). Bennett and her colleagues argue that Aboriginal-run agencies have been able to provide more culturally appropriate services to children, families, and communities, though in varying degrees (27).

The issue remains that although Aboriginal-controlled agencies have been granted more authority in providing services to their communities, Aboriginal children continue to be removed from their families and communities and are greatly overrepresented in the Canadian child welfare system. Cindy Blackstock and Nico Trocmé estimate that there are as many as three times the number of Aboriginal children in the care of provincial child welfare authorities today as there were attending the residential schools at their peak in the 1940s (1).

In Ontario, Aboriginal children represent merely 3 percent of the total child population (Sinha and Kozlowski 3). However, it is estimated these children represent 21 percent of all children placed in out-of-home care in the province (Sinha and Kozlowski 3). John Beaucage, Aboriginal adviser to the minister, highlights the difficulties in determining the exact number of Aboriginal children in care in Ontario, since not all families and children involved in child welfare choose to self-identify as Aboriginal and not all workers ask families if their children have Indian or band status despite requirements to do so (1). As such, these figures are likely much higher. Dr. Lauri Gilchrist of Lakehead University remarks, "Given the current child welfare statistics, the 'Sixties Scoop' has merely evolved into the 'Millennium Scoop'" (qtd. in Sinclair 67). Similarly, as Old Crow Chief Norma Kassi notes, "the doors are closed at the residential schools but the foster homes are still existing and our children are still being taken away" (qtd. in Truth and Reconciliation Commission 186).

DIFFERENTIATING BETWEEN NEGLECT AND EXPERIENCED POVERTY

The factors underlying the overrepresentation of Aboriginal children in the Canadian child welfare system are complex. Three cycles of the Canadian Incidence Study on Reported Child Abuse and Neglect (CIS) conducted in 1998, 2003 and 2008 demonstrate that Aboriginal children are more than twice as likely as non-Aboriginal children to be reported to child welfare services and removed from their homes due to neglect (Blackstock et al., *Wen:De* 8; Sinha, "Substantiating" 2083). However, when "neglect" is unpacked, it becomes clear that structural risk factors faced daily by Aboriginal families in Canada—such as poverty, substance abuse and poor housing—are strongly equated with parental neglect.

Vandna Sinha and her colleagues argue that although all provinces and territories recognize neglect as a form of maltreatment, no consensus exists about what constitutes neglect across jurisdictions; the way neglect is assessed varies across Canada. Neglect often consists of chronic situations that are not associated with a specific incident or event (Trocmé et al. 68). An example of physical neglect as defined by the CIS-2003 includes a child living in "unhygienic dangerous living conditions" (Trocmé et al. 68).

It is important to understand the risk factors that become equated with neglect in the context of the social and economic conditions faced by Aboriginal communities. These conditions are shaped by colonial policies and practices that "dispossessed people from traditional lands, disrupted functioning economic systems, suppressed First Nations cultures and languages, and separated generations of children from their parents" (Sinha 2083). Today, Aboriginal families in Canada live far below the general standard of living and experience poverty both on and off the reserve (Bennett 271-272). They are almost five times more likely to live in overcrowded homes because of the lack of affordable housing and are four times more likely to live in housing that is inadequate and requiring major repairs (Reading and Wien 8; Sinha et al., *Kiskisik Awasisak* 10). A large number of on-reserve homes are infested with mould and mildew as a result of overcrowding and improper ventilation, which has led to health problems such as severe asthma and allergies (Reading and Wien 8). Food security is also a prevalent problem as Aboriginal peoples are four times more likely to report experiencing hunger than non-Aboriginal Canadians (Bennett 272). Those living in more remote rural and reserve communities face considerable food insecurity as transportation costs of market foods in these areas are so high that healthy foods are unaffordable for most families (Reading and Wien 8). Access to safe drinking water continues to be a major concern on reserves across Canada. In 2011, 118 out of approximately 630 First Nations across Canada were on a drinking water advisory (Reading et al. 3).

Most children living in areas that are plagued by any one of these issues could be considered neglected by provincial child welfare standards. These economic and structural issues are further exacerbated by the intergenerational effects of colonial policies such as the residential school system and the Sixties Scoop, which separated generations of children from their families and, arguably, disrupted the transference of caregiving practices from one generation to the next (Fournier and Crey 90-91; Sinha et al., *Kiskisik Awasisak* 11). Intergenerational trauma has also been linked to negative individual behaviour—such as substance abuse, guilt, depression, and other psychosocial problems—which has undoubtedly contributed to present day involvement with child welfare services (Sinha et al., *Kiskisik Awasisak* 11).

Greenwood and de Leeuw argue that the child welfare system is practically predisposed to focus on Aboriginal mothers, who are much more likely to be lone parents caring for a higher number of children than their non-Aboriginal counterparts and face increased levels of poverty (177). These issues are justifications supporting the perpetuation of negative stereotypes, including the association of Aboriginal motherhood with social assistance. C.B. Radmore contends that this connection persists not because state policies have economically disenfranchised Aboriginal communities but because Aboriginal mothers are thought to be lazy and welfare dependent; they are perceived as unworthy of receiving financial aid (15). Furthermore, Randi Cull reminds us that the "drunken Indian" stereotype has serious repercussions on Aboriginal families, particularly on mothers who are already in precarious positions (151). When Aboriginal mothers experience addiction and substance abuse and the public and state ignore their complicity in the intergenerational trauma caused by colonial policies, issues of addiction become labelled as exclusively an Aboriginal problem.

A review released in the province of Ontario in December 2015 disclosed that the Motherisk Drug Testing Laboratory at Toronto's Sick Kids Hospital produced inadequate and unreliable results for hair-strand testing in thousands of child welfare cases across the country and has had serious implications for families; one positive result from the test was sufficient grounds for apprehending children and placing them in foster care. Between the years of 2005 and 2015, more than sixteen thousand people were required to have their hair strands tested at the request of child protection agencies. Hair tests were also used in six criminal cases leading to convictions (Gallant and Mendleson). Jonathan Rudin, program director for Aboriginal Legal Services in Toronto, highlights the importance of understanding the disproportionate impact that hair testing has had on Aboriginal peoples. He argues that at least one quarter of all families affected by the Motherisk failings are Aboriginal (Gallant and Mendleson). Although the Independent Motherisk Commission offers support and assistance to people affected by the results of the flawed tests, Rudin notes that the Commission can be particularly traumatizing for Aboriginal families (Porter). He asks that the Commission take the particular and unique circumstances of Aboriginal peoples into consideration: "Aboriginal people who have not only lost their children through child welfare but probably have a history of involvement in child welfare and likely residential schools—all those issues need to be considered" (qtd. in Porter N.p.). Although further data and information will undoubtedly emerge following investigations completed by the Commission, one thing remains clear: child protection agencies in the province who were requesting to test the hair samples of Aboriginal mothers were looking to prove that these women were impaired by drugs and alcohol, ultimately constructing them as unable to properly care for their children. It could be argued that these negative stereotypes, namely the "drunken Indian" construction, positioned Aboriginal women, particularly those with addiction problems, as more susceptible to this testing—once again attributing blame and scrutiny to the individual habitus of Aboriginal mothers.

CONCLUSION

Many Canadians believe that the separation of Aboriginal children from their families ended with the closure of the residential schools. However, as this chapter demonstrates, Aboriginal children are still being removed from their communities through policies enacted by the state, specifically evidenced within the child welfare system. We argue that the state is culpable for the ongoing symbolic violence experienced by generations of Aboriginal families. A brief historical overview of state-Aboriginal relations over the last century reveals a steadfast and concerning preoccupation with Aboriginal caregiving practices, which arguably involves the individualized habitus of the unfit Aboriginal mother. The habitus of the mother, including embedded inter-generationally transmitted dispositions, has become a dominant site for attributing blame for perceived child maltreatment. The difficulty in distinguishing neglectful mothering from experienced poverty and failed government policy, for example highlights the state's neoliberal focus of masking structural barriers as individualized problems. Furthermore, the ideological assumption that Aboriginal mothers lack adequate caregiving skills or that a particular race is deemed incompetent or incapable stems back to the valuation and persistence of white-Western patriarchy and assimilation, and a particular need to remedy the so-called Indian problem (Cull 146-151). The issue remains that the classification of Aboriginal caregiving as neglectful fails to consider the efforts made by many Aboriginal parents who, on a daily basis, manage their day-to-day realities, which are shaped by both historical and current structures of colonialism and racial oppression.

Though beyond the scope of this chapter, it is important to note that Aboriginal-led child welfare agencies are limited in their ability to develop and provide innovative and effective culturally based solutions and services to better the lives of children and families in their communities. As Harris-Short explains, these agencies "still have to operate under provincial mandate, apply provincial child welfare law, operate within the provincial governance structure and are ultimately accountable to the provincial ministry for maintaining provincial standards of care and protection" (116). Granting these agencies more say within these frameworks is merely a reform to an inherently colonial system, which continues to uphold the same colonial relations of power that worked to institutionalize Aboriginal children during the residential school era, during the Sixties Scoop and beyond, and constructed Aboriginal parenting as unfit and Aboriginal mothers as neglectful. The successful decolonization of Aboriginal child welfare can only be achieved when political and legal decision making authority over child welfare is fully restored to Aboriginal communities. Ultimately, it is our conviction that any real change must start with a radical transformation of the child welfare system and cannot end with reforms to a system that is inherently colonial in itself.

ENDNOTES

[1]We use the term Aboriginal throughout this paper. This term is used to describe a group of peoples whose ancestors were the original inhabitants of the land but whom are now governed by Euro-Western values, laws, and regulations. Our choice to use this specific term does in no way imply that we believe that all Aboriginal peoples are the same. We follow Paula Gunn Allen, who recognizes that there is a "wide diversity of tribal systems on the North American continent ... and they are as diverse as Paris and Peking" (qtd. in Hanohano 207).

[2]Referring to a concept developed by sociologist Sharon Hays, intensive mothering refers to the "dominant ideology of socially appropriate child rearing" in contemporary Western society (*Why Can't a Mother* 414). Tenets of intensive mothering are understood to be "child-centred, expert-guided, emotionally absorbing, labour-intensive, and financially expensive" (Hays, *Why Can't a Mother* 414).

[3]We initially use quotations around the concepts of neglect, as well as the dichotomies of good and bad, fit and unfit, adequate and inadequate to denote the degrees of subjectivity involved in

the interpretation of such terms and to acknowledge that they are social constructions. For readability and aesthetic purposes, we refrain from applying quotations throughout.

WORKS CITED

Baum, Kathryn Blaze. "Manitoba Vows to Strengthen Child Welfare Services." *Globe and Mail*, 27 Jan. 2015, www.theglobeandmail.com/news/national/manitoba-pledges-to-overhaul-child-welfare-system/article22651311/. Accessed 25 Jan. 2016.

Beaucage, John. "Children First: The Aboriginal Advisor's Report on the Status of Aboriginal Child Welfare in Ontario." *Ontario Ministry of Children and Youth Services*, 2011, pp. 1-28, http://www.children.gov.on.ca/htdocs/English/professionals/indigenous/child_welfare-2011.aspx. Accessed 10 May 2016.

Bennett, Marlyn. "Aboriginal Children's Rights: Is Canada Keeping its Promise?" *A Question of Commitment: Children's Rights in Canada*, edited by K. Covell and R. Howe, Wilfred Laurier University Press, 2007, pp. 265-286.

Bennett, Marlyn, et al. "Literature Review and Annotated Bibliography on Aspects of Aboriginal Child Welfare in Canada." 2nd ed. *First Nations Research Site of the Centre of Excellence for Child Welfare and The First Nations Child & Family Caring Society of Canada,* 2005, http://cwrp.ca/sites/default/files/publications/en/AboriginalCWLitReview_2ndEd.pdf. Accessed 26 May 2015.

Blackstock, Cindy, and Nico Trocmé. "Community-Based Child Welfare for Aboriginal Children: Supporting Resilience through Structural Change." *Social Policy Journal of New Zealand*, vol. 24, no. 1, 2005, pp. 12-33..

Blackstock, Cindy, et al. "Reconciliation: Rebuilding the Canadian Child Welfare System to Better Serve Aboriginal Children and Youth." *Putting a Human Face on Child Welfare: Voices From the Prairies*, edited by I. Brown et al., Prairie Child Welfare Consortium, 2007, pp. 59-87.

Blackstock, Cindy, et al. "Child Maltreatment Investigations among Aboriginal and Non-Aboriginal Families in Canada." *Violence against Women*, vol. 10, no. 8, 2004, pp. 901-916. *Research*

Gate, doi: 10.1177/1077801204266312.

Blackstock, Cindy, et al. *Wen:De We are Coming into the Light of Day.* First Nations Child and Family Caring Society of Canada, 2005.

Bourdieu, Pierre. *The Logic of Practice.* Stanford University Press, 1990.

Bourdieu, Pierre. *The Field of Cultural Production*, edited by R. Johnson, Columbia University Press, 1993.

Bourdieu, Pierre. *Pascalian Meditations.* Stanford University Press, 2000.

Cameron, Gary, et al. "Positive Possibilities for Child and Family Welfare: Expanding the Anglo-American Child Protection Paradigm." *Moving toward Positive Systems of Child and Family Welfare*, edited by G. Cameron et al., Wilfred Laurier University Press, 2007.

Chabot, Martin, et al. "Exploring Alternate Specifications to Explain Agency-Level Effects in Placement Decisions Regarding Aboriginal Children: Further Analysis of the Canadian Incidence Study of Reported Child Abuse and Neglect Part C." *Child Abuse & Neglect*, vol. 49, no. 1, 2015, pp. 97-106. *PubMed*, doi: 10.1016/j.chiabu.2015.04.012.

Contenta, Sandro, et al. "Why Are So Many Black Children in Foster Care and Group Homes?" *Toronto Star.* 11 Dec. 2014. Accessed 1 June 2015. https://www.thestar.com/news/canada/2014/12/11/why_are_so_many_black_children_in_foster_and_group_homes.html

Cull, Randi. "Aboriginal Mothering Under the State's Gaze." *"Until Our Hearts Are On the Ground": Aboriginal Mothering, Oppression, Resistance, and Rebirth*, edited by D.M. Lavell-Harvard and J. Corbiere Lavell, Demeter Press, 2006, pp. 141-156.

Fallon, Barbara, et al. *Ontario Incidence Study of Reported Child Abuse and Neglect-2013 (OIS-2013).* Child Welfare Research Portal, 2015, http://cwrp.ca/publications/OIS-2013. Accessed 16 Dec. 2015.

Fournier, Suzanne, and Ernie Crey. *Stolen From Our Embrace: The Abduction of First Nations Children and the Restoration of Aboriginal Communities.* Douglas & McIntyre, 1997.

Gallant, Jacques, and Rachel Mendleson. "Damning Review of

Motherisk Drug Testing Sparks Call for Second Probe." *The Toronto Star*, 18 Dec. 2015, www.thestar.com/news/gta/2015/12/17/review-of-motherisk-drug-testing-sparks-call-for-public-inquiry.html. Accessed 29 May 2016.

Go, Julian. "Decolonizing Bourdieu: Colonial and Postcolonial Theory in Pierre Bourdieu's Early Work." *Sociological Theory*, vol. 31, no.1, 2013, pp. 49-74. *Phil Papers*, doi: 10.1177/0735275113477082

Gosselin, Cheryl. "'They Let Their Kids Run Wild': The Policing of Aboriginal Mothers in Quebec." *"Until Our Hearts Are On the Ground": Aboriginal Mothering, Oppression, Resistance, and Rebirth*, edited by D.M. Lavell-Harvard and J. Corbiere Lavell, Demeter Press, 2006, pp. 196-206.

Greenwood, Margo, and Sarah De Leeuw. "Fostering Indigeneity: The Role of Aboriginal Mothers and Aboriginal Early Child Care in Responses to Colonial Foster-Care Interventions." *"Until Our Hearts Are On the Ground": Aboriginal Mothering, Oppression, Resistance, and Rebirth*, edited by D.M. Lavell-Harvard and J. Corbiere Lavell, Demeter Press, 2006, pp. 173-183.

Hanohano, Peter. "The Spiritual Imperative of Native Epistemology: Restoring Harmony and Balance to Education." *Canadian Journal of Native Education*, vol. 23, no. 2, 1999, pp. 206-226. *Research Gate*, www.researchgate.net/publication/234646118_The_Spiritual_Imperative_of_Native_Epistemology_Restoring_Harmony_and_Balance_to_Education. Accessed 27 Dec. 2015.

Harris-Short, Sonia. *Aboriginal Child Welfare, Self-Government and the Rights of Indigenous Children*. Ashgate Publishing Limited, 2012.

Hays, Sharon. *The Cultural Contradictions of Motherhood*. Yale University Press, 1996.

Hays, Sharon. "Why Can't a Mother Be More Like a Businessman?" *Maternal Theory: Essential Readings*, edited by Andrea O'Reilly, Demeter Press, 2009, pp. 408-430.

Jenkins, Richard. *Pierre Bourdieu*. Routledge, 1992.

Johnston, Patrick. *Native Children and the Child Welfare System*. James Lorimer & Company Limited, 1983.

Kline, Marlee. "Child Welfare Law, 'Best Interest of the Child' Ideology, and First Nations." *Osgoode Hall Law Journal*, vol.

30, no. 2, 1992, pp. 376-425.

Kline, Marlee. "Contemplating the Ideology of Motherhood: Child Welfare Law and First Nations Women." *Queen's Law Journal*, vol. 18, no. 2, 1993, pp. 306-342.

Kozlowski, Anna, et al. "First Nations Child Welfare in Ontario." CWRP Information Sheet #100E. *Centre for Research on Children and Families*, 2012, cwrp.ca/infosheets/first-nations-child-welfare-ontario. Accessed 11 May 2016.

Lawrence, Bonita. *"Real" Indians and Others: Mixed-Blood Urban Native Peoples and Indigenous Nationhood*. University of Nebraska Press, 2004.

Lugones, Maria and Elizabeth Spellman. "Have We Got a Theory for You! Feminist Theory, Cultural Imperialism and the Demand for "The Woman's Voice."" *Feminist Theory: A Reader*. 4th ed, edited by Wendy K. Kolmar and Frances Bartkowski, McGraw-Hill, 2013, pp. 17-24.

McRobbie, Angela. *The Aftermath of Feminism*. Sage Publications, 2009.

Milloy, John S. *A National Crime: The Canadian Government and the Residential School System, 1879 to 1986*. The University of Manitoba Press, 1999.

Monture-Angus, Patricia. *Thunder in My Soul: A Mohawk Woman Speaks*. Fernwood Publishing, 1995.

Porter, Jody. "Motherisk Commission Must Heed Aboriginal Concerns, Lawyer Says." *CBC News*, 4 Jan. 2016, www.cbc.ca/news/canada/thunder-bay/motherisk-commission-must-heed-aboriginal-concerns-lawyer-says-1.3385836. Accessed 29 May 2016.

Radmore, C.B. *The New "White Man's Burden": Legal and Press Media Discourses on MS.G., A Vilified Indigenous Mother*. Dissertation, Trent University, 2011.

Reading, Charlotte Loppie, and Fred Wien. *Health Inequalities and Social Determinants of Aboriginal Peoples' Health*. National Collaborating Centre for Aboriginal Health, 2009.

Reading, Jeff, et al. *Crisis on Tap: Seeking Solutions for Safe Water for Indigenous Peoples*. Centre for Aboriginal Health Research, 2011, http://ir.lib.uwo.ca/aprci/211/. Accessed 4 January 2016.

Reich, Jennifer A. *Fixing Families: Parents, Power, and the Child Welfare System*. Routledge, 2005.

Royal Commission on Aboriginal Peoples (RCAP). *Report of the Royal Commission on Aboriginal Peoples. Vol. 1. Looking Forward, Looking Back.* Indian and Northern Affairs Canada, 1996.

Sinclair, Raven. "Identity Lost and Found: Lessons From the Sixties Scoop." *First Peoples Child* and *Family Review*, vol. 3, no. 1, 2007, pp. 65-82, journals.sfu.ca/fpcfr/index.php/FPCFR/article/view/25. Accessed 10 Jan. 2016.

Sinha, Vandna, and Anna Kozlowski. "The Structure of Aboriginal Child Welfare in Canada." *The International Indigenous Policy Journal*, vol. 4, no. 2, 2013, pp.1-21, http://ir.lib.uwo.ca/iipj/vol4/iss2/2/. Accessed 10 May 2016.

Sinha, Vandna, et al. *Kiskisik Awasisak: Remember the Children. Understanding the Overrepresentation of First Nations Children in the Child Welfare System.* Assembly of First Nations, 2011.

Sinha, Vandna, Stephen Ellenbogen, and Nico Tocmé. "Substantiating Neglect in First Nations and Non-Aboriginal Children." *Children and Youth Services Review*, vol. 35, no.1, 2013, pp. 2080-2090.

Smith, Andrea. *Conquest: Sexual Violence and American Indian Genocide.* South End Press, 2005.

Sunseri, Lina. "Moving Beyond the Feminism versus Nationalism Dichotomy: An Anti-Colonial Feminist Perspective on Aboriginal Liberation Struggles." *Canadian Women Studies*, vol. 20, no. 2, 2010, pp. 143-148.

Swartz, David. *Culture and Power: The Sociology of Pierre Bourdieu.* The University of Chicago Press, 1997.

Swift, Karen and Henry Parada. "Child Welfare Reform: Protecting Children or Policing the Poor?" *Journal of Law and Social Policy*, vol. 19, 2004, pp. 1-17.

Swift, Karen and Marilyn Callahan. *At Risk: Social Justice in Child Welfare and Other Human Services.* University of Toronto Press, 2009.

Trocmé, Nico, et al. "The Experience of First Nations Children Coming into contact with the Child Welfare System in Canada: The Canadian Incidence Study on Reported Abuse and Neglect." *Wen:De We are Coming into the Light of Day*, edited by Cindy Blackstock, First Nations Child and Family Caring Society of Canada, 2005, pp. 60-86.

Truth and Reconciliation Commission of Canada (TRC). *Honouring the Truth, Reconciling for the Future: Summary of the Final Report of the Truth and Reconciliation Commission of Canada.* The Truth and Reconciliation Commission of Canada, 2015.

Vandenbeld Giles, Melinda. "From "Need" to "Risk": The Neoliberal Construction of the "Bad" Mother." *Journal of the Motherhood Initiative for Research and Community Involvement*, vol. 3, no. 1, 2012, pp. 112-133.

Walmsley, Christopher. *Protecting Aboriginal Children.* University of British Columbia Press, 2005.

Waterfall, Barbara. "Native Peoples and the Social Work Profession." *Canadian Social Policy: Issues and Perspectives.* 3rd ed. Edited by Anne Westhues, Wilfrid Laurier University Press, pp. 50-66.

Mothering in Prison

The Case of Spain's New External Mother Units[1]

SOPHIE FEINTUCH

INCARCERATED WOMEN have long been castigated not only for breaking the social contract by committing a crime but also for failing to embody the maternal and feminine qualities expected of them. In recent years, prison reforms and alternatives for female offenders— especially for mothers—have been increasing in many countries, including Spain, the US, Australia, Canada, and Germany (Penal Reform International). Yet the implications of new programs have not been fully studied, and their development begs new questions about the shifting landscape of mothering behind bars.

This chapter offers an analysis of the experience of mothering in one such new initiative, Spain's external mother units. These units represent a new step and go beyond the more typical internal prison nurseries that many nations established as facilities within prisons for mothers and their young children. No literature had addressed the external mother units prior to my research. Here, I argue that although these units offer a clear improvement to prior programs, their structure and programming (re)produce a white, Western, middle-class idealized vision of motherhood and rehabilitation—which is inconsistent with the background of most of the imprisoned women—and motherhood is used as a source of control.

Following a contextualization of the development of the Spanish units and a discussion of my methodology, I analyze how certain program elements impede the progressive intentions behind the units. I then explore the ways program facilitators (guards, volunteers, social workers, nursery school teachers, and administrators) speak of the incarcerated mothers, and provide insight into the justification for certain programs, the experience of mothering in prison, and the reproduction of class hierarchies. Finally, I examine the incarcerated women's views on the shift from prison nurseries to the new units, the challenges and negotiations that they undertake in parenting while incarcerated, and the ways they demonstrate resistance.

BACKGROUND

The issue of what to do with the children of incarcerated women arises throughout the world, and although approaches vary, most states offer some program or facility to allow women to care for their babies and young children inside the prison walls. This concern has grown in recent years, as global rates of female incarceration have continued to rise in the early twenty-first century, with a large proportion of these women being mothers (Penal Reform International). Although women still comprise a minority of prisoners around the world, their rate of incarceration rose 50 percent between 2000 and mid-2015, whereas overall imprisonment rates increased by only eighteen percent (Walmsley).

Incarcerated women tend to have committed drug-related and nonviolent crimes, receive fewer services than their male counterparts, and serve their sentences in inappropriate facilities (Penal Reform International). Scholarship has indicated that incarcerated mothers face a range of added difficulties. Women tend to be the sole or primary caregivers before incarceration, and imprisonment results in separation from children in most cases, as the majority of countries do not allow children above the age of three to live in prison nurseries (Robertson). Studies have shown these mothers often experience a high degree of emotional trauma from concern for their children, including feelings of guilt, anxiety, and shame (Taylor; Ferrero and Moe). Research has also highlighted that incarcerated mothers struggle to balance their identities of mother and prisoner (Granja et al.; Berry and Eigenberg). The image of the "good mother" demands certain behaviours and attributes that conflict with images of criminals and inmates, and although many women want to be "good mothers," according to Kate Luther and Joanna Gregson, "within the total institution of the prison or jail, they are not able to satisfy the prescriptive ideals of motherhood" (85).

Prison nurseries mitigate some of these issues, as they allow mothers to continue to play an active role in the lives of their young children (Jbara). In spite of the long history of children living in prisons, the topic has remained largely invisible, and little research has examined the impact of these facilities on mothers. A few studies have looked at the experience of women raising children in prison nurseries and have shown positive results (Shamai and Kochal; Carlson; Eloff and Moen). Other studies, though, have indicated some negative aspects of prison nurseries, including the difficulties of raising children in a strict, institutional setting and the traumatic separation of children from their mothers when children age out of the programs (Jbara; Shamai and Kochal).

Spain has always had some type of accommodation enabling young children to live with their incarcerated mothers, and modern prison nurseries developed in Spain around 1989. The nurseries allowed mothers to cohabitate with their children up to the age of three and provided daycare centres, medical attention, and activities for the children ("Mujeres en prisión"). No publications discussed the experience of mothering in the nurseries, but a few studies examined the psychosocial effects on children growing up in Spanish prison nurseries, highlighting safety concerns and insufficient space and stimulation, which affected women's ability to mother (Morago).

According to their founders of the external mother units, they were designed to offer a unique alternative to the nurseries that would rectify these problems and address other common gender-specific challenges for inmates (Yagüe). Prison and justice ministries are rarely known for their feminist politics. Yet in Spain in 2004, the governing socialist party (*Partido Socialista Obrero Español)* appointed Mercedes Gallizo, a woman known for pioneering a regional feminist movement, as the director of the Department of Prison Services. She, along with assistant director Concepción Yagüe Olmos, spoke of wanting to lower incarceration rates, support educational and rehabilitative programs, and avoid unnecessary separation between convicted mothers and their young children. In this spirit, and in light of a government mandate to remove children from women's prisons, they devised a plan to build six external mother units apart from prisons and integrated in cities and towns, specifically to meet the needs of this population.

In contrast to the previous prison nurseries, the units would provide individualized attention, including job training. In line with the profile of this population, the government constructed the units without bars or electric doors. In fact, the founders' intention was for the inmates to have opportunities to leave the units to accompany their children to school, take classes in the community, and potentially work. The mothers would also get some respite from the intense experience of mothering in prison by sending their children to community daycare centres as well as out with family or NGOs on weekends and holidays. Additionally, the program would stress agency and empowerment by involving inmates in the development of the units, which is rare in prisons. The program would also allow children to stay in some cases up to the age of six (rather than three, as in the prison nurseries), and all efforts would be made to have mothers and children leave together rather than face separation.

METHODOLOGY

This chapter is based primarily on qualitative research that I conducted between 2010 and 2013 in Spain. In 2010, I carried out semi-structured interviews with nineteen incarcerated women and ten staff and volunteers in the units that were then open: Palma de Mallorca (*Unidad de Madres de Palma de Mallorca*) and Seville (*Unidad de Madres de Sevilla*), and in the prison nurseries in Aranjuez (*Centro Penitenciario Madrid VI, Aranjuez*) and Soto del Real (*Centro Penitenciario Madrid V, Soto del Real*). I also interviewed Concepción Yagüe Olmos, the co-founder of the programs. In 2013, I interviewed two facilitators involved in the newly opened external mother unit in Madrid (*Unidad de Madres "Jaime Garralda,"* Madrid) and spoke again with a volunteer in the external unit in Palma and with Yagüe.

Staff selected the women I could interview, with my only insistences being that participation was voluntary and that I speak to both Spanish citizens and foreigners. All of the incarcerated individuals I interviewed in the units had one child under the age of three with them. Some had entered prison with their child, others were pregnant, and a final group had gotten pregnant in prison through conjugal visits. At the time of the 2010 interviews, approximately two hundred women resided in prison nurseries and external units; thus, I interviewed roughly 10 percent of this population. About half of the women in the centres were non-Spanish citizens—coming mostly from Latin America and Eastern Europe. Oppressed minority groups have a disproportionate presence in the court and prison population, and approximately a quarter of Spain's Spanish nationals in prisons are of Roma ethnicity.

I chose not to ask the women about their criminal records, but many spoke of their sentence lengths, which tended to be approximately nine years. This was longer than the average sentence in part because the units were initially open only to women with long enough sentences to be able to undergo the full rehabilitation program. Staff told me that the majority had been convicted of drug trafficking. I also did not ask about their ages, but the women all appeared between twenty-two and thirty-nine years old. Interviewees maintained varying degrees of contact with the fathers of their children, and the majority were in relationships with male partners, many of whom were incarcerated themselves in other Spanish prisons or abroad. All of the staff and volunteers were female, non-Roma, white, and Spanish citizens, ranging in age from thirty-six to sixty-eight. Although I did not ask the staff about their own children, several talked about being mothers themselves. Most could be considered middle class. Unlike most of the incarcerated women, all of the volunteers, social workers, teachers, and directors had pursued higher education. The two guards had high school diplomas.

When interviewing my subjects, I began by asking how many children they had, where they were from, and if they had been in other prisons with or without their children. I invited them to speak about their decision to bring their children with them, the experience of mothering in prison, their family situations, and their contact with any older children they had who did not live in the units with them. I asked about daily routines, the positives and negatives of the units, and how prison conditions affected their children. I also inquired about contact with the outside world and rehabilitation opportunities. I asked staff and volunteers about their decision to get involved in this work, their responsibilities, interactions with the children, and opinions of prison nurseries and the units. As certain themes emerged—such as women getting pregnant to come to the units or not taking advantage of opportunities—I tailored my questions to learn more about facilitators' views of the inmates.

After conducting my second round of interviews in 2013, I coded the data, allowing themes to surface. The semi-structured nature of the interviews allowed me to shift my focus to the topics of greatest importance for the participants themselves. The theoretical issues central to this chapter arose through conducting a discourse analysis of the transcriptions. Although I began my research primarily interested in why Spain was replacing prison nurseries with external mother units, themes from my interviews regarding how staff perceived incarcerated mothers and the challenges of mothering in the new units took on a new importance, and oriented my research toward a critical look at mothering in prisons.

Recognizing that all research is inevitably biased, scholar Donna Haraway has called for "situated and embodied knowledge," to avoid generating irresponsible and "unlocatable" knowledge (88). My status as a white, middle-class, educated, American young woman without children inevitably influenced my research process—from the way I approached the topic to how I related to participants, selected questions, and coded data. Although greater distance separated me from the incarcerated population, during my interviews, prison staff and volunteers spoke to me as their equal. Throughout, I have struggled with being an outsider in Spain, a stranger to the criminal justice system, and to the experience of motherhood. My intention here is to "make visible [my] own critical positioning within the structures of power," as implored by Linda McDowell, to allow for a greater identification of my biases and shortcomings in narrating the experiences of others (413). All interviews were conducted in Spanish, and all translations are mine. Interviews were conducted in confidentiality, and the names of interviewees except for that of Concepción Yagüe have been changed.

ANALYSIS OF THE INTENTIONS AND RAMIFICATIONS OF THE UNITS

Spain's external mother units offer a progressive alternative to either separating young children from their mothers or keeping children in prison. Simultaneously, the program includes structural and programatic elements that reinforce a certain model of mothering and impede the realization of the official goals of agency and autonomy. This section explores some of these elements.

SURVEILLANCE AND CONTROL BY CARING

Although the incarcerated women may leave the units and have more control over their children's eating and care routines, they encounter greater vigilance than in prison nurseries. The switch from bars to a security system in which guards watch through cameras and lock the women's apartments at night may provide a more appropriate structure for female inmates who have not committed violent crimes and their children, but it should not be confused with staff having diminished control. Paula,[2] the director of the unit in Palma de Mallorca, explained:

> The women are evaluated every day in every aspect. From the cleanliness of their room to how they're dressed to how they interact with other women to how they do their work—absolutely everything....They have a good quality of life because there aren't conflicts, there aren't fights. They get used to the fact that everything is resolved in an educated and socially acceptable manner.... Then there's an evaluation system. If you don't behave well, if you don't do certain things, if you don't follow the rules, you can be kicked out of the unit.

Regardless of whether the women were abusive or committed other crimes that might suggest they would put their children in harm, they fall under extreme surveillance, which undermines their autonomy in parenting. Although Yagüe claimed that removing the child is never used as a threat, mothers know that they can lose their children if they are dismissed from the program; their compliance is intrinsically linked to a fear of being separated from their children. This type of control functions similarly to Michel Foucault's interpretation of Bentham's Panopticon in *Discipline and Punish*. As with the Panopticon, the mothers are uncertain about whether they are under surveillance and thus begin monitoring themselves and internalizing the domination. The units do not require bars; rather, the structure implores the women to inscribe the power relations in themselves and obey out of uncertainty of being watched.

Other program elements contributed to the creation of an environment where inmates were expected not only to behave in certain ways but also to change their inner goals and values to be more aligned to the idealized mothering expectations. This type of inner control, which is integral to the program design, can best be understood through Annemieke van Drenth and Francesca de Haan's concept of "caring power." The concept links power as defined by Foucault as a set of dispersed, productive, social practices with the use of care as a technique. Caring power is a type of control that operates through a commitment to the wellbeing of others. Though secular in nature, caring power aims at inner transformation. It is most often associated with elite women who, through their work of caring for and reforming other women, develop new identities for themselves (van Drenth and de Haan).

The first element that allowed for caring power was the fact that the program was voluntary. Rather than relying on force, caring power seduces individuals into conformity and obedience by providing them with material benefits as well as with hope for a more promising future. The founders made the program voluntary to ensure that the women were willing to change. The women were not forced to participate, and in coming, they were afforded better conditions and more opportunities for rehabilitation and training than in traditional prisons. However, the women were thus expected to change their priorities and care for their children in certain ways in order to find redemption. As such, mothering became a form of control in the units.

Nonetheless, it is necessary to look at what is required of the women in exchange as well as the extent to which the program can be considered voluntary. Once all the external units were constructed, prison nurseries were to be abolished, and then a woman's refusal to participate in the rehabilitative program would result in separation from her children. And once mothers agree to participate in the program, they must exhibit complete compliance and conformity with program values. Paula stated the following: "We offer training, and, in the future, once they have training, work. That's the general idea. And then just some basic education, such as their ways of dressing, their behaviour, respect towards the guards and the other women." Women must comply with programming developed by authorities who have come from different backgrounds, including modifying their dress and behaviour.

MATERNALISM

Maternalism—the female version of paternalism—and the idea that the facilitators know best is most evident in the mothering school, which all women in the program are required to attend. The co-founders and staff believed the school to be necessary. Yagüe explained it in the following way:

> Our psychologists are going to maintain all of the programs on strengthening mother-child relationships, on parenting, on hygiene, and on nutrition. Why? Because we know that many of these women come with really strange and unhealthy habits with regards to nutrition. They're very apt to give their kids solid food during the first few months of life. Or give them lots of junk. Or not have an eating schedule.

Obligatory classes presuppose that all incarcerated mothers need parenting training, regardless of how much experience they already have in raising other children. Mothering practices vary based on systems of race and class in addition to culture.

According to Patricia Hill Collins, "Motherhood occurs in specific historical contexts framed by interlocking structures of race, class, and gender, contexts" (56). In the case of the new mothering school, developed by white, middle-class feminists, the school teaches a Western, middle-class ideal of parenting as the norm to which all mothers should aspire. In doing so, it ignores and invalidates the various cultural heritages and practices of the incarcerated women who are primarily poor and come from all over the world.

Along with the problematic assumptions inherent in mandatory parenting classes, logistical constraints at the time of my interviews and deeper societal beliefs caused the job training and other programming to further enforce a specific model for the women. Governmental financial constraints coupled with an ideology of promoting community collaboration led to NGOs providing much of the programming. This meant many of the courses that the co-founders had envisioned did not exist at the time of my interviews. Despite the original plan for the units to be open and women to take advantage of skill-building opportunities in the community, interviews revealed that it was difficult for women to access community courses and the courses offered within the units were taught by the NGOs involved. Adriana, a mother in the unit in Palma, described all of the available courses: "We have a dog grooming course, haircutting, English, yoga.... what else is there? Cooking.... We have a course on hygiene and health habits that the Red Cross gives.... There's a self-confidence workshop. Ah, Fridays we have a workshop with the psychologists, which is like a group therapy. A sewing workshop, too."

Speaking of programming in Spanish women's prisons, Elisabet Almeda writes that the average woman in prison "is precisely the type of woman who, in the majority of cases, has rejected the most conventional feminine role; in reality [the programming] responds to the standard expectations of middle-class women" (52). The co-founders intended to teach more lucrative skills, yet program reliance on external NGOs resulted primarily in classes that reinforce middle-class homemaking expectations, which are reminiscent of century-long traditions of women's prisons aiming to mould incarcerated women into better homemakers.

HOW PROGRAM FACILITATORS VIEW THE WOMEN

Beyond these structural elements, interactions between program facilitators and incarcerated mothers were fundamental in shaping the experience of the mothers in the new units. Program facilitators in the new units had been selected specifically for transfer from other prisons, and their testimonies indicated that they were invested in the project and committed to creating a different type of facility with new opportunities for imprisoned mothers and children. Yet in my interviews, similar to staff of the prison nurseries, they often spoke patronizingly about the women, and their discourses tended not to consider crucial aspects of mothering in prison. These portrayals illustrate not only current Spanish societal attitudes toward incarcerated mothers but also the critical role of class and race in positioning subjects and in interpreting motherhood.

Not all facilitators expressed the same opinions about the women with whom they worked, and some were also careful to not generalize. Speaking of parenting, for instance, the guard Silvia stated, "There are good mothers and bad mothers, just like on the street." Nevertheless, certain themes emerged in the discussions of the incarcerated women: their decisions to either bring their children with them or get pregnant in prison, their efforts to maintain contact with older children, and the ways they raised their children.

Facilitators tended to disparage the women's mothering abilities, revealing a judgment system based on white, middle-class standards of intensive mothering that require mothers to be selfless and self-sufficient at providing the care themselves. Andrea O'Reilly has argued that "this normative discourse of mothering polices *all* women's mothering and results in the pathologizing of those women who do not or cannot practice intensive mothering" (7). Despite cultural contradictions and diverse practices, varying particularly based on systems of race and class, intensive mothering ideology remains the normative standard by which all mothering practices are valuated. These standards are particularly difficult for mothers in prison, given that the "good mother" ideals are also based on an identity as a white, middle-class, heterosexual, married, non-offending woman and because of the difficulties of mothering while not having autonomy. The following sections illustrate some of the most pervasive themes that arose in the facilitators' depictions of the mothers and their relationships.

DEPENDENCY

Guards, social workers, and volunteers often criticized the mothers for being highly dependent on those around them, both for material goods and emotional support. For instance, the social worker Gabriela insisted that the incarcerated women "[had] to learn to solve their problems. Because up until now, we hear, 'My kid has this problem' and, 'I need this,' and the institution resolves all of their problems." As Merry Morash and Pamela Schram have indicated about the experience of mothering in the few existing prison nursery programs in the US, "Inmate-mothers become dependent upon the institution for survival and are unable to take responsibility for themselves or for their children" (81). In the new units, the mothers were theoretically allowed to go out, but at the time of my interviews, none had been able to work outside the units because of logistical issues, such as a lack of public transportation to the city centre and strict rules about needing to be in the unit whenever children were not in school. Moreover, the women adhered to a strict schedule and had little power over their space, time, or lives, prohibiting them from taking initiative, being independent, or earning money. Yet reflecting dominant expectations of mothering in isolation rather than sharing the work, Gabriela and others saw the mothers' reliance on the institution as a sign of incompetent mothering rather than as a barrier to independence created by the prison system (Green).

Notions of the women as dependent extended beyond the units' walls, as facilitators believed that many of the women had ended up in prison because of an earlier dependency on men, which they believed was an impediment to being a good mother. As the social worker Natalia explained: "One of the biggest issues for the women is their dependence on male partners. When they get to prison, the men are the first people they want to call. Last month, I had one woman here who got here and needed to deal with where her children were going to stay, but instead, she wanted to call her partner." Furthermore, when volunteers, especially those financially supported by their husbands, criticize incarcerated women for relying on men, they demonstrate how women in prison and other socially marginalized women are held to higher standards than middle-class individuals. Moreover, this discourse fails to recognize that the majority of incarcerated women are not, in fact, economically dependent on men; rather, they are responsible for the economic survival of their entire families. To label them as dependent on men is to obscure the ways in which they exhibit agency, maintain their families, and reinforce a maternalistic environment.

SELFISHNESS

Program facilitators commonly criticized the prisoners for being selfish, as Lourdes stated: "They're all so selfish. I love them, but they're immature and selfish. They think of themselves before anything else." When referring to women who decided to bring their young children to the units, facilitators employed competing discourses of the need for children to be with their mothers and the belief that women only came for their own gains. At times, facilitators expressed sympathy and recognized that the conditions facing the women on the outside were challenging and that prison was sometimes the "lesser of two evils" for the child. Nevertheless, women's decisions were often seen to be selfish because the external mother units signified improved living conditions. Gabriela stated the following: "There are people [who] want their kids with them because they know it's better for their kid to be with the mother, and that's where they should be. And others who think only of how it will benefit themselves."

Several guards and staff members espoused the belief that mothers are indispensable to their children's upbringing in any situation. Yet facilitators such as Gabriela expressed discomfort with the ways that the mothers benefitted from the units, which implied that any decision that served the mother was selfish and was no longer in the best interest of the child. This attitude reflects and reproduces expectations of selfless mothering, in which according to Dorothy E. Roberts, "a mother is a selfless creature.... Because society defines women as caretakers of children, it subordinates women's personal needs and desires" (105). By making decisions based on their own needs or desires, the women fail to embody the ideals of motherhood in the eyes of the program authorities.

In a few instances, facilitators argued that women had gotten pregnant specifically to qualify for the units. According to Sonia, a middle-aged woman who volunteers regularly in Palma, "There are mothers who have kids to improve their situation in prison. It's crazy because the kids last your entire life." Questioning women's decisions to get pregnant reproduces class and race differences in terms of motherhood expectations; only certain women must justify their choice. Being in prison places women under a gaze that judges and demands justification for all of their decisions.

DIFFERENTIATION

Program facilitators presented homogenizing images of incarcerated mothers as coming from poor backgrounds, being dependent on those around them, and needing help to overcome their pasts. These images served to differentiate the facilitators, who sometimes argued the women were more competent mothers. Lorena, one of the guards, stated the following:

> We give [the incarcerated mothers] baby food. We give them medicine, diapers. We find everything for them. The food comes prepared. They have the option to study. Me, for example, when I'm outside, I have to take care of my daughter and organize myself if I want to do something else. Or I have to give up the chance to study more and do other things because I have to take care of my daughter.

Facilitators define themselves in contrast to the prisoners. They identify as middle-class, nondeviant, white, "good mothers," defining themselves in opposition to the others. As with caring power, these constructions legitimate the roles of middle- and upper-class women in the prison system, establishing them as authority figures, if not "saviours." Here, the criticisms of program facilitators underscore the impact of white and middle-class intensive mothering ideologies. They both illuminate how the dominant group views mothers from marginalized populations and shape how facilitators treat incarcerated women. These comments evoke a discourse of care rather than of rights and justice, which has a significant effect on the rehabilitative nature of the program. Discussing women's prisons in the UK. Mary Bosworth has reported that the women prisoners are assumed to be less confident and autonomous than their male counterparts; "Overall, there was a sense that they needed to be looked after rather than punished" (58). Much like in Bosworth's study, my interviews demonstrate the persistence of an infantilizing discourse and how it justifies programs focusing on monitoring, caring for, and teaching inmates to overcome their pasts to acquire Western ideals of empowerment in addition to selflessness to be "good mothers."

INCARCERATED MOTHERS' CHALLENGES AND NEGOTIATIONS

Having examined how specific ideals of motherhood were used to control inmates in these new units, despite intentions to offer women more freedom and opportunities than in prison nurseries, I now turn to the impressions and experiences of the mothers. All of the incarcerated interviewees in the external units had previously been in prison nurseries; some had also been in women's prisons in Spain or abroad without their children. The interviewed mothers revealed that they overwhelmingly agreed that these units provided better living conditions for caring for their children. Women praised the safety reforms, increased staff attention, extra space, and additional activities. They worried less about their children's safety and also felt that mothering was easier. They were able to stay busy and get along, making it easier to care for their children. The women also found it empowering to be able to help design the units and expressed pride in the ways that they had gotten involved.

Despite these improvements, women in the units still have to negotiate the challenges of mothering under adverse conditions, including deciding to bring children to prison, maintaining contact with family, balancing identities of mother and prisoner, and managing power relations. These processes complicate the homogenous image presented by program facilitators and instead show diverse individuals struggling to make the best of their situation. The following sections depict some of the main challenges that the women confronted in the new units.

NEGOTIATING PARENTING DECISIONS AND GUILT

In contrast to staff remarks that attributed women's presence in the units to self-interest, women recounted that their decisions to bring their children to the units were complex. They considered many of the same factors as in prison nurseries, with the caveats that on the one hand, the units provide better conditions but on the other, the small number of facilities often increases distance from family. For some women, the decision to have their children with them was evident and stemmed either from the belief that children must be with their mothers, a lack of alternatives, or a desire to mother. In some cases, women described their decision to bring their children as a personal sacrifice: As Alicia said, "I would have preferred to serve my sentence alone, because being with my daughter means I [face] twice as many problems.... I have to worry about her...it isn't the same." Alicia's decision illustrates one of the paradoxes incarcerated mothers face; if they serve their sentence alone, they are portrayed as abandoning their children. Yet if they keep their children, they are depicted as selfishly improving their own conditions.

When considering the best interests of their children, some mothers spoke of guilt and concern for what their children would miss. Valentina entered prison when she was pregnant with her son, who was two years old at the time of the interview. She shared the following: "In the beginning when you have him, it scares you a bit because you think, "What future will he have? If he needs things, what am I going to do to be able to buy them for him?" But then, as time goes on, you can do different things.

At the beginning, it's the fear of not being able to give your son what he needs. That's the first fear." Despite more spacious and safer facilities, women in these new units still expressed guilt from knowing that their actions had resulted in their child's imprisonment, as in prison nurseries. Opportunities for children to attend daycare in the community and go on fieldtrips mitigates some of the losses involved with growing up in prison, but women still contend with not being able to provide their children within a "normal" environment.

Similarly, women still have to deal with the guilt of not being present for their families. Given that women tend to be primary caregivers and held to higher expectations to support their families than men, studies have shown that the severing of family relationships provokes a larger loss for them than for incarcerated men (Sharp and Eriksen). The units partially address this gendered burden of incarceration by allowing women with family nearby to visit regularly and others to be granted furlough to other parts of the country. Rocío, for instance, was from Palma de Mallorca, and she was able to go visit her mom every day after dropping her daughter off at daycare. In general, though, at the time of my interviews, maintaining contact with family appeared more difficult because with the transfer from prison nurseries to a handful of external units, distances increased between where women who had been previously residing in Spain lived and the units. Women's financial situations also hindered them from being able to maintain the contact that the program co-founders had envisioned. In fact, phone calls and mail were also more difficult at the time of my interviews, as companies had been less willing to provide inexpensive services to these smaller facilities.

NEGOTIATING FINANCIAL BURDENS

Although the program co-founders hoped the program would help break cycles of marginalization, money has continued to be a determining factor in women's ability to take advantage of the programming. Adriana, a Brazilian woman without any family in Spain to support her, explained that "You have to buy a lot of things. For instance, a cream for my child, trash bags, dish soap....

You need money to go out on furloughs, too." Not only were the incarcerated women poor, but the units exacerbated their financial problems because of their size, as Adriana said, "Here there are two jobs that pay. So people who live here need to have money from the outside."

When I asked Sunnee whether she kept in touch with her family in Thailand, she explained that calls were prohibitively expensive, and she struggled to obtain money: "I have no work here. I have no money. Only my guy, he works." Sunnee could only maintain contact with her family because of her boyfriend, who was also in prison but had more work opportunities. Staff critiqued dependency in women's relationships without acknowledging the role the institutions played in increasing it. In cases such as Sunnee's, having a partner was a strategy to get by. An intersectional approach can be useful for exploring the experiences and challenges of foreign women such as Sunnee in Spanish prisons. The concept of intersectionality reminds us that the notion of gender on its own is not enough to explore the complexities of women's lives. Individuals all have multiple, shifting locations and are subjected to multiple systems of oppression and privilege. An intersectional perspective allows for a recognition of the ways that issues of race, class, ethnicity, and nationality all interact with gender (Crenshaw). The co-founders and program facilitators were all women who were aware of the gender inequalities within the prison system. However, the program does not account for the ways non-national women serve a triple sentence. Foreign women have fewer opportunities to get work out of the units because of labour laws and more difficulty maintaining contact with family given that they cannot take furloughs outside of Spain and must instead rely on exorbitantly expensive phone calls. The development of the units was unable to address any of these issues faced specifically by non-Spanish women.

NEGOTIATING IDENTITIES

Embodying both roles of prisoner and mother proves challenging for women and complicates how they explain their situation to their children, which, at times, can provoke clashes in getting their children to respect and listen to them. For this reason, as well as to not upset their children and maintain intact their identities, some mothers choose to lie to their older children outside the units about where they are, as Alicia does in her example: "He thinks that his mother is working out of the country and that she comes to see him whenever she can travel. It's the very common excuse of the mothers in prison. We don't want our kids to suffer. But it's difficult." Other women choose to tell the truth. Lina's five-year old was living with her sister back in Colombia, and Lina had told her the whole truth: She's a kid, but since she's really intelligent, she knows the whole situation. And I think that's better than if I lied to her. She understands that I can't go out, that I'm here as punishment because I behaved badly, exactly the same as how I teach her she can't behave badly."

Negotiating the roles and identities of mother and prisoner is a daily stress in many women's lives. Women in the units have more freedom than in the prison nurseries, and life is less marked by prison routines. For instance, guards do not obligate women to line up outside their rooms each morning for roll call as they do in prison nurseries, and guards and inmates all dress in plain clothes and refer to each other by first name. However, the women still have to find a way to parent while having limited control over their lives. They spoke of having to fulfill a particular role for their children that contradicted their role as prisoners and to hide their pain and display strength. As Lina explained, "For instance, with [my son], I can't cry. Because he's older now, and he asks. So I can't. I have to be okay for him. If I were alone, I'd be crying all day long.... With him, I know what I have to do. I have to be happy, and I have to be okay."

POWER AND RESISTANCE

Women in the units are not only under the surveillance of staff but also under the gaze of one another, which often centres on their mothering practice. Interviews revealed that women judge each other's parenting skills and, at times, call others bad mothers while criticizing others for getting pregnant to come to the units. For instance, Rocío, a Spanish woman who did not have any other children, believed others might be taking advantage of the system: "There are people who think, 'I have a long sentence. I'll get pregnant and great, I'll be able to go there. And they have kids. I don't understand it, but I think there are people who think that way.'" As Foucault posits regarding Bentham's Panopticon, power is inherent to the structure, and any individual can function as the observer, regardless of motives. Reminiscent of broader societal practices of surveilling lower-class mothers, here women in turn monitor one another at all times.

In the face of mothering expectations and policing of all behaviours, imprisoned women must find ways to cope. Foucault has argued that resistance is inherent in all power relationships (*The History of Sexuality*). Women's testimonies revealed forms of covert resistance in the ways that some complied with the general expectations of the program without adopting the underlying ideology or allowing the facilitators to dictate their identities or values. Some women rejected the notion that they were bad mothers, negated the idea that facilitators always knew best or were better mothers, and refused to terminate discouraged relationships with men. Despite staff attitudes and an institution that ultimately works to erase prisoners' authority and legitimacy, some mothers expressed confidence in their parenting skills. Patricia, a woman in the unit in Seville whose family lived nearby insisted, "I don't need anyone telling me how to raise my daughter. I know what she needs. I've had four kids before her, and I will teach her what she needs to know." Some women noted that they were better prepared to equip their children with the values they would need than guards and volunteers who came from different backgrounds. This was not unanimous, but it does imply that some women reclaimed a sense of maternal authority and rejected the capacity of staff to impose their own ideologies. Hence, some women's relationships with their children became sites of resistance. Despite the challenges, constraints, and negotiations of mothering alone behind bars, some women also found a sense of authority in dealing with their children that was often lacking in prisons. In small ways, they found that their relationships offered space to legitimize their own values and prepare their children for their own realities.

Some women also stood up for their choices of male partners. For instance, Alicia argued that her boyfriend in the nearby men's prison had a "very positive" relationship with her son and stated, "My son obviously has his mother, but he's always been missing a paternal parent. And little by little, that's being filled. We wouldn't be able to do it without him." Rather than letting staff members' criticisms affect them, these women continued their relationships and appeared to reject notions that they were incapable of choosing good partners or that staff member knew what they needed. Through these actions, they retained autonomy, not succumbing to abandoning their own beliefs and desires.

CONCLUSION

In general, interviews revealed that the women in mother units formed a diverse group with different priorities, outlooks, and mothering ideals. Some derived power within their roles as mothers, whereas others appeared to find their obligations to their children oppressive. Yet even those who seemed enthusiastic about living for their children and learning homemaking skills arguably challenge hegemonic notions of good mothers being white, middle or upper class, married, without criminal records, and able to prioritize their children. Their heterogeneous ways of coping with multiple forms of social exclusion and trying to raise a child inside a prison ultimately complicate visions of how women experience and interpret motherhood.

When interpreting the aims and implications of the units, it is important to examine whom this program excludes. Rehabilitation programs directed at mothers of young children reinforce the notion that these women are more worthy of rehabilitation than women of older children or women who are not mothers. Once again, women obtain their value through their mothering.

Overall, the external mother units—and other reforms underway internationally—are positive developments. The greater focus on rehabilitation and awareness of gender inequalities in penal systems offers opportunities to fight cycles of marginalization. Spain's external mother units may be unique, but similar initiatives are developing elsewhere. For instance, the Drew House, founded in

New York in 2008, has been lauded as a good practice because it offers a unique residential alternative to imprisonment predominantly for women who have experienced homelessness, mental health issues, or substance abuse to live in a nonsecure setting with their children. The facility is staffed by practitioners and peers rather than custodial workers, and unlike many programs, the Drew House does not exclude women automatically for violent crimes. Alternatively, Preungesheim prison in Germany considers mothering as a work placement for women with work-release privileges, allowing them to spend their days at home caring for their children of all ages.

In an age when female incarceration is continuing to grow worldwide, such programs and more alternatives are certainly needed to reduce the detrimental effects of incarceration on individuals, families, and communities. Yet, as is the case in Spain, it is necessary to employ an intersectional approach and look at the impact of the classed positions of those in charge. Spain's efforts demonstrate how boundaries between prisoners and staff members based on class and power differentials encumbered solidarity efforts. The external units are not solely a feminist project but rather a middle-class feminist project that maintains dominant notions of how women should mother that do not necessarily align with all women's needs. They offer a step in the right direction but more is needed to challenge the role of criminal justice systems in systematically oppressing certain individuals and to move beyond the oppressive nature of dominant motherhood ideologies.

ENDNOTES

1This chapter is based on my master's thesis, which I completed at Central European University and the Universidad de Granada in 2013.

2All names from interviews are pseudonyms, and all Spanish-English translations of interviews and texts are mine.

WORKS CITED

Almeda, Elisabet. *Corregir y Castigar: El Ayer y Hoy de las Cárceles de Mujeres. (Correcting and Punishing: The Past and Present of Women's Prisons)*. Ediciones Bellaterra, 2002.

Berry, Phyllis, and Helen Eigenberg. "Role Strain and Incarcerated Mothers: Understanding the Process of Mothering." *Women and Criminal Justice*, vol. 15, no. 1, 2003, pp.101-119.

Bosworth, Mary. *Engendering Resistance: Agency and Power in Women's Prisons*. Ashgate, 1999.

Carlson, Joseph. "Prison Nursery 2000: A Five-Year Review of the Prison Nursery at the Nebraska Correctional Center for Women." *Journal of Offender Rehabilitation*, vol. 33, no. 4, 2001, pp.75-97.

Collins, Patricia Hill. "Shifting the Centre: Race, Class, and Feminist Theorizing About Motherhood." *Representations of Motherhood*, edited by Donna Bassin et al., Yale University Press, 1996, pp. 56-74.

Crenshaw, Kimberlé. "From Private Violence to Mass Incarceration: Thinking Intersectionally about Women, Race, and Social Control." *UCLA Law Review*, vol. 59, 2012, pp. 418-742.

Eloff, Irma, and Melanie Moen. "An Analysis of Mother-Child Interaction Patters in Prison." *Early Child Development and Care*, vol. 173, no. 6, 2003, pp. 711-720.

Feintuch, Sophie. "New Spanish Practice Aims to Break the Cycle among Mothers and Children." *Corrections Today*, vol. 72, no. 6, 2010, pp. 38-43.

Ferraro, Kathleen, and Angela Moe. "Mothering, Crime, and Incarceration." *Journal of Contemporary Ethnography*, vol. 32, no. 1, 2003, pp. 9-40.

Foucault, Michel. *The History of Sexuality. Volume I: An Introduction*. Pantheon Books, 1980.

Foucault, Michel. *Discipline and Punish: The Birth of the Prison*. Vintage Books, 1979.

Granja, Rafaela, et al. "Mothering from Prison and Ideologies of Intensive Parenting." *Journal of Family Issues*, vol. 36, no. 9, 2015, pp. 1212-1232.

Green, Fiona Joy. "Feminist Motherline: Embodied Knowledge/s of Feminist Mothering." *Feminist Mothering*, edited by Andrea O'Reilly, SUNY Press, 2008, pp. 161-176.

Haraway, Donna. "Situated Knowledges: The Science Question in

Feminism and the Privilege of Partial Perspective." *The Feminist Standpoint Theory Reader: Intellectual and Political Controversies*, edited by Sandra Harding, Routledge, 2003, pp. 81-102.

Jbara, Anne. "The Price They Pay: Protecting the Mother-Child Relationship Through the Use of Prison Nurseries and Residential Parenting Programs." *Indiana Law Journal*, vol. 87, no. 4, 2012, pp. 1825.

Luther, Kate, and Joanna Gregson. "Restricted Motherhood: Parenting in a Prison Nursery." *International Journal of Sociology of the Family*, vol. 37, no. 1, 2011, pp. 85-103.

McDowell, Linda. "Doing Gender: Feminism, Feminists and Research Methods in Human Geography." *Transactions of the Institute of British Geographers*, vol. 17, no. 4, 1992, pp. 399-416.

Morash, Merry, and Pamela J. Schram. *The Prison Experience: Special Issues of Women in Prison*. Waveland Press, Inc., 2002.

O'Reilly, Andrea. "Introduction." *From Motherhood to Mothering: The Legacy of Adrienne Rich's* Of Woman Born, edited by Andrea O'Reilly, SUNY Press, 2004, pp. 1-24.

Penal Reform International. *Global Prison Trends 2016*. Penal Reform International, 2016.

Roberts, Dorothy. "Motherhood and Crime." *Iowa Law Review*, vol. 79, 1993, pp. 95-141.

Robertson, Oliver. *Children Imprisoned by Circumstance*. Quaker United Nations Office, 2008.

Shamai, Michal, and Rinat-Billy Kochal. "'Motherhood Starts in Prison': The Experience of Motherhood Among Women in Prison." *Family Process*, vol. 47, no. 3, 2008, pp. 323-340.

Sharp, Susan F., and M. Elaine Eriksen. "Imprisoned Mothers and their Children." *Women in Prison: Gender and Social Control*, edited by Barbara H. Zaitzow and Jim Thomas, Lynne Rienner Publishers, 2003, pp. 119-36.

Taylor, Rachel. *Women in Prison and Children of Imprisoned Mothers*. Quaker United Nations Office, 2004.

van Drenth, Annemieke, and Francisca de Haan. *The Rise of Caring Power: Elizabeth Fry and Josephine Butler in Britain and the Netherlands*. Amsterdam University Press, 2000.

Walmsley, Roy. *World Female Imprisonment List*. 3rd ed. Institute for Criminal Research, 2015.

Yagüe Olmos, Concepción. "Mujeres en Prisión. Intervención Basada en sus Características, Necesidades y Demandas." ("Women in Prison: Intervention Based on their Characteristics, Needs, and Demands.") *Revista Española de Investigación Criminológica*, vol. 5, 2007, pp. 1-23.

2.
MEDICALIZATION AS SOCIAL CONTROL

"ADD," 2013, polyester resin, plaster, steel wool, wood, iron rod, rope, 174 x 33 x 44 cm.

Mea Culpa

NOA ARAD YAIRI

I AM NOT a bad mother. In fact, I think I am rather a good one. I know my children think so. But I feel I am responsible for everything and that ultimately I am to blame. This is how I think society sees me. I remember a friend once quoted her mother saying that if a girl is fat, it is her mother's fault.

I used to be a heavy smoker. Two packs a day. I was sure that when I became pregnant, I would quit. I didn't. I am hesitant to say I couldn't. I smoked three to five cigarettes a day during both my pregnancies. I actually confessed only to three.

My son, the younger of my two children, has ADD. I know it has a lot to do with genetic inheritance. We have plenty of the ADD genes on both sides of the family. So it is not only my fault. And environmental factors can influence the tendency and severity of the symptoms. Maybe I should have switched to organic food years earlier.

But then, I did smoke. Research has proven that smoking during pregnancy increases the chances of ADD/ADHD. So then I am to blame! From that point in time onwards, I have felt responsible for any misfortune that befell my son. His failure in an exam, his difficulty in learning musical notes, forgetting the key ... anything at all, I had my share in it. So I tried to assist him as much as I could, reminding him to take the key, the notebook, the sandwich, the guitar, helping him with his homework, and even cleaning the room for him. As he grew up, he had difficulties at school and didn't believe in his own abilities. Eventually his therapist said that I had overprotected him, and this had made him feel that he could hardly do anything on his own, which added to his sense of incompetence. So there it was—I was to blame yet again.

"ADD (detail)," 2013, polyester resin, plaster, steel wool, wood, iron rod, rope, 174 x 33 x 44 cm

"Bad Mothers" and the HIV/AIDS Epidemic in Saskatchewan, Canada

PAMELA J. DOWNE

INTRODUCTION: RACHEL[1]

RACHEL, one of the emotionally and physically strongest women I have ever met, started to cry. We had been talking about her two children and their importance in her life when she stopped, midsentence, and recalled the day that they were taken from her care: "When you lose your kids, the sky goes dark. Like the worst storm in the world is coming. It don't matter how much you love your kids, if you got HIV, you'll lose your kids, and the sky goes dark. But the sun is back there somewhere, eh? We got to remember that. I don't know how, though." For Rachel, a First Nations woman from northern Saskatchewan, motherhood is a site of loss, surveillance, and judgment. Although many, if not all, mothers encounter sorrow and scrutiny (Landsman; Thurer), for Rachel—and most mothers living with HIV and addiction—scrutiny and fear are intense and all-encompassing. The "bad mother" judgment overshadows the love and nurturance that also characterize Rachel's mothering: "No matter how much I love my kids, give them all I got, I will never be 'mom enough' for the white, straight world."

In this chapter, I explore how this bad mother judgment figures into and impacts the lives of women, such as Rachel, who are living with or affected by HIV/AIDS and injection drug use. Between 2008 and 2013, I partnered with AIDS Saskatoon—the central HIV/AIDS organization serving central and northern Saskatchewan—in a project that explored motherhood and maternal care in the context of HIV/AIDS. The genesis of this project dates to the early 2000s when AIDS Saskatoon was moving locations from an office in a strip mall on a major thoroughfare to a house in a residential and core neighbourhood of the city. In its new location, AIDS Saskatoon can provide a larger drop-in centre with more services: laundry facilities, computer stations, donated clothes area, as well as a larger and more comfortable lounge. This expansion in services resulted in an increase in the numbers of women and families who began to access the safe spaces and peer support that AIDS Saskatoon could now provide. The (then) education and prevention coordinator contacted me to ask if I could assist AIDS Saskatoon staff in understanding the priorities, needs, and strengths of these women and families. A collaborative and community-engaged project was developed and undertaken with women who access AIDS Saskatoon services. A community advisory committee representing eleven other organizations throughout the central and northern regions of the province that offer HIV-related services and supports provided guidance and feedback throughout the project. The overarching question that was explored through narrative interviews, program access interviews, and a photo voice component was the following: what does it mean to be a mother in the context of HIV/AIDS? The women who participated in this research answered this question in nuanced and complex ways, but one response rang out with resounding clarity: being a mother living with or affected by HIV/AIDS means being subject to and engaging with the bad mother label.

REPRESENTING HIV/AIDS IN SASKATCHEWAN

Saskatchewan has the highest HIV rates in Canada. When this research was conducted, the provincial rates were almost three times that of the national rate. The epidemic is distinctly Indigenized, with the highest rates occurring among First Nations and Métis Peoples. Indeed, according to Health Canada, the rate of new infections on First Nations reserves in Saskatchewan is almost eleven times higher than national rates, representing a higher incidence than that of Rwanda and Nigeria (Vogel 793), and deaths from

HIV are four times higher than the national average (Salloum). Although HIV/AIDS is not seen by most Saskatchewan residents as affecting their own community, there has been a fairly significant public profiling of the epidemic and the media headlines paint a grim picture (McDowell et al. 4). Ken MacQueen's 2015 feature article in Maclean's magazine, for example, declares that "Third World levels of HIV infection rates in one of the world's wealthiest countries are a national disgrace" whereas Geoff Leo of the CBC news decries the "real Canadian crisis of African HIV rates" on the prairies. In the Saskatoon biweekly community magazine *Planet S*, readers learn that "AIDS Still Sucks" because although it was believed that mother-to-infant transmission of the infection was under control (indeed, no HIV-positive babies were born in Saskatchewan in the previous four years), three babies were born HIV positive in 2015 (Malone).

The HIV epidemic is not, of course, a standalone health issue. Anthropological studies of HIV/AIDS have led the way in identifying the interconnections among HIV and other conditions by advancing our understanding of syndemics—the synergistic relationship among several biological and/or sociocultural conditions that exacerbate burdens of illness and experiences of despair (Singer 204). In both urban and rural Saskatchewan, HIV/AIDS is intertwined with addictions, hepatitis C, as well as poverty and structural inequities that First Nations and Métis peoples disproportionately endure. The most common modes of HIV transmission are injection drug use and heterosexual sex, and although rates of testing are increasing, there are still significant degrees of stigma and fear associated with seeking out HIV care (DeJesus et al. 570; Kennedy et al. 74; Reis 420). The picture has become more complicated and concerning since the provincial HIV strategy expired in 2014 (limiting the available budget). Moreover, healthcare is a provincial responsibility, but First Nations healthcare falls within a federal portfolio and there is, therefore, no clearly defined HIV-related leadership, which results in health regions trying to deliver more services with leaner resources while caught in between provincial and federal mandates.

In the public representation of the epidemic, the most common images and photographs that accompany news articles are of syringes, usually shown to be discarded in heaps in public areas. Not only do these images foreground the connection between HIV/AIDS and injection drug use, they also cast drug use as a wider threat to society because of the supposed danger associated with discarded syringes. Of course, if handled properly, publicly discarded syringes do not pose a high risk to those who encounter them; few—if any—cases of HIV infection are traceable to the handling of a publicly discarded needle. In February 2015, the Canadian Paediatric Society reaffirmed its position that "It is extremely unlikely that HIV infection would occur following an injury from a needle discarded in a public place" (Moore, and Canadian Paediatric Society 207). Despite this, however, the images of syringes accompany these news articles more than any other graphic and this fuels unfounded stories about the HIV-related dangers that result from discarded needles used by those who inject drugs (Goldstein 141).

Alongside the emphasis on drug use are common references to families and children. In Geoff Leo's CBC news report, for example, an infectious disease specialist is quoted as describing the situation on reserves as one in which "you'll get a mother who is injecting with a daughter who is injecting with an uncle and a cousin." Although this description may not be inaccurate, it positions the mother as the primary actor in the chain of needle sharing and HIV transmission. In her 2015 report in the *Canadian Medical Association Journal*, Lauren Vogel similarly notes that in First Nations communities "There are stories of families sharing needles—grandmothers and mothers shooting up with children and cousins—and of people dying of HIV on reserves without ever receiving a diagnosis" (793). Mothers are referenced centrally here, and it may not be an overextension to suggest that when narrative descriptions such as these are coupled with images of stockpiled syringes, mothers become culpable not only for their own and their family's addiction and HIV infections but also for the dangers that the discarded syringes are thought to pose to the community more broadly.

The central casting of mothers in the media reports draws a critical response from the mothers themselves. Holding up the 7 July 2006 issue of *Newsweek* magazine that featured the story

"AIDS at 25," Rachel expressed dismay over the photograph of a pregnant woman on the cover. "It's like this all the time, eh? Women who got HIV are seen as poison. Poisoning our babies, all the babies. We're just, I don't know. Bad poison moms." The articles in this award-winning issue of the magazine focus more on the empowerment of women and the challenges of caregiving than on representations of maternal culpability. Yet in light of the focus on mothers that emerges in other news reports, Rachel's initial response to the magazine cover was to interpret it as a condemnation of mothers and as an imposition of the bad mother label. When I asked her for other examples of representations of maternal culpability—"moms as bad poison"—she pointed to a poster on the wall of AIDS Saskatoon's drop-in centre. The poster—produced in the late 1980s by Clement Communications—an American public relations company that distributed programs and materials to help organizations communicate with their intended audiences—depicts an African-American baby girl (maybe six to nine months of age) and the primary caption reads: "She has her father's eyes and her mother's AIDS." Only the baby is featured on the poster (the mother is absent), but intending mothers are clearly the audience targeted for the message: "Before you become pregnant, find out if you need to be tested." The website of the National Library of Medicine (associated with the Institutes of Health in the United States) explains that this poster was designed to make an emotional appeal to women (African-American women in this case) and to suggest that women have a responsibility beyond themselves to be tested for HIV. In Rachel's reading of the poster, the focus on responsibility slipped into culpability:

> All us moms are is threats to the babies. The mother isn't even there. You can't see her. She's just, like, the virus in the baby. Just like [the *Newsweek* cover], all the focus is on ... what the mom is giving to the baby. Nobody sees that the mom loves the babies. Nobody sees how good the moms are. Nobody sees what us moms go through or what we're dealing with. It's like, you know, we're just bad for the babies. That's all we are.

In the above interview excerpt, Rachel includes herself in, and therefore identifies with, the group of mothers who are held culpable for the potential HIV-related harm to children, families, and communities, and are, at the same time, rendered invisible. As she noted, what is missing from many representations of the HIV epidemic is a focus on the women themselves and the successful mothering in which they engage. To be an HIV-infected or at-risk mother, especially when coupled with injection drug use, is to be cast almost exclusively as a source of risk and danger; in Rachel's words, "bad poison." Of course, this is not limited to public media representations. Scholarly work is rife with examples of child-centric castings of women and mothers. For example, in her widely cited book on women, families, and HIV/AIDS in the United States, Carol Campbell argues that "mothers who are IDUs [injection drug users] must be discussed because of the close relationship between injection drug use and pediatric AIDS" (152) and presumably not because the mothers themselves deserve discussion in their own right. There are some important works that counter and repair the invisibility and blame that accompany these kinds of child-centric castings of mothers infected with, and affected by HIV—Susan Boyd's ("The Journey to Compassionate Care") critique of medical models of addiction and her call for compassionate care for mothers who use drugs comes to mind—but even a cursory analysis of the available literature on mothers and HIV reveals a clear pattern. There is much less emphasis on mothers' well-being and much more emphasis on both the risks of maternal transmission to babies and the culpability of mothers for children's ill-health and stress. This constitutes a significant form of mother blame that is borne heavily and negatively by the women who participated in the AIDS Saskatoon research.

In total, thirty women ranging in ages from eighteen to sixty-four years participated in the research. Twenty-six women are Aboriginal—Métis, Cree, Dene, or Saulteaux—and four women identify as white. Twenty-eight women had children of their own (the children ranging in ages from eight months to thirty years of age), and ten of these women also had grandchildren. Two other women are among the primary caregivers to their sister's or cousin's children, and identify as "one of the moms." All but five of the women have had children removed from their care because of drug use and housing insecurities. Indeed, safe housing is one of the most pressing challenges faced by the research participants, only seven of whom have lived in their current residence for more than one year. Many of the women move frequently between Saskatoon and the communities (usually more northern communities) where their extended families live and to which they commonly refer as "home." HIV and hepatitis C are ongoing conditions in the lives of the research participants, all of whom are either infected with, at risk for, and/or intimately affected by these chronic viruses.

BAD MOTHERS, MOTHER BLAME, AND "MOTHERISK"

In the introduction to their edited volume on mother blame, Vanessa Reimer and Sarah Sahagian argue that there is a prevailing and cultural obsession with bad mothers in North America where the bad mother label is "dangerously adaptable" to almost any circumstance and context (3-4). The label emerges where blame exists and as Reimer and Sahagian point out, mother blame is omnipresent: "the world is structured to persecute mothers. Mothers are blamed for everything" (3). Paula Caplan, one of the most influential feminist scholars of mother blame, agrees. In her work as a clinical psychologist in a healthcare setting, Caplan notes that "no matter what was wrong, no matter what the reason for the family's coming to the clinic, it turned out the mother was always assumed to be responsible for the problem" (592). Blame slides easily into vilification, and bad mothers emerge.

In the context of HIV/AIDS, mother blame and vilification abound. A Saskatchewan-based study presented 160 participants with four vignettes, each describing a pregnant women with one of the following medical conditions: HIV/AIDS, obesity, lung cancer, and diabetes. As the researchers expected, the woman described in the HIV/AIDS vignette "received less approval of her pregnancy and lower ratings of her parental fitness, even after the health of the child was controlled" (Lawson et al. 678). Combined with the racism that Aboriginal mothers encounter, these negative judgments of maternal fitness are exacerbated. Cindy Baskin and Bela McPherson point out that there are certain women who are particularly susceptible to the labels of "bad mothers," "unfit," and "undeserving," (111), and—as Rachel's comments attest—Aboriginal women who use drugs and are living with or affected by HIV are among them. Karen Swift pointed out over twenty years ago that Aboriginal families have long been viewed as "the other" by Canadian and American child welfare institutions with little, if any, accommodation for the historical uprootedness, disruptions, and oppression faced by First Nations and Métis peoples (147). For generations, the intersection of poverty, addiction, and racism has placed Aboriginal families in highly vulnerable positions.

Mother blame, then, is bound tightly to social inequity, particularly that faced by Aboriginal peoples in Canada. It extends beyond First Nations and Métis communities, of course, with women who are poor, single, and marginalized on the basis of race, culture, sexuality, age, and/or ability (among other forces of inequity) being held individually responsible for the social and historical structures that restrict their opportunities and limit their resources. The stigma of mother blame is often experienced most acutely by marginalized women while they are in public spaces such as grocery stores, doctors' offices, and social service offices (Seccombe et al 854). This publicly encountered stigma can lead women to avoid those places in order to evade public censure; this, in turn, fuels stereotypes of these mothers as bad mothers who do not seek out services or buy necessary groceries for their children.

The implicit and explicit mother blaming that occurs in the context of HIV/AIDS in Saskatchewan (and elsewhere) speaks to a moral panic about HIV and drug use that has its roots in the criminalization of addiction generally (N. Campbell)—maternal addiction and drug use specifically (Boyd, *Hooked*, *Mothers and Illicit Drugs*; Stengel)—in the restrictive focus on individual agency in the prevention of HIV (C. Campbell; Farmer), and in an ethnocentric understanding of child endangerment and neglect (Krane and Davis; Swift). This is not to say that children are not deserving of our scholarly attention, concern, and political support. Of course they are. But I argue that the assertion—confronted by all research participants and succinctly summarized earlier by Rachel—that HIV positivity and drug-related risks automatically result in the unredeemable status as bad mothers is detrimental to women's individual and collective wellbeing. I now turn to consider the experiences of two women in the AIDS Saskatoon study who live with and confront the bad mother label.

ISABEL

When we first met, Isabel was fifty-four years old. AIDS Saskatoon was a "second home" to her—a safe place where she would bring her seven-year-old grandson, Mark, to watch TV while she visited with staff and friends. Isabel had been awarded custody of Mark when Isabel's daughter was arrested for drug possession and deemed to be guilty of child neglect. However, because of Isabel's positive HIV status and her own history of drug use, regular visitations from child and family services were required. On one occasion, the visit came without warning on a cold winter afternoon. Isabel had known that she would be late from work that day and had confirmed that her cousin, who lived across the crescent from Isabel's small rental house, would be at home. When Mark arrived home from school that afternoon to find his uncle and several friends drinking in the back room, he knew to head over to their cousin's house. "I remember the day the social workers came to check up on us. Mark was on [cousin] Serena's stoop kicking at her screen door because she always had it latched," Isabel explained.

> They called me, saying "you left him all alone" and "he had no place to go." But none of that was true. My cousin was there, she was just slow to get to the door. But, no. They said he was outside alone, unsupervised, and they said that's, like, neglect. So they just took him away. When I go to meet with them the next day, they wouldn't even talk to me in private. They stood out in the waiting room and right in front of everybody, and the place was real packed, so right there they told me that they was going to do another home assessment and until that got done and approved, Mark had to stay in emergency foster care.

As our discussion continued, Isabel indicated that the subsequent home assessment focused centrally on her HIV status.

> They go asking me "When did you get it?" "How did you get it?" "What are you doing about it?" It was the third degree. They asked about my daughter, how often she uses. About my cousin, how often she uses. About me, how often I use. They just assumed we all are still using. Well, I'm not. But they just assumed it. And then when I tried to tell them that Mark wasn't left alone that afternoon, that he had my cousin and his uncle there, they just started quizzing me about who had HIV. It didn't make no sense to me so I started crying. They were painting me all wrong. Like a bad drug mother. I'm a good *kohkum* [grandmother]. I'm not like how they were painting it.

As a First Nations woman from a northern reserve, Isabel grew up and learned to mother in an environment in which a cultural mandate for collective caregiving exists. Although there is a great deal of diversity across Canada's First Nations, Memee Lavell-Harvard and Kim Anderson note that one general commonality is the community cooperation in regards to caregiving: "interdependent supportive networks of kin have shaped Indigenous motherhood; the legacy of which continues to influence our collective experience today" (6). The imposition of what Sharon Hays calls the "intensive mothering mandate" (15) that lays virtually sole responsibility for child nurturance and care onto one mother figure—in Isabel's case, the grandmother—is an oppressive and culturally marginalizing experience for many Aboriginal women. Isabel was genuinely confused by the allegation of neglect because it rested on a single-mother model, which is foreign to Isabel's understanding of collective- and kin-based care, despite a colonial history that promoted a Eurocentric model of patriarchal and private motherhood.

Isabel's choice to use the Cree word *kohkum* for "grandmother" strategically marks her culturally specific understanding of her mother role. She rejects the bad mother picture painted by the overemphasis on her HIV status and history of drug use, and she chooses, instead, to state simply and emotionally that she is a good *kohkum*—caring for Mark by ensuring that there was kin care available for him after school. Echoing Rachel's earlier concerns, Isabel expressed great frustrations that the care she consistently and lovingly provided to her young grandson (as well as to her adult daughter) were so readily overshadowed by the picture child and family services painted of her as an HIV-infected and drug experienced Aboriginal woman. Drawing on Paula Caplan's work, Vanessa Reimer and Sarah Sahagian argue that "mothers are not only blamed for anything that goes wrong in their children's lives, but they are also frustratingly unappreciated when they do things 'right'" (4). For the women participating in this research, this is a common experience. Twenty-five of the thirty participants have had children permanently or temporarily apprehended into provincial care, and each of these twenty-five women expressed frustration that their HIV status and history of drug use were used to label them as bad mothers, a label that negated the successful and loving mothering they provided to their children.

VALERIE

Valerie brought an orchid to our first interview. It was a warm summer day, so she emphasized that it was safe for the fragile flower to be carried from her apartment one block away to the office at AIDS Saskatoon where we were meeting. "I did my research," she explained. "Orchids are real sensitive and real hard to keep alive. But LOOK!" She outstretched her arms to show me a beautiful and thriving flower. Valerie was nurturing this plant in order "to prove" that she was responsible. She had lost custody of her eighteen-month-old son because of her chronic drug use and HIV as well as hepatitis C positive status. Valerie is a young Cree mother who grew up in Saskatoon-based foster homes. She first learned that she was HIV positive during a prenatal hospital visit when she agreed to HIV, hepatitis C, and drug screening tests.

> When the test results come back, one of the nurses told me to "get ready to kiss the baby goodbye." I didn't know what to do. [The doctor], he told me to start taking the antivirus drugs to protect the baby. And he says: "This is your chance to lower your motherisk and do right by your kid." I'm like, "motherisk? What's that?" And he goes "That's you. You're motherisk." He said it just like that, too: "You're

> motherisk." I'm like, I don't know, I was just, you know. Really? I know I was only eighteen, but I was real happy to be having a baby, to be having a family. A family that I never got growing up. When I told my real mom that I was pregnant, it was the first time we had spoken in years. It was bringing us back together but then all I hear was "motherisk" and HIV and HPC, you know?

The term "motherisk" is increasingly used in HIV and hepatitis C related healthcare interactions. In the 101 interviews conducted across the three components of this research project, nine separate descriptions of motherisk were provided by participants. All of these nine participants encountered the term in their clinical interactions when discussing their drug use, and three of the participants described the term being used in their dealings with Child and Family Services. This is not entirely surprising given that the term "motherisk" was introduced through the Hospital for Sick Children's Motherisk program, which—before it was closed because the testing was found to be lacking scientific validity (Lang)—conducted drug and alcohol testing to be used in child protection and criminal proceedings when maternal (and subsequently paternal) drug use was suspected. For Valerie, the term produced an epiphany: the motherhood that she anticipated as a source of family and joy was now a source of risk, surveillance, and looming child apprehension.

> "I got so scared. I didn't go to my doctor's appointments 'cause I didn't want to hear the word 'motherisk' no more," Valerie whispered as she held tightly to the orchid. "I didn't want them treating me like I'm some kind of mother monster, you know? I kept it together until [her son] was born. And they let me keep him, but I just couldn't get rid of the feeling that I was doomed. I felt doomed to be a shitty motherisk mom. So, I started using again. Then they took him away."

Research has repeatedly shown that stigmatizing labels, such as "motherisk," perpetuate and actually exacerbate self-loathing, drug use, mistrust of police and social services, as well as rejection and avoidance of healthcare (Gustafson 277; Moulding et al. 250; Rutman et al. 229). Internalized mother blame often expresses itself as self-blame, which is well illustrated in Valerie's description of herself. At first, she did little to refuse her casting as a bad and risky mother. The "shitty motherisk mom" label was one that undermined her self-assessment and led to feelings of doom. She described herself as "depressed and sick," unable to care for her son and, in her estimation, she was "totally useless." Valerie's case is similar to that of many other research participants for whom the bad mother label emerged as a medicalized and culturally based attribution. Although similar findings are well represented in the literature, the effect that such an attribution has on dissuading women from seeking the HIV-specific care that they and their families need has received only limited attention, yet it stands out in the AIDS Saskatoon study as one of the most important findings. Certainly for Valerie, her health was adversely affected by the sense of doom that the motherisk label wrought.

Fortunately, when temporary custody of her son was granted to her aunt in another Saskatchewan city, her aunt would call Valerie when the baby was awake and cooing. Her aunt was reassuring: "she says to me, you know, I'm here for you too, my girl. I got you too. And the more I talked to her, and heard [the baby] sounding real good, the more I believed in myself. I could do this." Valerie subsequently began attending parenting classes, adhering to the methadone maintenance addiction program, and doing all that she could—including buying house plants—to prove that she was responsible enough "to show them that even though I might have been a shitty mom at first, I've come a long way. I'm ready to be a mom. I'm not going to say a 'good mom' because I don't think nobody could be a good mom the way that everybody expects. But I'm ready to be a *real* mom to my boy."

CONCLUSION

My aim in this chapter has been to explore how bad mothers emerge from judgments of women living with or affected by HIV/AIDS and injection drug use. The construction of mothers as implicated in, and culpable for, the provincial HIV profile is one that permeates news reports and public discussions. Bad mother attributions also emerge from and circulate within institutional contexts—including child and family services and medical clinics—that foster ethnocentric understandings of maternal care and intensive mothering as well as a moralizing rejection of the fact that HIV-infected and -affected women can manage their addictions in a responsible way while caring for their children. The climate created by these kinds of public discussions and institutional context leads Aboriginal mothers who are living with, or affected by HIV and injection drug use to experience mother blame and vilification. This, in turn, allows allegations of bad mothering—risky and neglectful mothering—to surface and circulate. As Britta Wigginton and Michelle Lafrance astutely note: "The marking of the 'bad mother' holds significant material consequences. In the context of drug use, this label can affect women's custody rights and the extent of professional intervention imposed on their child rearing" (31). In the context of drug use, HIV, and racism, this label seems inescapable, as so well reflected in Rachel's lament that she believes that she would never be "'mom enough' for the white, straight world."

However, as the three mothers whose experiences I have drawn centrally on in this chapter illustrate, the label can be effectively refused and challenged. Rachel is not shy about expressing her criticism of the materials that depict mothers as the faces of HIV or that reduce mothers to cases of pediatric HIV. She is an outspoken advocate for a more robust and inclusive representation of mothering, and Aboriginal mothering specifically. Similarly, Isabel understands that although she is subject to the "third degree" inquiry and surveilling, she refuses the connotations of the bad drug mother by reasserting her identity as a *kohkum* who relies on a heritage of collaborative and collective childcare. And, Valerie, initially so devastated by the HIV diagnosis and "motherisk" label, received the kind of reassurance and support from her aunt, which now enables her to invoke the label "real mother" to offset and refuse the allegation of risky motherhood. Resistance is not without its own risks: risks of being perceived as difficult and defiant; risks of negative parental fitness assessments; risks of adverse health consequences from avoiding medical appointments; and risks of exacerbated stigma. However, the kind of resistance in which the research participants engaged allows them to counter the bad mother label by reasserting their connection to extended kin and longstanding Aboriginal approaches to intergenerational care. In addition to being culturally grounded coping strategies, such women as Rachel, Isabel and Valerie reframe their own positions as mother to mitigate and even directly reject being cast as bad mothers. This kind of resistance indicates that the bad mothers, whom mother blame gives birth, are not always docile and voiceless; they are often dedicated, loving, and concerned mothers, highly deserving of support.

ENDNOTE

[1]All names of research participants used in this chapter are pseudonyms.

WORKS CITED

Baskin, Cyndy, and Bela McPherson. "Towards the Wellbeing of Aboriginal Mothers and their Families." *Mothers of the Nations: Indigenous Mothering as Global Resistance, Reclaiming and Recovery*, edited by Memee Lavell-Harvard and Kim Anderson, Demeter Press, 2014, 109-129.

Boyd, Susan. *Mothers and Illicit Drugs: Transcending the Myths*. Toronto: University of Toronto Press, 1999.

Boyd, Susan. "The Journey to Compassionate Care." *With Child: Substance Abuse During Pregnancy: A Woman-Centered Approach*, edited by Susan Boyd and Lenora Marcellus. Fernwood, 2007, pp. 10-19.

Boyd, Susan. *Hooked: Drug War Films in Britain, Canada, and the United States*. University of Toronto Press, 2008.

Campbell, Carole. *Women, Families, and HIV/AIDS: A Sociological Perspective on the Epidemic in America*. Cambridge University Press, 1999.

Campbell, Nancy. "'Why Can't They Stop?' A Highly Public Misunderstanding of Science." *Addiction Trajectories*, edited by

Eugene Raikhel and William Garriott, Duke University Press, 2013, pp. 238-262.

Caplan, Paula J. "Don't Blame Mother: Then and Now." *Maternal Theory: Essential Reading*, edited by Andrea O'Reilly, Demeter Press, 2007, pp. 592-600.

DeJesus, Maria, et al. "Attitudes, Perceptions and Behaviours towards HIV Testing among African-American and East African Immigrant Women in Washington, DC: Implications for Targeted HIV Testing Promotion and Communication Strategies." *Sexually Transmitted Infections*, vol. 91, no. 8, 2015, pp. 569-575. doi: *10.1136/sextrans-2014-051876*

Farmer, Paul. *Pathologies of Power: Health, Human Rights, and the New War on the Poor*. University of California Press, 2003.

Goldstein, Diane E. *Once Upon a Virus: AIDS Legends and Vernacular Risk Perception*. Utah State University Press, 2004. Print.

Gustafson, Diana L. "Non-Resident Mothers: Refining Our Understandings." *Mothers, Mothering, and Motherhood Across Cultural Differences*, edited by Andrea O'Reilly, Demeter Press, 2014, pp. 273-297.

Hays, Sharon. *The Cultural Contradictions of Motherhood*. Yale University Press, 1996.

Kennedy, Caitlin, et al. "Safe Disclosure of HIV Serostatus for Women Living with HIV who Experience or Fear Violence." *Journal of the International AIDS Society (JIAS)*, vol. 18, supplement 5, 2015, pp. 74-82. *JIAS*, www.jiasociety.org/index.php/jias/article/view/20834/html. Accessed 22 Jan. 2016.

Krane, Julia and Linda Davis. "Mothering and Child Protective Practice: Rethinking Risk Assessment." *Child and Family Social Work*, vol. 5, no. 1, 2000, pp. 35-45.

Landsman, Gail. "Reconstructing Motherhood in the Age of "Perfect" Babies: Mothers of Infants and Toddlers with Disabilities." *Signs: Journal of Women in Culture and Society*, vol. 24, no. 1, 1998, pp. 69-99.

Lang, Susan E. *Report of the Motherisk Hair Analysis Independent Review. Ministry of the Attorney General*, 2015, www.attorneygeneral.jus.gov.on.ca/english/about/pubs/lang/. Accessed 15 Feb. 2016.

Lavell-Harvard, D. Memee and Kim Anderson. "Indigenous

Mothering Perspectives." *Mothers of the Nations: Indigenous Mothering as Global Resistance, Reclaiming and Recovery*, edited by D. Memee Lavell-Harvard and Kim Anderson, Demeter Press, 2014, pp. 1-11.

Lawson, Karen, et al. "Judgments Regarding the Acceptability of Childbearing and Parental Fitness Made Towards Women Living with HIV." *AIDS Care*, vol. 25, no. 6, 2013, pp. 676-679.

Leo, Geoff. "HIV Rates on Sask. Reserves Higher than Some African Nations." *CBC News*, 3 June 2015, www.cbc.ca/news/canada/saskatchewan/hiv-rates-on-sask-reserves-higher-than-some-african-nations-1.3097231. Accessed 27 Jan. 2016.

MacQueen, Ken. "Saskatchewan's HIV Epidemic: Third World Levels of HIV Infection Rates in One of the World's Wealthiest Countries are a National Disgrace." *Maclean's Magazine*, 22 July 2015, http://www.macleans.ca/news/canada/saskatchewans-hiv-epidemic/. Accessed 22 Jan. 2016.

Malone, Geraldine. "AIDS Still Sucks." *Prairie Dog Magazine*, 1 July 2016, www.prairiedogmag.com/2016-01-07/aids-still-sucks/. Accessed 15 Jan. 2017.

McDowell, M., et al. *Taking the Pulse of Saskatchewan 2012: Health, Wellbeing and Saskatchewan Families*. Social Sciences Research Laboratories, University of Saskatchewan, 2012.

Moore, D.L. and the Canadian Paediatric Society. "Needle Stick Injuries in the Community." *Paediatric and Child Health*, vol. 13, no. 1, 2008, pp. 205-210. *Canadian Paediatric Society*, www.cps.ca/documents/position/needle-stick-injuries. Accessed 31 Jan. 2016.

Moulding, Nicole T., et al.. "Untangling Self-Blame and Mother-Blame in Women's and Children's Perspectives on Maternal Protectiveness in Domestic Violence: Implications for Practice." *Child Abuse Review*, vol. 24, no. 4, 2015, pp. 249-260.

Reimer, Vanessa and Sarah Sahagian. "Contextualizing the Mother-Blame Game." *The Mother-Blame Game*, edited by Vanessa Reimer and Sarah Sahagian, Demeter Press, 2015, pp. 1-18.

Reis, Edward. "What Part of HIV Prevention Conversations Don't We Understand?" *Culture, Health and Sexuality*, vol. 10, no. 4, 2008, 417-422.

Rutman, Deborah, et al. "Perspectives of Substance-Using Women and Service Practitioners: Reflections from the Margins." *Unbecoming Mothers: The Social Production of Maternal Absence*, edited by Diana L. Gustafson, Haworth Press, 2005, 227-249.

Salloum, Alec. "Rates of HIV Deaths in Saskatchewan." *Regina Leader-Post*, 15 Dec. 2015, leaderpost.com/news/local-news/rates-of-hiv-related-deaths-in-saskatchewan-more-than-four-times-national-average. Accessed 29 Dec. 2015.

Seccombe, Karen, et al. "'They Think You Ain't Much of Nothing': The Social Construction of the Welfare Mother." *Journal of Marriage and the Family* 60.4 (1999): 849-865. Print.

"She She Has Her Father's Eyes and Her Mother's AIDS." Clement Communications. *National Library of Medicine, Profiles in Science*, 1988, profiles.nlm.nih.gov/ps/retrieve/ResourceMetadata/VCBBGQ. Accessed 18 Feb. 2016.

Singer, Merrill. *Introducing Syndemics: A Critical Systems Approach to Public and Community Health*. Jossey-Boss, 2009

Stengel, Camille. "The Risk of Being 'Too Honest': Drug Use, Stigma, and Pregnancy." *Health, Risk, and Society*, vol. 16, no. 1, 2013, pp. 36-50.

Swift, Karen J. *Manufacturing 'Bad Mothers': A Critical Perspective on Child Neglect*. University of Toronto Press, 1995. Print.

Thurer, Shari L. *The Myths of Motherhood: How Culture Reinvents the Good Mother*. Houghton Mifflin, 1994.

Vogel, Lauren. "HIV in Saskatchewan Merits Urgent Response." *Canadian Medical Association Journal*, vol. 187, no. 11, 2015, pp. 793-94. *Canadian Medical Association Journal*, www.cmaj.ca/content/187/11/793. Accessed 15 Jan. 2016.

Wigginton, Britta and Michelle N. Lafrance. "How Do Women Manage the Spoiled Identity of a 'Pregnant Smoker'? An Analysis of Discursive Silencing in Women's Accounts." *Feminism and Psychology*, vol. 26, no. 1, 2016, pp. 30-51.

The Risky Mother

The Medicalization of Mothering

ALEXANDRA CAMPBELL

THE RELATIONSHIP between mothering, science, and biomedicine is not new. Scholars have long noted and described the many ways in which mothering is shaped by scientists, doctors, and other experts. Motherhood is becoming an experience that occurs more and more in relation to biomedical discourse (Malacrida; Artis; Bruer). Rima Apple's seminal text, *Perfect Motherhood: Science and Childrearing in America,* charts the erosion of mothering "instinct"—a notion that had underwritten mothering prior to the nineteenth century—and the emergence of "experts" who are increasingly viewed as "holding answers to healthful appropriate childcare" (9). There is a proliferation of childrearing books, parenting magazines, websites, and more, alongside advice from paediatricians and other health workers, all of which direct mothers to heed expert advice. Feeding, bathing, attachment, and development are all monitored through wellness checkups, nurse visits, and so forth.

What is new in the past decade is the intensification of scientific preoccupation with mothering, which is now permeated with a profound discourse of "risk." Mothering is increasingly viewed as fundamental to the life chances of the children that a woman mothers. No longer is there simply a concern with how a mother physically cares for her children, as in how she bathes them, gets them to sleep, and feeds them. A body of scientific research is emerging that converges on the physical and emotional health of the mother—her gestating, lactating, and emotional body is now valourized and held responsible for a plethora of individual and societal ills.

I intend to focus on two burgeoning areas of scientific interest: fetal origins research and attachment theory, the latter of which neuroscience has newly invigorated. At the centre of research proliferation in these areas is the woman-as-mother's body. The mother's body is reduced to a set of epidemiological risk factors as the quality of her in utero environment is assessed as the gestating mother, as in fetal origins research. Her emotional ability to attach securely to her children is assessed through neuroscience and attachment theory. These factors are connected to an array of chronic diseases, emotional disturbances, behavioural problems, educational failure, poverty, and more.

THE LENS OF MEDICALIZATION

Examining the scientific research on mothering through a lens of medicalization helps us to think through consequences of such a body of knowledge. As Irving Zola has long argued that although it seems a benign and an apolitical process, medicalization is a pernicious form of social control. It is insidiously camouflaged as purely scientific and, crucially, as a benevolent and an altruistic process (502). Scholars have noted that women's bodies and emotions have been particularly vulnerable to projects of medicalization. Issues such as eating disorders, pregnancy and childbirth, and menopause are powerfully understood through the paradigm of biomedicine, which casts women and their bodies as pathological and in need of intervention (Morgan 84-86).

Situating the paper in the context of medicalization makes it possible to examine the regulatory effects of scientific mothering, which also serves to spotlight growing legitimated surveillance and interventions as mothers' bodies transform into risks to be managed. This chapter is not so much concerned with the veracity of the claims made by scientists and social scientists on mothering; rather, it is interested in thinking through some of the consequences of the medicalizing process as mothers endure the growing scrutiny of doctors, healthcare workers, legal entities, and larger societal judgments while a broad range of social problems are reduced to defective mothering.

Below, I detail a selection of fetal origins research and neuroscience attachment theory, which increasingly find their way into popular culture. In so doing I draw attention to the regulatory effects of scientific mothering. Drawing on a Foucauldian framework, I explore how such discourses give rise to the concept of the good-bad mother. I also examine how these meanings operate in and through the bodies of mothers, given the implication that mothering, at its heart, is a radically risky phenomenon.

SCIENTIFIC MOTHERING

Fetal Origins Research

In 2010, *Time* magazine published an article by Annie Paul titled "How the First Nine Months Shape the Rest of Your Life." The article's byline asks the following questions: "What makes us the way we are? Why are some people predisposed to be anxious, overweight, or asthmatic? How is it that some of us are prone to heart attacks, diabetes or high blood pressure?" The article's main tenet is that life as a fetus is one of the key determinants of one's physical and emotional health. It asserts that conditions in the womb are of considerable consequence, as in utero environments shape our susceptibility to disease, our appetite, metabolism, intelligence, and even our temperament and levels of happiness.

Drawing on the body of knowledge known as "fetal origins," Paul's article introduces examples of pivotal research in this field to a lay audience—including work examining nutrition during pregnancy, exposure to pollutants, drugs, and infections, as well as the mother's overall health, stress level, and state of mind during pregnancy. In so doing, the article persuasively argues that nine months of gestation constitute the most "consequential period of our lives, permanently influencing the wiring of the brain and the function of organs such as the heart, liver, and pancreas" (51).

Fetal origins research, with its roots in epidemiology and epigenetics, explores the links between in utero environments and a range of short-, medium-, and long-term effects on the life of the fetus. Researchers in the field argue that human epidemiologic research and animal model data indicate that during critical periods of prenatal and postnatal mammalian development, nutrition and other environmental stimuli influence developmental pathways and thereby induce permanent changes in metabolism and chronic disease susceptibility (Waterland and Michaels 363). By examining the function or expression of gene code, researchers focus on the epigenetic effects of such stimuli at a molecular biological level (Lupton 99).

Emerging from the research are connections between a broad range of adverse environmental conditions in utero and an array of negative health effects during the subsequent lifetime of an exposed child (Newnham and Ross). Studies examining the diet and weight status of mothers have suggested links between obese and overweight women and premature birth, gestational diabetes, and further complications at birth increasing the risk of stillbirth (Yao et al. 457.e1). Moreover, examining the effects of nutrition on gene expression, research suggests that there are longer-term effects— including an increased propensity of the child, and even its descendants, to conditions such as diabetes, cardiovascular disease, high blood pressure, obesity, or metabolic syndrome (Landecker 176-177). Nutritional deprivation during the prenatal period has also been linked to addiction (Franzek et al. 433) and schizophrenia (Kirkbride et al.).

Prenatal maternal stress has been theorized as changing the genetic material of the fetus, rendering it more likely to develop mental illness (Lupton 99). Other studies suggest that stress deleteriously results in early programming of brain functions, with permanent changes in neuroendocrine regulation and behaviour in offspring (Mulder et al). Perinatal exposure to viral infections has been connected to behavioural and pharmacological changes in the adult offspring, notably implicated in the development of schizophrenia (Zuckerman and Weiner), which is also linked to maternal lead exposure (Opler et al.).

The effects are not limited to health, however; economists, for instance, have become increasingly interested in expanding the fetal origins hypothesis as they investigate a broader range of fetal "shocks" and conditions linking them to later-life effects on outcomes, including test scores, educational attainment, income, and health (Almond and Currie 154). Collectively, these data (and I have described only a small fraction of current research) add to a body of research that scrutinizes practically every aspect of a pregnant mother's life, such as the air that she breathes, the food and drink she consumes, the chemicals she is exposed to, the emotions she feels, and so much more. All are regarded as pivotal to the long-term physical, emotional, and economic health of her offspring (Paul).

In the *Time* article, Paul quotes the Nobel prize–winning economist Amaryta Sen in arguing that prenatal experience "sows the seeds of ailments that afflict adults," which, as Paul continues to write, "makes the womb a promising target for intervention, raising hopes of conquering public health scourges like obesity and heart disease through interventions before birth." (52). The social control consequences are not difficult to discern: mothering behaviour during pregnancy becomes valourized as a legitimate time for medical supervision and biomedical intervention. Deborah Lupton notes that pregnant women have long been under intense examination, their every behaviour examined for its effect on a baby's health (93). Yet the increased understanding of the role of the placenta—no longer understood as a barrier separating mother and fetus—has led not only to a proliferation of scientific research but also to an intensification of scrutiny. Long-term effects of bad mothering are construed as having effects well into future generations.

Research by Elizabeth Armstrong and Ernest Abel on fetal alcohol syndrome (FAS) is instructive in exposing not only the social control implications of such research but also the function of wider social and cultural structures that undergird it. Fetal alcohol syndrome—understood as a pattern of physical and psychological anomalies in children born to alcoholic women—was not a recognized condition until the 1970s. By the 1990s, it had been transformed into a major public health concern (276). In their research, Armstrong and Abel explore how wider social concerns and anxieties, such as child neglect and abuse, and the victimization of children, intersected with emerging scientific discourses. Thus, FAS was understood through the lens of child endangerment.

Greatly exaggerating the prevalence and impact of FAS, the media, drawing on so-called experts and biomedical discourses, raised awareness of the issue. Within the biomedical community, there was diagnostic and expertise expansion, culminating in the unproven premise that any amount of alcohol consumption is a threat to the fetus (Armstrong and Abel 277). A surgeon general advisory that counselled women not to drink while pregnant was issued in 1981. In addition, a point-of-purchase warning about drinking when pregnant, along with public education campaigns to educate the public about the dangers, effectively turned drinking while pregnant into a major risk in the public's imagination.

Indeed, the image of a drinking or drunk pregnant woman elicits strong reactions, as she is imagined as callously indifferent to the health of her unborn (Longhurst 79). Framed in terms of personal responsibility, women who drink when pregnant—or who are seen to engage in other risky behaviours such as using illegal drugs, smoking, or not getting prenatal care—are harshly judged by a society that scrutinizes a range of maternal behaviours (Knowles 115), even as those behaviours are reduced to individual health choices. Researchers have catalogued the formal sanctions brought against women who have been prosecuted for child neglect, such as fetal abuse, manslaughter, and homicide (Ruhl; Dubow; Marrus; Paltrow and Flavin). The increasing jurisdiction of medical authority is also apparent. Some women have been ordered by U.S. courts to undergo a range of medical interventions against their wishes, such as cervical surgeries, blood transfusions, and Caesarean sections, whereas others are detained in hospitals or psychiatric units to receive enforced medical treatment for drug addiction (Paltrow and Flavin 306-309).

Undergirding these prosecutions are medical discourses that link a mother's health behaviours to a range of devastating outcomes for an unborn child. Although personhood initiatives in the United States, which have worked to create "fetus rights," have no doubt contributed to these sanctions (Dubow), it is crucial to appreciate the ways in which medicalization lends legitimacy to this phenomenon. The conviction of a South Carolina woman who used crack cocaine in the third trimester of her pregnancy, and who was sentenced to eight years imprisonment when the baby was born with cocaine metabolites in its system, illustrates the authority of such fetal origins narratives (Marrus 302).

Early research on prenatal cocaine exposure in the 1980s led to the popular belief that crack babies, a term coined to describe children exposed to cocaine, faced a range of physical, mental, and emotional disabilities. Widely accepted within lay and medical communities as a major public health emergency, the crack baby phenomenon was turned into a moral panic that led to babies being removed from homes and to arrests and prosecutions (Fitzgerald). Analyzing the media coverage of this epidemic, Mariah Blake highlights some of the alarmist popular accounts, encapsulated in the remarks of Charles Krauthammer, a columnist for the *The Washington Post*, who writes that crack babies are doomed to "a life of certain suffering, of probable deviance, of permanent inferiority" (qtd. in Blake). Blake notes that the public braced for the day when this "'biological underclass' would cripple our schools, fill our jails, and drain our social programs." And yet longitudinal research into the effects of prenatal cocaine exposure has shown that these predictions have not been realized and that poverty, not cocaine use, is predictive of development and overall cognition (Hurt, et al., "A Prospective Comparison" and "Children With and Without Gestational Cocaine Exposure").

Despite this, the South Carolina case cited above is but one example of a widespread movement to legally sanction women who have been found to have used drugs during their pregnancies. A new law in Tennessee, enacted in July 2014, is the first law in the United States to explicitly authorize the arrest and incarceration of a woman who has used drugs while pregnant, with the provision that she may avoid criminal charges if she submits to a state treatment program (Bassett). The first woman to be charged under the law, twenty-six-year-old Mallory Loyola, was arrested and charged with misdemeanour assault after she and her newborn baby tested positive for methamphetamine use (Feenay).

It is clear that women of colour and those living in poverty feel most the burden of such legal interventions. Paltrow and Flavin's 2013 analysis of arrests of, and forced interventions with, pregnant women between 1973 and 2005 reveals that the vast majority of women in their study were economically disadvantaged, with 71 percent of the women qualifying for indigent legal representation. Moreover, "Of the 368 women for whom information on race was available, 59 percent were women of color, including African Americans, Hispanic American/Latinas,

Native Americans, and Asian/Pacific Islanders; 52 percent were African American" (311).

The attention on individual women who are overwhelmingly from deprived social groups is perhaps not surprising, given the medicalizing imperatives that underpin fetal origins research and the focus on epigenetics. Medicalization valourizes the individual, as it attributes the causes of ill health and disease to individual biology and health behaviours. Here, maternal behaviours are primed as the cause for a range of fetal health outcomes, which ignores the broader socioeconomic context of a mother and her baby. Instead, attention is paid to an individual mother's lifestyle choices, because mothering and associated behaviours are linked in the scientific discourse to the child's short- and long-term health. Imagining the problem, thus, classifies women in a way that legitimates the interventions of both medical and legal institutions. In turn, this permits an individualistic account of social failure, even as it negates structural inequalities, poverty, inadequate education, and so on.

NEUROSCIENCE AND ATTACHMENT

Whereas fetal origins research and theory studies the gestating woman, attachment theory, and associated neuroscience research, has, at its core, the mother's emotional capacity to attach to her child. Grounded in ethology and developmental psychology, John Bowlby's early research in the area of attachment links an array of problems to "unattached children," who are considered to have lacked love and affection. Undergirding Bowlby's theory is the concept of "monotropy"—the belief that babies have an innate biological need to develop a unique and vital attachment with one primary person, usually the mother. The mother was conceived as being reciprocally preprogrammed to respond sensitively to a myriad of the child's signals or social releasers (Bowlby, "Attachment and Loss"). Bowlby has conceived of the breakdown of such a monotropic attachment, or the absence of one entirely, as potentially catastrophic for a child. An array of social and individual problems has been connected with such maternal deprivation—from juvenile delinquency, antisocial behaviour, and affectionless psychopathy (an inability to show affection or concern for others), to a range of development and emotional delays as well as high levels of morbidity and mortality (Bowlby, "Forty-Four Juvenile Thieves").

Published in a 1952, the World Health Organization report *Maternal Care and Mental Health* offers a detailed account of maternal deprivation's deleterious effects as well as ways to prevent it. Bowlby's extensive body of research underscores the notion that children's experiences of interpersonal relationships are crucial to their psychological development (Rutter 549). This contention has not gone away. Indeed, although attachment theory is not new, I suggest that contemporary efforts have invigorated this kind of research—moving toward systematically understanding and substantiating the underlying biology of attachment. Research in neuroscience, in particular, is leading the way, as the brain's neural plasticity is understood to be especially susceptible to damaging experiences in a person's infant and toddler years.

Renewed focus on attachment has been animated by new scientific methodologies to catalogue the physiological effects of early interactions and deprivation. In particular, the interplay between psychological and physiological processes and their relationship to the short- and long-term consequences in the developing child have come into focus. Biomedical technologies, in particular, have been central to this project. As Megan Gunnar et al. note, "Improved measuring techniques allow assessment of brain activity and neuroendocrine activity, in addition to autonomic nervous system activity" (355). Magnetic Resonance Imaging scans (MRIs) that examine neural structure and function of institutionalized versus noninstitutionalized children, for instance, have sought to demonstrate the significance of "rearing environments" on deficits in language, lower IQ, and executive functioning (Sheridan et al.). The ability to measure cortisol elevations using salivary cortisol has also opened up the possibilities for research, since physical and psychological events are claimed to produce elevations in this hormone when humans are stressed (Gunnar et al. 356).

Perhaps some of the most well-known studies involve contrasting the scans of brains of children who have been raised in "normal" settings and those marked by abuse and neglect. In these images, the normal brain is significantly larger than the brain of the child who has experienced extreme neglect (Sheridan et al.). Research by Teicher et al., for example, which examines brain scans to show the effects of childhood maltreatment, has found specific changes in regions in and around the hippocampus, including lower volume. The authors contend that such exposure to childhood stress, which affects "hippocampal subfield development," makes maltreated children more vulnerable to depression, addiction, and posttraumatic stress disorder later in life (563).

The notion that love and nurture are hardwired into the brain is compelling. Biomedical discourses are exceptionally persuasive. As new ways to map, to measure, to observe, and to know the brain emerge, attachment theory is afforded a new veneer of legitimacy. Moreover, it is imagined that this emerging knowledge tells us much about how parents (usually mothers) should interact with their children. Innumerable popular parenting books, which explicitly employ research in neuroscience and developmental psychology, place acute emphasis on the mother-child bond. In Sue Gerhardt's popular book, *Why Love Matters: How Affection Shapes a Baby's Brain,* the author contends that the first two to three years of a child's life are crucial, as various systems for managing emotions are put into place. For Gerhardt, without basic emotional skills, children may grow up to be emotionally incompetent. The research highlights the role of the hormone cortisol; specifically a connection between childhood spikes of this hormone and problems with depression, anxiety, and even violence and aggression later in life. In a similar vein, the prolific psychologist and writer Oliver James, whose work is explicitly founded on neuroscience and attachment research, focuses attention on the first three years of a child's life. He pays particular attention to the quality of the relationship between a mother and her offspring. Oliver's bestselling texts—*How They F*** You Up* and the sequel *How Not to F*** Them Up*—focus on the "science of parenting" and seek to show how early parenting (mothering, in particular) is linked to a range of mental and emotional disturbances—including depression, anxiety, schizophrenia, aggression and violence. In so doing, he theorizes the longer term effects of mothering as he describes the impact on educational achievement and career success later in life.

Circulated through popular discourse, the proliferation of attachment and neuroscience research inspires, much like the fetal origins research, a host of social policies that tend to focus on and intervene in the lives of families from those same vulnerable communities described above. John Bruer's text, *The Myth of the First Three Years*, documents the way in which new brain science is employed as a high level justification for the emergence of social programming that seeks to intervene in families during their most vulnerable years. Intervening in child-parent relationships in problem families is legitimated by such research and on the assumption that early experiences lead to irreversible changes in the brain. Early intervention programs in the UK (e.g., Sure Start) and the U.S. (e.g., Head Start), which are founded on these assumptions, are considered key to ensuring that at-risk children can overcome the damage inflicted on their developing brains by problematic home lives. Rob Reiner from the Rob Reiner Foundation, for example, has encapsulated this interventionist project in the following way:

> If we want to have a real significant impact, not only on children's success in school and later on in life, health relationships, but also an impact on reduction in crime, teen pregnancy, drug abuse, child abuse, welfare, homelessness, and a variety of other social ills, we are going to have to address the first three years of life. (qtd. in Bruer 8)

Thus, the belief is that programming will ameliorate the damage of defective parenting. Implicit in this is the notion that early intervention in the family lives of the underclass will prevent "costly dysfunction" before it starts (Butler, "Policymakers Seduced by Neuroscience"). Much of the findings in neuroscience that work their way into popular parenting texts and are foundational to social policies are highly contested. For example, as Bruer persuasively points out, there are many problematic assumptions about the brain and its plasticity, which suggest that changes in the brain that occur when dealing with adversity in early childhood are irreversible and always reflect permanent damage (21-22).

The simplistic view of brain development, which gives privilege to the mother-child bond over the family's place in society, valourizes a deterministic, an ahistorical, and an asocial position in which structures of poverty and racism are underplayed as a context for dysfunction. As similarly described in the preceding section, the body of research legitimates and even seems to demand that attention be paid to the quality of mothering. Maladjusted children and those diagnosed with behavioural disorders and delays add to the medicalization of mothering, as the child comes to be viewed as a symptom of bad mothering (Singh 1200). There are innumerable policy initiatives that seek to intervene directly in the lives of targeted families, specifically to deal with bad childrearing. Parent-child interaction therapy (PCIT), as an example, aims to address "the negative parent-child interaction patterns that contribute to the disruptive behavior of young children. Through PCIT, parents learn to bond with their children and develop more effective parenting styles that better meet their children's needs" ("Child Welfare Information Gateway"). These types of programs treat the parent and child together. They make explicit the idea that bad parenting is the cause of problems ranging from inattention and behavioural problems to depression and self-injurious behaviour. They are also explicit that child-parent intervention is the solution to them (Pincus et al.). The social and economic context is relegated as a risk in favour of an analysis that places the mother at the heart of the problem: she is cast as both the origin and the answer to entrenched, structural inequities.

THE DISCIPLINED MOTHER

Fetal origins research and attachment theory, strengthened by neuroscience, contribute to the medicalizing of mothering and the emergence of "scientific parenting," but there are other discourses at work that collaborate and reinforce this process. The lactating mother has long been at the centre of public health initiatives. Efforts are made to encourage breastfeeding and to increase its prevalence by focusing in particular on women in marginalized communities (see Blum). Even how much a mother talks to her child is of scientific concern, with a host of studies that seek to show the long-term deleterious effects of women in the lower-class speaking fewer words to her offspring (Suskind).

I have described above how the state targets mothers, at the centre of the research, for various forms of intervention, including criminal action. This type of regulation, repressive in nature, overwhelmingly focuses on marginalized women who bear the brunt and judgment of social and penal policies. What is more, the radical inequalities— thoroughly implicated in the social ills that are so readily connected to defective mothering—are habitually neglected or at best underplayed.

However, as Foucault (*Power/Knowledge*) reminds us, power is not simply repressive: it is productive. In his work on disciplinary power, Foucault suggests that contemporary power operates in and through bodies, which are socially constructed through systems of discursive practices in specific institutionalized settings. Focusing on the relationship between knowledge and power, Foucault argues that knowledge about bodies is always inextricably enmeshed with power. Knowledge is not objective and indifferent to politics but rather is produced in specific historical and social contexts. With his focus on the production of knowledge, Foucault's work underscores the ways in which knowledge is constituted through various systems of representation, and how such knowledge produces the body itself. In short, bodies are not simply natural entities, but rather they are produced within discourse, and thus they are radically historicized, subject to the different regimes of power/knowledge of the time (Hall 78). Indeed, as Foucault notes, each society has its so-called regime of truth, and the types of discourse that it accepts as valid in the acquisition of truth (Foucault, "Power/Knowledge" 131).

Viewed in Foucauldian terms, then, the knowledge provided by the natural and social sciences are constitutive as opposed to being reflective of an objective, material reality. Power/knowledge brings into circulation certain truths about the body, which are not only produced through discourse but are further managed and regulated by it while the body is divided, classified, and reinscribed by power/knowledge. Under perpetual scrutiny, knowledge of bodies, in aggregate, contributes to the formulation of standards and norms, against which individuals are judged (Nettleton 118-119). The capacity of normalization to regulate conduct is immense. The judges of normality, as Foucault counsels, are everywhere and include "the teacher-judge, the doctor-judge, the educator-judge, the social worker-judge; it is on them that the universal reign of the normative is based" ("Discipline and Punish" 304).

The efficacy of normalization as a technique of power, however, lies in its internalization. The judges' gaze may be everywhere, the surveillance perpetual, but it is the internalization of power/knowledge that shores up disciplinary power. As Foucault encapsulates, normalization necessitates "an inspecting gaze, a gaze which each individual under its weight will end up interiorizing to the points that he is his own overseer, each individual thus exercising this surveillance over, and against himself. A superb formula: power exercised continuously" (Foucault "Power/Knowledge" 155). This framework for understanding power is especially useful when examining projects of medicalization. Biomedical understandings of the body are the framework through which our bodies have become culturally intelligible (Harding 145). This opens up the possibility for intervention and surveillance, for as a condition of being normal and acceptable members of society, we tacitly agree to "being surveyed and measured by a calculating medical eye" (Finklestein 14). Medical expertise interacts with self-care and self-help, and our bodies are managed and regulated in accordance. Such a process is apparent in relation to mothering, as running alongside scientific discourses is a proliferation of pregnancy and parenting manuals, magazines, and other discursive resources that disperse these medical narratives throughout society.

Lupton details the ways in which pregnant women are counselled to avoid using tobacco, alcohol, caffeine, and to not consume fish and soft cheese; they are counselled to avoid BPA plastics, radiation from X-rays, too much vitamin A, lying on their backs in late pregnancy; and they are admonished to get enough sleep, folic acid, vitamin B, and omega 3 fatty acids (96). Moreover, pregnant women are encouraged to engage in a host of behaviours—such as researching pregnancy books to ensure that they are informed; participating in prenatal screening and testing to check for fetal abnormalities; exercising regularly; resting at work if it's physically demanding; engaging in relaxing activities; being aware of mental health problems; seeking counselling or help before and after the birth; and on and on. Once the baby is here, visits from health workers and lactation consultants, wellness checkups, and postpartum appointments extend the monitoring: mothers are checked for postpartum problems that may inhibit mother-infant bonding. Childcare books counsel women on how to bond with their babies.

These everyday discourses work their way into the lives of mothers, many of whom actively seek out such advice, disciplining their bodies as they monitor and self-police. Mothering is a wholly embodied phenomenon, and such routine bodily practices— encouraged by health care experts, parenting books, magazines, and so on—give rise to perpetual regulation, self-surveillance, and the constitution of an appropriately normalized mother identity.

GOOD MOTHER-BAD MOTHER

The deployment of scientific discourses is, crucially, constitutive of an ideal mothering archetype. Such expert knowledge produced within the natural and social sciences— psychology, economics, and so on—collectively marks out the boundaries of risky mothering. Risk should be understood here as a social and moral technology, regimenting and cajoling mothers to act in specific ways in the present to avoid future catastrophe. Mothers receive constant reminders that they and their offspring are at risk, which gives rise to a "regime of truth" that powerfully regulates and governs what is considered desirable and normal.

In the shadow of the ideal and good mother lurks the bad mother. Engaged in risky behaviours, the bad mother is always and already the object and focus of medicalization and normalization, as described above. The at-risk or bad mother is increasingly imagined as someone who is sick—addicted or depressed or emotionally unstable and so on—and who requires medical supervision and intervention. Should she resist, then other forms of control are legitimated, as the consequences of bad mothering are made apparent. The spectre of the bad mother who fails to contend with risk appropriately is a critical mode of social control, for she is an internalized figure that serves as a point of comparison for mothers to assess the quality of their own mothering (Malacrida 116).

Robyn Longhurst's research details the myriad ways that women contend with risk, and underscores, too, the importance of their being seen to do so. The regulatory discourses of medical workers, family members, friends, and even strangers encourage continual self-appraisal and discipline not only because women internalize the narratives of good mothering but also because they want to elude being viewed as a reviled figure. Other research shows that many mothers feel enormous guilt and failure if they do not live up to mothering ideals (Stearns). They constantly monitor themselves and their practices to assess their success and failure (Malacrida 116). Pregnant women express enormous anxiety and feelings of guilt if they have transgressed behavioural norms that may put their unborn child at risk, and they seek out experts to ensure optimal health and development of the child (Lupton 100).

The wider cultural obsession with risk management creates the conditions for the manufacturing of an endless list of risky mothering behaviours, which settle as truths. Aggregated data is transformed into sets of often-inconsistent guidelines in which every conceivable part of a mother's life and experience has turned into a risk to be managed. The dramatization of what could happen if precautionary measures are not taken underlies these guidelines, as stories of crack babies, fetal alcohol syndrome, obese children and adults, and so forth, litter the cultural landscape.

The everyday management of risk is an embodied one. Women avoid drinking alcohol and ingesting drugs, exercise just enough, eat a healthful diet, avoid risky activities, visit their health workers, and so. These corporeal practices are in a sense a performative condition (Butler, "Gender Trouble") of ideal mothering, and their enactment and repetition give rise to a maternal subjectivity marked by interminable anxiousness about the future of a mother's offspring. As new scientific claims are made, frequently contradicting previous instructions,[1] mothers, who bear the burden of avoiding harm, feel the burden to manage new risks. Risk management performances support a culture of intensive mothering, which Sharon Hayes describes as a "child centered, expert guided, emotionally absorbing, labor intensive, financially expensive ideology in which mothers are primarily responsible for the nurture and development of the sacred child in which children's needs take precedence over the individual needs of their mothers" (46). The symbol of the bad mother connected to so much social and individual failure helps to make natural and to essentialize this ideology, as mothers' needs are erased by the discourse of fetal and child endangerment (Bordo 77).

CONCLUSION

On the surface, the directives and advice flowing from scientific research on mothering seem only beneficial and educational. Yet the regulatory effects on women, in particular, are difficult to ignore. A failure to comply with certain medical directives can result in criminalization and formal sanctions, as described above, but medicalization compels women to self-regulate. As the figure of the bad mother is internalized as a disciplining category, women are compelled to self-scrutinize and self-police. Lupton's research indicates that middle class women are much more likely to be vigilant about taking steps to protect their unborn child. Although women living in poverty, single mothers, and women of colour are most vulnerable to formal state interventions, all women are subject, in Brian Turner's terms, to "normative coercion" (xiv).

The regulatory capacity of medicalization is immense. Contemporary scientific assertions on mothering are especially forceful, given the prominence and authority currently accorded to neuroscience and epigenetic research. These discourses contribute to and fortify a wider culture hospitable to biomedical claims, yet these truths are not totalizing. Although the emergence of new, sometimes contradictory, truths can leave mothers feeling bewildered as they impossibly navigate and integrate contrary advice, these shifts expose fissures in the production of knowledge.

Within neuroscience, Bruer's work has been pivotal in highlighting the disagreements within the field over claims about the lifelong neural effects of early experience. Other research on attachment and sleep raises questions about the links between stress and later emotional and behavioural development (Gradisar et al.), whereas Hurt et al. debunk claims about in utero cocaine use and the crack baby, imagined as forever doomed. Alcohol ingestion while pregnant is also contested within the scientific literature, with some studies suggesting that no amount of alcohol is safe (Flak et al.), whereas other longitudinal studies suggest that there are no adverse effects of low to moderate drinking (Eriksen et al). These examples serve to highlight the fractures in knowledge, making space for the interrogation of "truths" in the process of resisting the force of medicalization.

The narratives of mothers' experiences of expert knowledge indicate that some women, at least, do actively integrate and often reject scientific discourses. Research related to social class, race, and breastfeeding, for example, reveals that although a powerful cultural association exists between breastfeeding and good mothering, it is not uniform across race and class (Carter 517). Linda Blum's examination of how mothers of different classes aspired to or rejected the intensive mothering ideology and mainstream cultural imperative to breastfeed is especially revealing. It shows the ways in which scientific narratives are internalized, adapted, or refused. Other movements are emerging which seek to demedicalize pregnancy and birth, with women choosing to give birth with the assistance of midwives either at home or in birth centres. In popular culture, stories of free-range parenting are emerging, which serve to counter the intensive parenting trend in the U.S. (Wergin). An Internet parody showcasing the contradictory parenting advice mothers receive recently went viral (Dube), which indicates, again, that mothers are not simply passive bodies, but they actively engage with scientific narratives, and in a way that can be disruptive and subversive.

Shining a light on these acts of resistance is important if we are to mount a resistance to medicalization. A critique of medicalization does not necessarily imply a rejection of science (Garry 262), but resisting institutionalized practices that reduce mothers to an epidemiological risk factor is critical. Modern motherhood is marked by the perpetual anxious management of risk, and it is an extraordinary burden on women. It encourages a mode of mothering that is intensive and utterly absorbing and that requires enormous self-sacrifice as scientific mothering conflicts with other central values in Western culture (Bell 47). At the same time, social failure is reduced to the failure of mothers to be "good," thus inviting analyses and policies that reinscribe the figure of the bad mother, which both regulates from the outside and inside.

ENDNOTE

[1]It is beyond the scope of this paper to innumerate the many contradictions within the scientific literature pertaining to "scientific mothering," but it is clear that mothers navigate a slippery set of instructions, as advice related to an array of maternal behaviours—from alcohol consumption limits when pregnant (no clear scientific evidence) to when to introduce peanuts to infants—exists.

WORKS CITED

Almond, Douglas, and Janet Currie. "Killing Me Softly: The Fetal Origins Hypothesis". *The Journal of Economic Perspectives*, vol. 25, no. 3, 2011, pp. 153–172. *American Economic Association*, doi: 10.1257/jep.25.3.153.

Apple, Rima. *Perfect Motherhood: Science and Childrearing in America* Rutgers University Press, 2006.

Armstrong, Elizabeth, M., and Ernest Abel. "Fetal Alcohol Syndrome: The Origins Of A Moral Panic." *Alcohol and Alcoholism*, vol. 35, no. 3, 2000, pp. 276-82. *Oxford Journals*, doi: dx.doi.org/10.1093/alcalc/35.3.276 276-282.

Artis, Julie. "Breastfeed at Your Own Risk". *Contexts* vol. 8, no. 4 (2009): 28–34.

Bassett, Laura. "Tennessee Enacts Law To Incarcerate Pregnant Women Who Use Drugs." *The Huffington Post.* 13 Apr. 2013, www.huffingtonpost.com/2014/04/30/tennessee-to-incarcerate-_n_5241770.html. Accessed 25 Jan. 2016.

Bell, Susan E. "Intensive Performances of Mothering: A Sociological Perspective." *Qualitative Research*, vol. 4, no. 1, 2004, pp. 45-75.

Blake, Mariah. "The Damage Done: Crack Babies Talk Back." *Columbia Journal Review*, September-October 2004.

Blum, Linda. *At the Breast: Ideologies of Breastfeeding and Motherhood in the Contemporary United States*. Beacon Press. 1999.

Bordo, Susan. "Bringing Body to Theory." *Body and Flesh: A*

Philosophical Reader, edited by Donn Welton, Blackwell, 1998, pp. 84-97.

Bowlby, John. "Forty-Four Juvenile Thieves: Their Characters and Home Life." International Journal of Psychoanalysis, vol. 25, 1994, pp. 107-127, http://psycnet.apa.org/psycinfo/1945-02692-001. Accessed 16 Jan. 2017.

Bowlby, John. "Maternal Care and Mental Health." *Academic Medicine*, vol. 26, no. 4, 1951, journals.lww.com/academicmedicine/Citation/1951/07000/Maternal_Care_and_Mental_Health_.34.aspx Accessed 22 Jan. 2017.

Bowlby, John. *Attachment and Loss*. Basic, 1969.

Bruer, J. *The Myth of the First Three Years: A New Understanding of Early Brain Development and Lifelong Learning*. Free Press, 1999.

Butler, Judith. *Gender Trouble: Feminism and the Subversion of Identity*. Routledge, 2006.

Butler, Patrick. "Policymakers Seduced by Neuroscience to Justify Early Intervention Agenda." *The Guardian*, 6 May 2014, www.theguardian.com/society/2014/may/06/policymakers-neuroscience-justify-early-intervention-agenda-bruce-perry. Accessed 16 Jan. 2017.

Carter, S. K. "Good, Bad, and Extraordinary Mothers: Infant Feeding and Mothering in African American Mothers' Breastfeeding Narratives." *Sociology of Race and Ethnicity*, vol. 1, no. 4, 2015, pp. 517-531, www.asanet.org/research-publications/journals/content/good-bad-and-extraordinary-mothers-infant-feeding-and. Accessed 16 Jan. 2017.

"Child Welfare Information Gateway." *Parent-Child Interaction Therapy*. 27 May 2016, www.childwelfare.gov/pubs/f-interact-bulletin/. Accessed 16. Jan. 2017.

Dube, Rebecca. "Exhausted New Mom's Hilarious Take on 'Expert' Sleep Advice Goes Viral." *TODAY*, 23 Apr. 2013, www.today.com/parents/exhausted-new-moms-hilarious-take-expert-sleep-advice-goes-viral-6C9559908. Accessed 26 May. 2016.

Dubow, Sara. *Ourselves Unborn: A History of the Fetus in Modern America*. Oxford University, Press, 2011.

Eriksen, H-L Falgreenet, et al. "The Effects of Low to Moderate Prenatal Alcohol Exposure in Early Pregnancy on IQ in Five-Year-

Old Children." *BJOG: An International Journal of Obstetrics & Gynaecology*, vol. 119, no. 10, 2012, pp. 1191-1200. *PubMed*, doi: 0.1111/j.1471-0528.2012.03394.x.

Finkelstein, Joanne L. "Biomedicine and Technocratic Power." *The Hastings Center Report*, vol. 20, no. 4, 1990, pp. 13-16. *Wiley*, doi: 10.2307/3562760.

Fitzgerald, Susan. "'Crack Baby' Study Ends with Unexpected but Clear Result." *Philly Inquirer*, 22 July 2013, http://articles.philly.com/2013-07-22/news/40709969_1_hallam-hurt-so-called-crack-babies-funded-study. Accessed 25 Jan. 2016.

Flak, Audrey L., et al. "The Association of Mild, Moderate, and Binge Prenatal Alcohol Exposure and Child Neuropsychological Outcomes: A Meta-Analysis." *Alcoholism: Clinical and Experimental Research*, vol. 38, no. 1, 2013, pp. 214-226. *Wiley*, doi: 10.1111/acer.12214.

Foucault, Michel. *Discipline and Punish: The Birth of the Prison*. Vintage, 1979.

Foucault, Michel. *Power/Knowledge: Selected Interviews and Other Writings, 1972-1977*. Pantheon, 1980.

Franzek, Ernst J., et al. "Prenatal Exposure to the 1944-45 Dutch 'Hunger Winter' and Addiction Later in Life." *Addiction*, vol. 103, no. 3, 2008, pp. 433-438. *Research Gate*, doi: 10.1111/j.1360-0443.2007.02084.x.

Garry, Ann. "Medicine and Medicalization: A Response to Purdy." *Bioethics*, vol. 15, no. 3, 2001, pp. 262-269. *Wiley*, doi: 10.1111/1467-8519.00236.

Gerhardt, Sue. *Why Love Matters: How Affections Shapes a Baby's Brain*. Taylor and Francis. 2004.

Gradisar, M.K., et al. "Behavioral Interventions for Infant Sleep Problems: A Randomized Controlled Trial." *Pediatrics*, vol. 137, no. 6, 2016. *Research Gate*, doi: 10.1542/peds.2015-1486.

Gunnar, Megan R., et al. "Attachment, Temperament, and Adrenocortical Activity in Infancy: A Study of Psychoendocrine Regulation." *Developmental Psychology*, vol. 25, no. 3, 1989, pp. 355-363. *Research Gate*, doi: 10.1037//0012-1649.25.3.355.

Hall, Stuart. "Foucault: Power, Knowledge and Discourse."- *Discourse Theory and Practice: a Reader*, edited by Margaret Wetherell et al. Sage, 2001, pp. 72-80.

Harding, Jennifer. "Bodies at Risk: Sex, Surveillance and Hormone Replacement Therapy." *Foucault, Health and Medicine*, edited by Robin Bunton and Alison Petersen, Routledge, 1997, pp. 134-150.

Hurt, Hallam, et al. "Children with and without Gestational Cocaine Exposure: A Neurocognitive Systems Analysis." *Neurotoxicology and Teratology*, vol. 31, no. 6, 2009, pp. 334-341. *NCNI*, doi: 10.1016/j.ntt.2009.08.002.

Hurt, Hallam, et al. "A Prospective Comparison of Developmental Outcome of Children with In Utero Cocaine Exposure and Controls Using the Battelle Developmental Inventory." *Journal of Developmental & Behavioral Pediatrics*, vol. 22, no. 1, 2001, pp. 27-34, journals.lww.com/jrnldbp/Abstract/2001/02000/A_Prospective_Comparison_of_Developmental_Outcome.5.aspx?trendmd_shared=0. Accessed. 16 Jan. 2017.

Kirkbride, James B., et al. "Prenatal Nutrition, Epigenetics and Schizophrenia Risk: Can We Test Causal Effects?" *Epigenomics*, vol. 4, no. 3, 2012, pp. 303-315. *NCBI*, doi: 10.2217/epi.12.20.

Knowles, Caroline. *Family Boundaries: The Invention of Normality & Dangerousness*. Broadview, 1996.

Landecker, Hannah. "Food as Exposure: Nutritional Epigenetics and the New Metabolism." *BioSocieties* vol. 6, no. 2, 2011, pp. 167-194. *NCBI*, doi: 10.1057/biosoc.2011.1.

Longhurst, Robyn. "Pregnant Bodies, Public Scrutiny: 'Giving' Advice to Pregnant Women." *Embodied Geographies: Spaces, Bodies and Rites of Passage*, edited by Elizabeth K Teather, Routledge, 1999, pp. 77-90.

Lupton, Deborah. *The Social Worlds of the Unborn*. Palgrave, 2013

Malacrida, Claudia. *Cold Comfort: Mothers, Professionals, and Attention Deficit Disorder*. University of Toronto, 2003.

Marrus, Ellen. "Crack Babies and the Constitution: Ruminations about Addicted Pregnant Women after Ferguson v. City of Charleston." *Villanova Law Review*, vol. 47, no. 2, 2002, pp. 299-340, http://digitalcommons.law.villanova.edu/vlr/vol47/iss2/1/. Accessed 22 Jan. 2017.

Morgan, Kathryn. "Contested Bodies, Contested Knowledges." *The Politics of Women's Health*, edited by Susan Sherwin, Temple University Press, 1998, pp. 83-12, openlibrary.org/books/

OL20280854M/CONTESTED_BODIES_CONTESTED_KNOWLEDGES_WOMEN_HEALTH_AND_THE_POLITICS_OF_MEDICALIZATION. Accessed 22 Jan. 2017.

Mulder, E.J., et al. "Prenatal Maternal Stress: Effects on Pregnancy and the (Unborn) Child." *Early Human Development*, vol. 70, no. 1-2, 2002, pp. 3-14, www.ncbi.nlm.nih.gov/pubmed/12441200. Accessed 22 Jan. 2017.

Nettleton, Sarah. *The Sociology of Health and Illness*. Polity, 1995.

Newnham, John P., and Michael G. Ross. *Early Life Origins of Human Health and Disease*. Basel: Karger, 2009. P.

Oliver, James. *They F*** You Up: How to Survive Family Life*. Bloomsbury, 2002.

Oliver, James. *How Not to F*** Them Up: The First Three Years*. Vermilion, 2011.

Opler, Mark, et al. "Prenatal Exposure to Lead, Aminolevulinic Acid, and Schizophrenia: Further Evidence." *Environ. Health Perspect.* vol. 116, no. 11, 2008, pp. 1586-1590. *Environmental Health Perspectives*, doi: 10.1289/ehp.10464.

Paltrow, Lynn. M., and Jeanne Flavin. "Arrests of and Forced Interventions on Pregnant Women in the United States, 1973-2005: Implications for Women's Legal Status and Public Health." *Journal of Health Politics, Policy and Law*, vol. 38, no. 2, 2013, pp. 299-343. *Journal of Health Politics, Policy and Law*, doi:10.1215/03616878-1966324.

"Parent-Child Interaction Therapy with At-Risk Families." *Child Welfare Information Gateway*, U.S. Department of Health and Human Services, Children's Bureau, 2013, https://www.childwelfare.gov/pubs/f-interactbulletin/. Accessed 22 Jan. 2017.

Paul, Annie Murphy. "How the First Nine Months Shape the Rest of Your Life." *Time*, 22 Sept. 2010, time.com/84145/how-the-first-nine-months-shape-the-rest-of-your-life/. Accessed 22 2017.

Petersen, Alan R., and Robin Bunton. *Foucault, Health and Medicine*. Routledge, 1997.

Pincus, D. B., Choate, M. L., Eyberg, S. M., & Barlow, D. H. "Treatment of Young Children with Separation Anxiety Disorder Using Parent-Child Interaction Therapy". *Cognitive and Behavioral Practice*, 12, 2005, pp. 126-135.

Ruhl, P. Lealle. "Disarticulating Liberal Subjectivities: Abortion and Fetal Protection." *Feminist Studies*, vol. 28, no. 1, 2002, pp. 37-60. *JSTOR*, doi: 10.2307/3178494.

Rutter, Michael. "Clinical Implications of Attachment Concepts: Retrospect and Prospect *." *Journal of Child Psychology and Psychiatry*, vol. 36, no. 4, 1995, pp. 549-571. *Wiley*, doi: 10.1111/j.1469-7610.1995.tb02314.x.

Stearns, Cindy. "Breastfeeding and The Good Maternal Body." *Gender & Society* vol. 13, no. 3, 1999, 308-325, journals.sagepub.com/doi/abs/10.1177/089124399013003003. Accessed 22 Jan. 2017.

Sheridan, M. A., et al. "Variation in Neural Development as a Result of Exposure to Institutionalization Early in Childhood." *Proceedings of the National Academy of Sciences*, vol. 109, no. 32, 2012, pp. 12927-2932., doi: 10.1073/pnas.1200041109.

Singh, Ilina. "Doing Their Jobs: Mothering with Ritalin in a Culture of Mother-Blame." *Social Science & Medicine*, vol. 59, no. 6, 2004, 1193-1205, www.ncbi.nlm.nih.gov/pubmed/15210091. Accessed 22 Jan. 2017.

Suskind, Dana. *Thirty Million Words: Building a Child's Brain.* Dutton, 2015. Print.

Teicher, M.H., et al. "Childhood Maltreatment Is Associated with Reduced Volume in the Hippocampal Subfields CA3, Dentate Gyrus, and Subiculum." *Proceedings of the National Academy of Sciences*, vol. 109, no. 9, 2012, pp. 563-572. *NCBI*, doi: 10.1073/pnas.1115396109.

Turner, Brian. "Foreword: From Governmentality to Risk, Some Reflections on Foucault's Contributions to Medical Sociology." *Foucault, Health and Medicine*, edited by Alan R. Petersen and Robin Bunton. Routledge, 1997, pp. ix-xxii.

Waterland, Robert A., and Karin B. Michels. "Epigenetic Epidemiology of the Developmental Origins Hypothesis." *Annual Review of Nutrition*, vol. 27, no. 1, 2007, pp. 363-388, www.ncbi.nlm.nih.gov/pubmed/17465856. Accessed 22 Jan. 2017.

Wergin, Clemins. "The Case for Free-Range Parenting." *New York Times*, 20 Mar. 2015, www.nytimes.com/2015/03/20/opinion/the-case-for-free-range-parenting.html. Accessed 22 Jan. 2017.

Yao, Ruofan, et al. "Obesity and the Risk of Stillbirth: A Population-Based Cohort Study." *American Journal of Obstetrics and*

Gynecology, vol. 210, no. 5, 2014, pp. 457e1-457e9. *NCBI*, doi: 10.1016/j.ajog.2014.01.044.

Zola, Irving. "Medicine as an Institution of Social Control." *Sociological Review*, vol. 20, no. 4, 1972, pp. 487-504. *Wiley*, doi: 10.1111/j.1467-954X.1972.tb00220.x.

Zuckerman, Lee, and Ina Weiner. "Maternal Immune Activation Leads to Behavioral and Pharmacological Changes in the Adult Offspring." *Journal of Psychiatric Research*, vol. 39, no. 3, 2005, pp. 311-323. *NCBI*, doi: 10.1016/j.jpsychires.2004.08.008.

Hospital Archive

RELA MAZALI

SHE WAS IN her midthirties, with two boys and an IUD. They were making ends meet for their kids and themselves without any savings to speak of. Partly, because they started out with none and paid rent and got by on whatever they made. And partly because after ten years of his travelling abroad on the job and her never joining him, given the costs, she had finally gone along on a couple of trips, when they expanded his high-tech senior manager's business trips into short vacations. And partly, too, because only part of her workweek generated income, while the other part (very slowly) generated art, which meant they were paying for after-school caretakers till the kids were about eight (when they learned to mostly respect the hours of artwork she did at home). At the time, some of her art had just made it into a few public venues but made no income. That was the setup, and the two of them were definitely okay but struggling. Both and each. To make things a little easier. To make things. To make something of self (his, hers) separately.

She wanted an abortion. She was clear about it immediately and calmly. Another baby was out of the question at this stage. She knew what it meant to her, how life-changing and all-engulfing and time-swallowing each baby had been. How two infants, two years apart, had kept her sleepless and exhausted for about five years straight. How hard it had been and how hard and guilt-infested it still was to carve out artwork hours and to keep them from succumbing to much more justifiable paidwork or motherwork hours. And no, motherwork wasn't all there was to mother, but there was a whole demanding lot of it. And sometimes, some of it—of the downright work—was even fun or funny or tender or satisfying. And sometimes it was smotherwork.

In any case, she had no patience with the U.S.-TV-style dramatization that constructed abortion as unavoidably, agonizingly ambivalent. Or with guilt or mourning of any kind for the nonborn. She firmly didn't want to mother a child she would have to resent, even if she also fell in love with her. Or him. She knew—no ambivalence—that she wanted an abortion.

She could have gone straight to a private clinic. She didn't know exactly how to go about finding one, but she did know, vaguely, that they should be findable. There had to be lots of them because they provided reliable, routine services to many thousands of women every year. She also knew that even though the law of the land made legal abortions conditional on the approval of a state-appointed committee, unapproved and (therefore) technically illegal ones were very common, completely safe and tacitly condoned. By the time she was thirty-something, in the early 1980s, she knew very well that the law was Israel's frequently unenforced lip service to the orthodox Jewish parties wielding a swing vote in the government. She hadn't thought much and didn't think much at the time about the lip service. She registered the extremely loose enforcement of this law of Israel's land as an expedient political compromise. A manoeuvre giving both sides (a significant) part of what they were after; the orthodox religious parties got an official, state law and a degree (or at least a façade) of legal power over women's fertility and sexuality. The nonreligious parties, both on the right and on the left, got a placated constituency of a majority of nonreligious women who (behind the façade) were allowed a considerable degree of control over their fertility and bodies and sexuality. Any woman with access to sufficient funds and adequate information could get a medically sound, responsible abortion with no legal repercussions. It seemed like a relatively liberal, workable arrangement. She barely noticed and didn't really register the built-in discrimination. She did note, though, that while not at all poor, she was far from rich and would be much better off reducing the not-to-be-sneezed-at expense of a private abortion. So she decided on a legal (and accordingly) subsidized one.

Her sick-fund dues were paid regularly. She was fully insured through one of the state-subsidized labour-union funds that still provided good medical coverage in Israel, in the early 1980s. She was consistently healthy save an occasional flu. She hardly ever needed or used any medical services. This was the one thing she had needed or wanted in years now. She was confident that she had a right to have an abortion subsidized by the fund. That is, a legal one. And she was confident that she had a right to make autonomous decisions about her pregnancy, her future, her family's future, her body and whether or not it would serve to lodge and feed an additional embryo. The state and the state-backed sick fund owed her that right. She was also sure the committee would approve, given her age (well over thirty), her history of high-risk pregnancy and the specific, somewhat increased risk of pregnancy with an intact IUD.

She didn't know how to go about locating "the committee" or submitting her request. She did know that it had to happen fast. And this was quite a few years before the web started making "how-to" information much more accessible to literate and Internet-literate people. So she went to the neighbourhood sick-fund clinic to enquire. She didn't need a doctor, and she didn't want to go through the usual forty-five-minute-to-almost-two-hour wait for one, tensely guarding her turn against the constant contest, customary in almost any line in Israel in the early eighties. All she needed was some basic technical information, which the clerk at the reception desk should be able to provide. There was a line at the reception window too, opposite two wooden benches, which were placed along the wall of the small, crowded anteroom. "Are you last?" was the standard greeting used on entering the room; usually answered either with a nod or with a finger levelled in the direction of someone else and a terse, "He is" or "She is." Even at reception and not just outside the doctor's door, an occasional entrance greeting stated, "I'm just a question," claiming a supposed right to skip the line and quickly obtain a piece of focused information. Almost invariably, a small volcano erupted at "Just a question," in angry retorts and reprimands and people rising from wooden benches (if they'd been lucky or early enough to get a seat) to physically assert their places in line and sometimes shoving and pushing, in the overcrowded space where she'd come to ask how you apply for an abortion. The clerk commanding the line was a tense little man whose service provision was chronically sour faced. "How would I know?" he answered extra loudly when she finally stood in front of him, "*I've* never had an abortion." Speech throttled by the audacity and the farce, she turned and left.

A day or so later, a woman she'd met recently through a mutual friend, told her with (to her) surprising ease and openness that she'd just had an abortion approved last week, based on marital status; she was unmarried. That, she said, made approval automatic. And being underage. Automatic. And having filed for divorce if you were married. Filing was enough. You didn't have to go through with the divorce.

In her midthirties, she only vaguely registered the subtext. That is, the prioritization and policing and production of "legitimate," in-wedlock Jewish babies, via the somewhat loose, but selective enforcement of the law of Israel's land.

"The committee," she learned from this woman, was multiple committees; a separate, autonomous, but presumably closely regulated crew at each hospital. And there was, she was told, a small, specialized hospital not too far from her house that actually specialized in abortions. It would probably be quicker to go through the process there. She called information for the phone numbers of two or three hospitals including the small specialized one and made it through hours of busy signals to a human voice at each number, which she asked how and when to apply to the committee. It met just once a week, she heard each voice say. And there was another line: a waiting list. She made an appointment for the closest date, which—as predicted—was at the small hospital.

The social worker was shocked. That—the shock—was distinct and evident at the preliminary, intake interview. Then, after the interview, when she walked into a room and came before the committee, it turned out to be the social worker and two men. She was startled and disoriented. So the social worker, who hadn't bothered to explain, wasn't a (presumably) supportive or an (presumably) understanding and empathetic screening professional and woman, preparing her for a review of her case. She was the review, the crew. Both preliminary and final. The two men didn't bother to explain anything either or to introduce themselves and she, obediently, didn't ask. It wasn't her place. They were the committee. She was the supplicant.

Her polite acquiescence was automatic. A quick involuntary reflex. Her resistant energies, her detached observation, her strategizing were totally exhausted. Exhaustively pledged to what she had come for. Hyper-braced to play her part before the committee, her mind was blank on all other matters. Correct comportment and deferent compliance were her default. Before questions asked or objections raised. She was thoroughbred. Deviations came to mind only later, often *after* they had been foreclosed. They said she needed extra time and enough reflection to make out the contours of the situation, to recognize the unexpected moves it harboured. To recognize her own as expected, tamed. Which was why she didn't even *think* to ask. She thought of it only later. That she could have asked, that it would have been within her rights, that it wouldn't have been unreasonable, that she should have asked, should have contested this lack of basic, decent, human etiquette, this complete disregard. For her.

Once it was over, their failure to start by providing their names and titles seemed so audacious that she mistrusted her memory of it. Maybe they did—introduce themselves—and she was just so tense and apprehensive that she didn't remember? Maybe it was her lapse, not theirs? Could they really have been so unprofessional? So totally indifferent to applicants' personhood? And applicants' rights? The upshot, in any case, was that she didn't know who they were and, possibly more important, what they were; which official titles had qualified them for membership in the crew. She guessed they were doctors, or maybe a doctor and a psychologist or a psychiatrist, or maybe, although she thought this might be taking it too far, a doctor and a lawyer. She wasn't sure why the doctor was the constant. Maybe because they were in a hospital.

The social worker looked—to her, from her midthirties—like an old woman and, in addition, like a very timid one. She actually used a whisper to wrap up the intake interview, "I strongly advise you to avoid repeating what you've just disclosed." Disclosed, that is, after hearing that her age (well over thirty), her history of high-risk pregnancy and the specific, somewhat increased risk of pregnancy with an intact IUD, were all irrelevant. Insufficient. Unfortunately, the aging woman had said, using the adverb softly, not authoritatively, projecting herself as a confidante and ally, unfortunately, she was ineligible. In Israel's mid-1980s, none of these facts, nor all of them combined, qualified as grounds for a legal (and accordingly) subsidized abortion. "If you insist, you'll need to sign *a written statement* to that effect," she said in the same low, conspiratorial voice, "and I very strongly recommend that you refrain from doing that." That she refrain, in other words, from coming before the committee and stating that she was pregnant by someone other than her husband.

It was a lie. She wasn't. But she was completely thrown to discover she was ineligible and she was also completely determined. On a surge of mounting indignation she manufactured a lie. Not premeditated. Not Plan B. It materialized, instantaneous, when needed. A sudden joy! Glee. She wasn't lying for her life and she knew it. She wasn't destitute. She had options. Of this she was constantly aware. She wasn't even sure, looking back later, that she would have lied like she did, that she would have been able to—so lightly and lightning fast—if she were utterly desperate. The lie-inducing nebula was adamant and angry and entitled. All of a sudden it was fully entitled. And, at its edges, wry and playful. She had a right and she knew it and she would act to ensure it, even if the institution moved to deny it. It felt daring. She felt daring. Resourceful, powerful. Once spoken, she found herself enjoying the lie and its gamble and the unexpected look of shock on the face of the social worker. She felt strong in her now-discovered capacity to shock. She hadn't meant to. In the split second before she deciphered the shock, she'd actually assumed that a social worker would already have heard hundreds of confessions like this. When the shock turned into "I strongly advise," she felt strong again in her capacity to stay the course, to persist in shocking against solemn, official, care-professional wisdom. When pressed and without consciously noting it, she had quickly divined the subtext of the escape clauses, their prioritization of what religion and the state considered legitimate paternity. She had conjectured that a declaration of adultery would very likely force their hand.

The visible shock and the apparently worried, whispered prescription placed the older woman in a culture and a set of codes that she, for her part, had rejected and pretty methodically shed. From her stand of relative freedom, she felt an undercurrent of disdain, almost pity, for the alleged authority she was facing. She sensed the cumulative strength of the complicated but stable open marriage she had crafted with her partner (defined by the authorities as "husband"), of the sound, strong relationship that allowed her to whip out this particular lie which, at other points in her life, could easily have been a truth. She savoured the fast, confident ease with which she opted for publicly, officially declaring her (falsified) infidelity, culminating in a signed statement before the committee. And the distinct absence of any fear that this document, her declaration, would come back to haunt or harm her.

She knew what the social worker was getting at. She knew that the orthodox religious courts that implemented divorce law and controlled divorce in Israel could ban a proven adulteress (after her divorce) from both husband and "possessor." She knew that a woman's adultery could be used in court to deny her child custody. And knowing all this and knowing her partner and knowing the history and timbre of their established, particular contract, she also knew that none of this threatened her. She knew she was safe—not from divorce, which was always a possibility—but from that kind of violence.

In the shocked, troubled social worker, she saw a woman whose mind was restricted in stale presuppositions about what people would or wouldn't do, could or couldn't do, about what would be too fearsome or shameful to do or to say. And, more important perhaps, about the inevitable, unavoidable risks of such saying or such doing. Unknown and unknowable to the social worker, she had stopped sharing these suppositions quite a while ago. It had been over a decade since she'd finally and decisively refused to go on taking for granted what, it seemed, was still taken for granted by the older woman. On the other hand, and unrecognized by her in her midthirties, she probably knew much less than the social worker of the unimagined, destructive results of doing what isn't done and saying what isn't said. She could be confidently reckless.

She did recognize though, through the intoxication of power, that she might have felt considerably more vulnerable if the lie hadn't been a lie. Her petition for committee approval, even if it wasn't destitute and desperate, would have felt much more vulnerable if she'd been telling a truth. The insulating layer of untruth let her put less—of her—at stake. It felt mischievous to perform disclosure of a frightened desperation without giving them a truth. It felt marginally amusingly in control to know for sure that they had no way of extracting it. Despite the authority they wielded. Despite her supplicant stand.

They were well aware that they were being lied to. That is, as a rule, by many of those petitioning them. Many women had prior knowledge, often more extensive than hers was, of the escape clauses and the escape scripts that fit them. In a few, specific cases, the committee knew, or at least strongly suspected, that they were being lied to, even if they couldn't prove it. But in many, the vast majority, of such cases, they tended to stick to the cues and the script and accede the liar's request. Strong suspicions aside.

Decades after the facts, given extra time and enough reflection, she tried to make out the contours of the situation, to recognize what it harboured. What is it that they're doing then, she asked herself. What are they doing when they pay lip service and go through the motions? When they know they're coercing or inviting people to lie and they know, as a rule, that people are lying, even if they don't know precisely which? What are they doing when they pretend, as a rule, to believe people they suspect of lying and when they let them get away with it? Obviously they're not after truth. Which, in hindsight, made her sense—back then—of an insulating layer of untruth totally beside the point; an illusion of safety that she had clung to, of no relevance to the committee. They were uninterested.

What were they, what *are* they, interested in? The statistics? That is, the control enacted through gestures of deference performed by thousands and thousands of women? The cumulative theatre of deference? Even if most of the petitions are granted? Ninety-eight percent, to be precise, she discovered more than thirty years later when a study of the committees was reported on page one of the Hebrew daily, *Haaretz*, on 9 June 2016, in an article by Ofra

Edelman, titled: "Even in 2016, Women Forced to Lie to Abortion Committees." As researcher Noya Rimalt told the journalist, "At the end of the day, the vast majority of abortions are performed through evading, not enforcing, the law." So what then? Are they staging a morality play of power? Upholding an appearance of upholding the law.

She could see, in fact she had seen all along, that even as mere lip service, recognized as such by both the power and the petitioner, the motions gone through by each woman effected her isolation. Shut her into secrecy, exacted an obligation to heretofore keep her lie hidden from state agents. At least for a time, she knew, the lip service circumscribed each liar within the confines of her lonely personal risk.

In hindsight, from well into the second millennium, she could re-read and reinterpret the lip service. Still a relatively liberal, workable arrangement ensuring both legal-bureaucratic power and a placated constituency. But also, no less, an expressly privatized and privatizing one, deflecting the force of a broadly shared social need and a fundamental right into individualized, socially stratified coping strategies. Rather than feeding a resistant energy joining those who shared the need and the right, it was siphoned off into each guarded lie and life that could now be gotten on with.

When she came before the committee in her midthirties, it of course held the power to approve or deny her a legal, subsidized abortion. But back then, she held and she felt she held a complement power to view them critically, even scornfully, to reject their legitimacy, although she couldn't reject their dominion. To bend the rules and lie to their faces in full knowledge that this was just. That she was right. In a "political arena," described by Hedva Eyal, "whose power isn't necessarily drawn from public exposure but rather from clandestine action and its access to abortions in spite of the restrictive law." She was already nearing the end of her sixties when Eyal noted this in her review of a book by Delila Amir on the legal and social history of abortions in Israel. The review, published in Hebrew on page forty-two of *Haaretz Books*, on June 9 2016, was titled, "Time to Talk about One of the Most Silenced Subjects in Israel."

The complement power of lying she sensed at her disposal three-plus decades earlier subsumed an intact, solid ownership of what it was that was not-a-lie, what it was that was being distorted. And the minute details of the distortion. Yes, she was pregnant. Yes, it was unintentional. Yes, she'd been using birth control. Yes, it was an IUD. Yes, it had been reliable for many years and periodically renewed by a doctor as required by the prescription. Yes, they had each other's standing consent to have sex with, and often affection for, other partners. Yes, they unfailingly let each other know when they exercised it. Yes, there were long periods of time when neither of them exercised it. Yes, some of her sexual partners had had the capacity to ejaculate sperm. No, the most recent one hadn't. No, none of the others had been very recent. No, she wasn't and couldn't be pregnant by any of them. A full reality check of all this was readily available, she knew, compliments of her partner, a.k.a. husband, who would listen to the details of her lie and share the same ownership of what it was that was not-a-lie and what it was that was being distorted. And the exact same details of the distortion.

Just knowing this was stabilizing; that he inhabited the same reality and knew the same knowledge, as unknown and invisible as these were to anyone besides the two of them. Just knowing this provided her with a bedrock of fact, made what was not-a-lie tangible. True.

About a decade after she came before the committee, a brief, back page item in the paper reported a fire at the small hospital that specialized in abortions, with no casualties save the entire hospital archive (the components of which were still stored on paper in the mid-1980s to the mid-1990s). She heard a celebratory laugh. Hers. Sudden, alien, almost a bark. The room had never occurred to her before. Lined, she now imagined, floor to ceiling with metal shelves. Along the walls and then again at intervals in between them. The folder had never occurred to her. Cardboard, she guessed. Standing stuffed among the others, presumably arranged according to date or first letters of last names or both. Repository of the physical traces of the action she'd taken to protect her right back in her midthirties. The paper page she had signed in two copies (or was it one?) underneath a false statement in her own wording and her own handwriting—okayed by the committee after she'd recited it aloud—of the non-husbanded paternity of a microscopic fetus. The bark emitted by her vocal chords exposed the threat. It had been there after all. Stowed away, all these years, in the shelf-lined room, embodied in the paper evidence through which state power could side with and consolidate male-spouse power, if circumstances ever turned badly against her. The laugh registered her relief that now, by some fluke that looked like divine justice, it had (apparently) been incinerated.

Fat Blame and Fat Shame

A Failure of Maternal Responsibility

KELSEY IOANNONI

THE BAD MOTHER is all around us, and she takes the blame for societies' ills. Whether she is the welfare mother who cannot afford to put healthy food on the table, the organic mom who restricts their child's food intake, or the mom who overindulges their child's food requests, the weight of their children lies on the shoulders of mothers. Mothers are typically responsible for making dinners, packing lunches, prepping snacks, and even acting as role models of health and fitness for their children (Jackson et al.). And for whatever does not go according to plan, these mothers take the blame.

This chapter highlights the swelling field of literature around obese and overweight children and mother blame. In it, I review literature in the area of motherhood studies, fat studies, and child health care to address the following question: how do researchers in fat studies and motherhood studies describe maternal responsibility when it comes to children's weight? I argue that mothers of "overweight" or "obese" children are considered bad mothers for having failed to adequately fulfill their supposed moral and maternal responsibility of feeding, nurturing, and regulating their children and their children's weight. As such, I argue that having overweight children is representative of a failure in maternal responsibility.

This chapter is rooted in the nexus of fat studies and motherhood studies. As Sandra Solovay and Ester Rothblum argue, fat studies is "an interdisciplinary field of scholarship marked by an aggressive, consistent, rigorous critique of the negative assumptions, stereotypes and stigma placed on fat and the fat body" (2). Jan Wright further points out that fat studies emerged from traditions similar to feminist and women's studies. She also argues that the preoccupation with weight and body size has been important to many social theorists, but specifically feminists for several decades. This field attempts to combat the dominant ideologies surrounding "obesity," which allows for the marginalization, pathologization, mistreatment, abuse, and discrimination of a significant segment of the population that transcends demographic boundaries (Gard and Wright).

Throughout this chapter, I explore the relationship between bad mothering and weight. The language I use to describe weight is fluid. Although the words are not necessarily used interchangeably in their truest form, for this chapter I understand "fat," "obese," and "overweight" to mean the same thing. These terms are problematic, as they focus on a biomedical model of understanding body types, marking obesity and overweight as deviating from what is considered healthy and normal. These terms require significant interrogation. However, although I do find these terms to be problematic,[1] in an effort to be consistent with the research reviewed herein, I will use the terms interchangeably, based on the relevant research.

THE GOOD MOTHER, BAD MOTHER DICHOTOMY

Molly Ladd-Taylor argues that there is no good mother without having a bad mother to which she can be compared. In her work on mother worship and mother blame, Ladd-Taylor highlights the invisibility of the good mother in contemporary mainstream politics and notes how this is a significant deviation from past representations of motherhood. Mother blame, according to Ladd-Taylor, escalated after the 1940s—with prominent images of overbearing mothers keeping their children too close and accusations of stay-at-home mothers being responsible for the production of homosexual or delinquent sons, or of black mothers causing the unemployment of black men. Many of these images are still prevalent and many more have been added: mothers are now blamed for children's sexual activity, drug use, youth violence, and, as this chapter highlights, their weight. Therefore, the bad mother, according to Ladd-Taylor, holds symbolic power. A clear example of this is the ever-prevalent image of the black, welfare mom, or the crack-addict mother. Motherhood, and specifically the so-called good mother, represents class privilege.

Other motherhood scholars, such as Paula Caplan, highlight how mothers are typically blamed for the psychological or emotional problems of children. Caplan highlights the existence of both "Good Mother Myths" and "Bad Mother Myths." The Good Mother Myths set the standards of motherhood that no woman can match. Caplan gives the example of the misconception of mothers always being 100 percent naturally nurturing, an unrealistic expectation that is not extended to fathers. The Bad Mother Myth, however, as Caplan notes "allow[s] us to take mothers' neutral or bad behaviour—because mother[s] are human, so we do bad things—or even mothers' good behaviour, and transform it into further proof that mothers are bad" (594). These myths about mothers are not mutually exclusive.

Shari Thurer furthers this argument and notes that "the current ideology of good mothering is not only spurious, it is oblivious of a mother's desires, limitations, and context, and when things go wrong she tends to get blamed" (332). This ideology of good mothering can be extended through Caplan's argument—in effort to maintain power, society needs the bad mother to act as a scapegoat for societal ills. For example, children's weight is blamed on the mother instead of looking at societal problems that foster increases in weight, such as access to healthy food.

Current standards for good mothering are so elusive, and in constant contradiction, that they cannot be attained. One of the major myths of motherhood that Thurer outlines is that a child's wellbeing is imperatively, and almost entirely, moulded by the quality of upbringing the child receives, which lies almost exclusively on the shoulders of mothers. These myths of motherhood defy common sense, and the stakes of being a mother are very high.

Linking the responsibility of a child's weight with the good mother, bad mother dichotomy is not a new phenomenon. Michael Gard and Jan Wright, in their work challenging scientific research on obesity, highlight the work of German psychiatrist Hilde Bruch.

Bruch was one of the first modern scholars to attribute the blame of childhood obesity to mothers. Mothers of obese children, according to Bruch, lie about how much food they give their children and are generally bossy and neurotic. Bruch argues the following:

> The giving and receiving of food was a tie of great significance in the relationship between a mother and her fat child, one which had retained, in a way, the same significance which food normally plays in early infancy.... Mothers of fat children are singularly unable to permit their children a normal unfolding of their personalities. These children are overstuffed not only with food; all other aspects of their physical care are greatly and anxiously exaggerated.... mothers live out their own problems and frustrations in these children. (qtd. in Gard and Wright 75)

Susie Orbach moves Bruch's arguments forward in her work *Fat is a Feminist Issue*, in which she describes compulsive eating, and in turn fatness, as an expression of the relationship between mothers and daughters. As women are socialized to become mothers, the role of providing for the family in the home, such as meal preparation and feeding children, is one of their central jobs. Orbach argues that the home is one of the only spaces in which women hold social power. One of the crucial roles in motherhood, Orbach argues, is for a mother to help ease her daughter into the female social role, and daughters learn to model feminine behaviour from their mothers. However, the world in which mothers are socializing their daughters is one of unjust and unequal power relationships between men and women, and exposing daughters to these power relations reproduces inequality. In an effort to prepare daughters for the inequality of the real world, Orbach argues that mothers, from an early age, hold back their daughters' desire to be autonomous and productive people, and instead focus their daughters' energy into caring for others.

This process of leading daughters into adulthood can pose problems for the mother, according to Orbach. By attentively feeding her daughter, the mother fulfills her need to be a "good mother" by being continuously nurturing. Although mothers want their daughters to leave them, as they have been preparing them for such departure, they also do not them to leave, as it triggers the end of motherhood, which Orbach says leads to powerlessness.

How does this relate with overeating and, in turn, fatness? Orbach says that feeding and nurturing play a crucial role in mothering—a mother must make sure her daughter is properly fed but not overfed, that her daughter looks healthy, and that her daughter is prepared to take on the nurturer role as a mother herself. In essence, the mother must reproduce the role that she has been socialized into. For the daughter, however, choices around food mark independence as she ages, and if the mother's nurturance is then cut off, the daughter turns to eating in search of comfort, love, and support. Orbach argues that "in overfeeding herself, the daughter may be trying to reject her mother's role while at the same time reproaching the mother for inadequate nurturing; or she may be attempting to retain a sense of identity with her mother" (20).

Orbach's work blames mothers for improperly wielding the only form of social power that women hold: control over the domestic domain. This maternal blame is in stark contrast to attempts around the period in which Orbach is writing, to push women out of the domestic domain and to expand their social, political, and economic power. Orbach herself is a psychotherapist, and her work on fatness and mothers focuses on psychological processes of overeating, which neglects the social construction of the ideology of good mothering and a so-called healthy weight. She places the responsibility of weight problems on the mother.

SHIFTING THE STIGMA: MOTHERS AS FAILED ROLE MODELS

The idea that mothers of overweight or fat children are bad mothers is further explored in the work of Debra Jackson and her colleagues. They interviewed a series of mothers to discuss their experiences as mothers to overweight or obese children and found four key themes among them. 1) They felt judged and blamed for their children's weight. They understood their children's weight as reflecting negatively on them as parents and felt guilty about it. 2) Mothers also felt frustrated and uncertain about how to help their overweight children and expressed discomfort in discussing obesity with their children, further entrenching the stigma associated with weight. Additionally, 3) they understood themselves to be in the position of reluctant role models. They expressed concern about having to model healthier choices for their children, as role modelling is seen as a maternal responsibility. One participant expressed resentment that her fitness was a part of her maternal responsibility. 4) Finally, the mothers were unsure of how to proceed with their obese or overweight child, and were concerned about the potential social and medical costs of obesity that are often reported by doctors and the media. Mothers of girls were particularly concerned about their daughters finding healthy romantic relationships in the future.

Olivia Southwell and John Fox add to this discussion a theoretical understanding as to why mothers minimize their children's weight. Citing studies that show how parents minimize their perceptions of their children as overweight or obese, the authors suggest that this minimization is, in part, due to reluctance on the part of mothers to take the blame or associated stigma of having overweight children. I argue that mothers' minimization could serve as an attempted form of resistance against bad mothering claims. By downplaying the realities of their children's weight, mothers suggest that this supposed problem is not actually a problem, and they have then, in fact, not transgressed the supposed boundaries of good mothering.

After questioning whether or not mothers of fat children could actually demonstrate resilience as they already have overweight or obese children, Southwell and Fox conclude that some mothers do demonstrate resilience through implementing weight management strategies. In this sense, resilience interfaces with control over children's eating habits. Less resilient mothers are more permissive with their children's food, which demonstrates a lack of control over their children's eating. The authors highlight that mothers experience emotional drain in navigating the dynamics of being a good mother to children, by feeding and nurturing them, and by being a good mother in society, represented through non-obese children, and these two ideals contradict each other.

Southwell and Fox speak of two different kinds of mothers by employing the good mother, bad mother dichotomy. They argue that mothers' perceptions of themselves, and how they feel they are perceived by society, influence their feeding practices for their children. Mothers see the weight of their children as indicative of their worth as mothers, and they engage in strategies to try to manage such perceptions, such as minimizing the actual weight of their children.

Southwell and Fox's concept of resilience can be otherwise interpreted as succumbing to the pressures of social control. By exercising supposed resilience through the implementation of weight management strategies, mothers, I argue, are reaffirming the stereotypes of the good mother by trying to control their children's weight so that they are not stigmatized as the a bad mother. Yet research on proper weight and body mass index (BMI) among children is built on somewhat flimsy science (Gard and Wright; Flegal). By trying to avoid the stigma of bad mothering through weight management, mothers reinforce stereotypes around weight and fatness.

In her article "Childhood Obesity: Is Parental Nurturing to blame?" Julie La Rocca looks at the relationship between the BMI and percentages of fat in mothers, fathers, and their children. Her study concludes that mothers have a stronger influence on their children's weight as well as more concern over their children's eating behaviours. In her study, both sons and daughters have fat percentages that relate to the mothers' BMI but not the fathers'. La Rocca indicates that girls tend to have a higher BMI if either of their parents are overweight. She suggests that parents should teach proper eating habits at the beginning of a child's life and that there should be more regulation for obese mothers while they are pregnant so as not to give birth to children with a risk of becoming obese.

Both academically and culturally, mothers take the blame for the weight of their children, as demonstrated in the work of Bruch, Orbach, and La Rocca. In contrast to many of the claims presented by these authors, researchers, such as those mentioned above, demonstrate the strain experienced by mothers in efforts to resist claims of bad mothering when their children are overweight or obese. Although these claims present different arguments, the tension in the arguments is not inconsistent. Whereas LaRocca argues that children are more likely to be obese if their mothers have a high BMI, Southwell and Fox highlight the tension mothers feel in modelling to their children healthy weight and BMI, as they feel that they bear that responsibility. Whereas LaRocca suggests more forms of social control, such as the regulation of obese and pregnant mothers, Southwell and Fox highlight the stigma attached to fat children, which is transferred to the mother in the figure of the "bad mother." Both arguments highlight the role of mothers in the weight management of their children.

It is evident in the research conducted by Jackson and her colleagues that mothers with obese or overweight children feel that that they are responsible. This responsibility takes many forms: mothers of obese or overweight children feel they have failed in their maternal responsibility to adequately nurture their children and to model a specific form of health to their children. This double failure, of maternal and personal responsibility, puts mothers at the forefront of blame for the weight of their children. This double failure is reinforced, for example, by La Rocca's research, which suggests that mothers are indeed to blame. La Rocca centres her analysis on the influence of mothers on their children's eating patterns. She argues for better eating habits to be taught to children by their mothers. La Rocca also suggests that there needs to be more regulation of obese mothers while they are pregnant in effort to not produce children who are at risk of becoming obese. This is an incredibly alarming suggestion, as pregnant women already face intense regulation over their reproductive bodies. How would such regulation be enforced? What does this regulation look like?

La Rocca's analysis lacks any acknowledgment of the socioeconomic and cultural factors that may influence an increase in BMI, which is further evident in her discussion of increasing obesity among ethnic minorities. Although she mentions that geographic location and socioeconomic status may factor into the reasons why such an increase exists, she ultimately concludes that "unfortunately, many ethnic minority cultures place strong emphasis on large, high fat, social meal ... [and] the majority of these cultures consider having a full figure as attractive and normal" (4). Again, the responsibility of weight management and for abiding by specific Western ideals of beauty is placed on the individual. Instead of discussing issues of poverty or understanding different cultural ideals, La Rocca blames non-Western culture for betraying Western norms of the thin ideal.

FATNESS, MEDIA, AND THE "NEW MOMISM"

The "new momism," as Susan Douglas and Meridith Michaels discuss, "is a set of ideals, norms, and practices, most frequently and powerfully represented in the media, that seem on the surface to celebrate motherhood, but which in reality promulgate standards of perfection that are beyond your reach" (620). New momism is rooted in Sharon Hays's concept of intensive mothering, where she describes an ideology of intensive mothering in which: 1) childrearing is critical and the mother is the central caregiver; 2) appropriate childrearing is "child-centred, expert-guided, emotionally absorbing, labour intensive, and financially expensive" (414); and 3) paid work and childrearing cannot be compared.

The professionalization of motherhood greatly contributes to the virtually unattainable expectations on mothers. Douglas and Michaels note the following:

> Intensive mothering insists that mothers acquire professional-level skills such as those of a therapist, pediatrician ("Dr. Mom"), consumer products safety inspector, and teacher, and they lavish every ounce of physical vitality they have, the monetary equivalent of the gross domestic product of Australia, and, most of all, every single bit of their emotional, mental, and psychic energy on their kids. (620-621)

In addition to a focus on the expertization of motherhood incorporated into cultural images, the media as an institution serves to reinforce the image of the bad mother, especially in reference to children's weight (Boero; Mitchinson). Representations of good motherhood are abundant in mainstream media, and it would be near impossible to list all of the characteristics that a mother must possess to be considered a good mother.

Tanya Zivkovic and her colleagues argue that mothers, not fathers, are primarily blamed both legally and morally for obese children: "current neoliberal models of governance deepen the critical focus on children as they recast responsibility as more of an individual or family matter and less of a collective or social responsibility protected by the State" (378). The authors look at media reports in three Australian newspapers over a three-month period and show that child obesity is a prominent topic, especially when framed around the question of responsibility (380). The newspaper stories ignore factors outside of maternal responsibility, such as socioeconomic status.

Furthermore, May Friedman, who is critical of the blame game around weight and motherhood, seeks to unmask the scrutiny around parenting and fatness in her research on child obesity and child welfare. She highlights how the abuse of fat bodies is pervasive in the media and how the images of fat children are often pictures of "headless fatties," (17) wherein children are only pictured from the neck down. This is dehumanizing for fat children and reduces them to problems in need of solution.

According to Friedman "the policing of fat children and their parents rest on two common sense medical truths that are central to the rhetoric of 'obesity': first, fat is unhealthy, and second, fat is reversible" (18). The news media sensationalizes scientific claims about obesity and children, and positions the humiliation of fat children as reflective of bad parenting. This is an interesting contrast, as fat adults are held responsible for their weight, and fatness is seen as individual failure; however, fat children are seen as a reflection of parental failure and more specifically, as evidenced throughout this chapter, maternal failure. Children are viewed as passive victims whose weight is an issue of child welfare. Friedman describes this victimization in the following way:

> [The] derision and humiliation that fat children experience in both the public and private spheres are evidence of their status as victims of bad parenting rather than, as with fat adults indication of their own failing ... literature invokes the humiliation that fat children face as evidence of pa-

> rental failure, signs of neglectful and uncaring caregivers unconcerned with their children's health and welfare (19).

It is clear that the ideology of the new momism pushes mothers to obtain a standard of motherhood that is, in fact, unattainable. The media reinforces the standards of the new momism through impossible representations of motherhood and positions mothers of fat children as bad mothers. The ideology propagated through the media reinforces the impossibilities of being the idealized good mother.

THE SOCIAL CONSTRUCTION OF GOOD MOTHERING AND HEALTHY WEIGHT

The tension between maternal responsibility to feed and nurture children and the need to demonstrate maternal competence, or to be the good mother, does not exist in a contextual vacuum. Instead, the preponderance of maternal blame is connected to the crisis of the supposed obesity epidemic and, in turn, to the changing nature of women's roles in society. As Thurer highlights in "The Myths of Motherhood," the way in which motherhood is performed varies by the context and the time period in which the mother is located. Motherhood, then, is culturally derived (334). Although the performance of motherhood and the constitution of a good mother have shifted, so too have the standards of appropriate weight, which has fueled the rhetoric around the obesity epidemic.

Natalie Boero discusses the way in which the obesity epidemic is connected to the changing roles of women in society, specifically the working mother. She argues that "as with other historic and contemporary examples of mother blame, evaluating the fitness of mothers based on the size of their children obscures larger structural issues of racism, economic inequality, fat phobia, and sexism among others" (113). Similarly, Gard and Wright describe the "couch potato" imagery that perpetuates fatness as occurring because of laziness, excessive television or videogames, and poor individual decisions. Discussing mother blame, Boero furthers this argument and notes that the sedentary lifestyle typically associated with overweight children is portrayed by the media as the primary cause of childhood obesity. Implicit in this imagery is blame on mothers, specifically the working mother, who is too busy to prevent her children from engaging in these self-destructive habits.

It is interesting to highlight the parallels between the concept of "maternal fitness" and "health fitness" when discussing claims of overweight, obesity, and bad mothering. Both maternal fitness and health fitness, I argue, are social constructions, which are statuses that are often unattainable (Douglas and Michaels; Caplan; Thurer). As Caplan highlights in her work on mother myths, the Good Mother Myths set an unattainable standard of motherhood. Any behaviour by a so-called good or bad mother can be transformed to represent bad mothering.

The particular societal ill discussed in this chapter—overweight and obesity among children—is also a social construct, specifically through the use of the BMI to assess health. BMI is an ever-changing standard of health measurement, and what constitutes as obese has been changing throughout the years (Gard and Wright). What this means is that the actual weight-to-height ratio assigned to BMI categories has not changed, but the meaning of the BMI scores has. Importantly, Gard and Wright note that BMI is wholly inaccurate for children, yet this is the standard used to measure health fitness and, as argued elsewhere in this chapter, to blame mothers.

The constitution of maternal fitness and health fitness is ever changing. As the standards of appropriate weight and good mothering continue to shift, the ability of women to attain these standards remains out of reach.

CONCLUSION

At the beginning of this chapter, I posed the question: how do researchers in fat studies and motherhood studies describe maternal responsibility when it comes to children's weight? In doing so, many key themes emerge when looking at the literature on mother blame and overweight or obese children. There is, however, a degree of tension present among these themes. This research is multidisciplinary and ranges from biomedical views (La Rocca), to psychoanalytic views (Orbach), and to sociological perspectives, which are not necessarily in concert with each other. The following themes emerge from the literature in reference to maternal responsibility: role modelling as maternal responsibility, feelings of judgment and blame, the moral responsibility of feeding and nurturing, and mothers' requirements in the regulation of children's weight.

La Rocca argues that parents who eat healthy will better model healthy eating patterns for their children and are less likely to have overweight children. Jackson and her colleagues relate that mothers feel intense pressure in their mothering responsibilities and in having to be role models for their children. La Rocca suggests that mothers have a strong influence on both the weight of their children and concern over their eating habits, which may be connected to the responsibility felt by mothers to ensure that they do not bear the stigma and blame for having an overweight child. La Rocca's argument encourages surveillance and self-surveillance. The mothers are blaming themselves as the specialists are placing the blame for having fat children on maternal failures, instead of on institutions such as capitalism, consumerism, and the media, which further highlights the role expertization plays in governing what is considered to be good mothering. When experts tell mothers that their behaviour is wrong and that they are at fault, these messages become internalized.

Zivkovic and her colleagues highlight how it is the moral responsibility of mothers to feed their children; however, this responsibility requires that they do not break social convention by feeding their children inappropriate amounts of food. Drawing on Hays's intensive mothering, the authors suggest that beliefs around motherhood can create a dichotomy of the good-bad mother, which is perpetuated further by the children's weight. In the *Good Mother Myths*, Caplan describes the good mother as a mother who is 100 percent nurturing. However, as evident in the literature on children's weight, this is only good mothering so long as the mother does not produce an overweight child, or else she becomes a bad mother (Southwell and Fox). All of these authors are critical to the debate on the impact of surveillance, internalization, expertization, and the media on the ways in which fat children represent maternal failure.

In modern society, children are viewed as an investment and as a reflection of their parents. As highlighted by Hays's concept of "intensive mothering," as well as Douglas and Michael's concept of "new momism," mothers spend the majority of their time and effort investing in their children's success. A fat child then reflects poorly on the mother, who often becomes the bearer of blame (Jackson et al.). The requirements of intensive mothering are taken even further. Mothers must police diets, ensure consistent and nutritional meals, enforce physical activity, and provide discipline over eating habits of children (Friedman).

Whether the blame stems from mothers being overweight themselves (La Rocca), mothers working outside the home (Boero), or mothers being poor role models of health and fitness (Jackson et al.), their children's weight, and that weight's responsibility, greatly contributes to creating the dichotomous good-bad mother.

Such mother blame is indicative of a complete failure in recognizing the complex causes of obesity that exist outside of mothering responsibilities. Caplan argues that blaming the mother positions her as the scapegoat for societal problems, which distracts from larger social problems, such as poverty, racism, and sexism. Boero highlights this as well by arguing that evaluating the fitness of a mother based on her child's size hinders discussion of larger sociocultural, economic, and political discussions of oppression. Neoliberalism frames this discourse of responsibility, as placing the sole blame of childhood obesity on the failures of mothers shifts focus away from larger social problems that contribute to marginalization, such as socioeconomic status and poverty, which could thereby influence weight.

Yet although good motherhood is virtually unattainable—in much the same way normative weight may be unattainable—mothers still bear the blame and stigma associated with overweight or obese children. Children's weight has become another litmus test of good mothering and having overweight or obese children represents a failure of good mothering.

ENDNOTE

[1]Obesity is a biomedical term for understanding weight, which

roots people's weight in a medical model of understanding health (specifically in relation to BMI), while 'overweight' pits people against the social construction of a 'normal' weight category. Both terms are problematic. Alternatively, many fat activists have reclaimed the word 'fat' as a descriptor of their bodies, as it is a descriptor rather than a judgment-fueled health term.

WORKS CITED

Boero, Natalie. "Fat Kids, Working Moms, and the Obesity "Epidemic": Race, Class and Mother Blame" *The Fat Studies Reader*, edited by E, Rothblum and S. Solovay, York University Press, 2009, pp. 113-120.

Caplan, Paula. "Don't Blame Mother: Then and Now." *Maternal Theory: Essential Readings*, edited, A. O'Reilly, Demeter Press, 2007, pp. 592-600.

Douglas, Susan, and Meredith Michaels. "The New Momism" *Maternal Theory: Essential Readings*, edited by A. O'Reilly, Demeter Press, 2007, pp. 617-639.

Flegal, Katherine, Brian Kit, Heather Orpana, and Barry Graubard. "Association of All-Cause Mortality With Overweight and Obesity Using Standard Body Mass Index Categories," *Journal of American Medical Association*, vol. 309, no. 1, 2013, pp. 71-82.

Friedman, May. "Mother Blame, Fat Shame, and Moral Panic: "Obesity" and Child Welfare." *Fat Studies: An Interdisciplinary Journal of Body Weight and Society*, vol. 4, no. 1, 2015, pp. 14-27. *Taylor & Francis Online*, www.tandfonline.com/doi/abs/10.1080/21604851.2014.927209. Accessed 18 Jan. 2017.

Gard, Michael and Jan Wright. *The Obesity Epidemic: Science, Morality and Ideology.* Taylor & Francis Inc., 2005.

Hays, Sharon. "Why Can't a Mother be More Like a Businessman?" *Maternal Theory: Essential Readings*, edited by A. O'Reilly, Demeter Press, 2007, pp. 408-430.

Jackson, Debra, Lesley Wilkes, and Glenda McDonald. "'If I Was in my Daughter's Body I'd be Feeling Devestated': Women's Experiences of Mothering an Overweight or Obese Child." *Journal of Child Health Care*, vol. 11, no. 1, 2007, pp. 29-

39. *Sage Journals*, http://journals.sagepub.com/toc/chca/11/1. Accessed 18 Jan. 2017.

Ladd-Taylor, Molly. "Mother-Worship/Mother-Blame: Politics and Welfare in an Uncertain Age." *Maternal Theory: Essential Readings*. Ed. A. O'Reilly. Bradford: Demeter Press, (2007). 660-667. Print.

La Rocca, Julie. "Childhood Obesity: Is Parental Nurturing to Blame?" *The Internet Journal of Allied Health Sciences*, vol. 7, no. 1, 2009, pp. 1-5.

Mitchinson, Wendy. "Mother Blaming and Obesity: An Alternative Perspective." *Obesity in Canada: Critical Perspectives*, edited by J. Ellison, D. McPhail et al., University of Toronto Press, 2016, pp. 187-217.

Orbach, Susie. *Fat is a Feminist Issue*. Berkley Books. 1990.

Solovay, Sandra, and Ester Rothblum. "Introduction." *The Fat Studies Reader*, edited by E. Rothblum and S. Solovay, New York University Press, 2009, pp. 1-7.

Southwell, Olivia, and John R.E. Fox. "Maternal Perceptions of Overweight and Obesity in Children: A Grounded Theory Study." *British Journal of Health Psychology*, vol. 16, no.3, 2011, pp. 626-641. *Research Gate*, doi: doi: 10.1348/2044-8287.002002.

Thurer, Shari. "The Myths of Motherhood." *Maternal Theory: Essential Readings*, edited by A. O'Reilly, Demeter Press, 2007, pp. 331-344.

Wann, Marilyn. "Forward: Fat Studies: An Invitation to Revolution." *The Fat Studies Reader*, edited by E. Rothblum and S. Solovay, New York University Press, 2009, pp. i-xxvii.

Wright, Jan. "Biopower, Biopedagogies, and the Obesity Epidemic." *Biopolitics and the "Obesity Epidemic": Governing Bodies*, edited by J. Wright and V. Harwood, Routledge, 2009, pp. 1-14.

Zivkovic, Tanya,et al. "In the Name of the Child: The Gendered Politics of Childhood Obesity." *Journal of Sociology*, vol. 46, no. 4, 2010, pp. 375-392. *Sage Journals*, http://journals.sagepub.com/doi/abs/10.1177/1440783310384456. Accessed 18 Jan. 2017.

III.
CULTURAL REPRESENTATIONS OF BAD MOTHERS

Nonavee Dale, "Protection," 2014, pencil on paper, 11 x 14 inches.

Malas Madres in Contemporary Latin American Literature

Representing Ill-Fated Motherhood in Myriam Laurini's *Qué raro que me llame Guadalupe*

MARÍA ALONSO ALONSO

THE FIGURE OF the *mala madre* is an important element in the cultural fictions of some Latin American countries. Latin American literary production has been noticeably marked by fluctuation between the image of the good and the bad mother. This dichotomy, which is influential in most social contexts, relegates those labelled as *malas madres* to a marginalized position. In Mexico, the omnipresent *La Virgen de Guadalupe* is juxtaposed against historical and folkloric characters, such as *Malinche* or *La Llorona*, to shape the representation of liminal women within a seemingly patriarchal society. For this reason, and in order to explore the figure of the bad mother in Latin American literature, the following pages offer an analysis of *Qué raro que me llame Guadalupe* (*How Strange That My Name is Guadalupe*),[1] a novel by the Argentina-born and Mexico-based author Myriam Laurini. The text invites the reader to consider, through its harsh language and shocking descriptions, the consequences of the dehumanization and commodification of women as well as the reasons behind the neglect of their children.

In an outwardly misogynistic society, much like the Hispanic one,[2] women and men exert their activism from within the arts. Literature is one of the channels through which readers can have access to different practices of resistance and empowerment. Since the 1990s, a new generation of Latin American authors has revolted against Boom literature[3] to address, through the use of a hyper-realist narrative style, the violence and moral corruption of a system that has been suffocating the Latin American continent.

For this new generation of post-Boom authors, there is no room for magic, folklore, or fantasy in literature anymore; there is no reason for the use of a baroque language or overcomplicated metaphors in their texts. This new generation speaks directly to and about characters born from the cloaca of the new world order while they illustrate the most grotesque and heartless side of our era.

Laurini's *Qué raro que me llame Guadalupe* is framed by this new wave of Latin American fiction, since it offers a thought-provoking picture of the human degradation that surrounds the lives of marginal women. The novel follows the arrest of Guadalupe, also known as Bere. This sixteen-year-old sex worker is suspected of having killed her newborn son, her pimp, as well as one of the little girls who was being sexually enslaved in *El Universo*, the name of the brothel where they all lived. Through the statement that she makes to her lawyer once she is imprisoned, together with a series of flashbacks that explain the social and economic context of the protagonist's unfortunate life, Laurini shows that motherhood under these circumstances is problematic. The author ensures that the reader knows from the very beginning that Bere was exploited for sexual purposes at the age of nine, under her mother's nose, in the brothel she was born into. There, she worked for their procurer, Puroloco, who is believed to be her father and the father of the baby that she murdered. Through this complicated network of family relations, *Qué raro que me llame Guadalupe* assists the reader in showing the consequences of reifying women by a society in which even the female body is subject to be commodified, something that inevitably poses a challenge to the healthy raising of children.

LATIN AMERICAN WRITERS STRIKE BACK AGAINST PATRIARCHY THROUGH LITERATURE

This new wave of post-Boom writing seen in contemporary Latin American literature is, to a high degree, led by women, which implies the emergence of a distinctive female consciousness within literature owing to the reconsideration of traditional culture. Diamela Eltit, Selva Almada, Carmen Boullosa, Ana Paula Maia and, of course, Myriam Laurini belong to this group of writers who demand, from their activism, a differing voice within Latin American literature. Thus, patriarchal values are challenged through a series of narrative strategies in contemporary literary production.

The incursion of a feminist consciousness within the Latin American literary canon, a predominantly male one, is productive. For Francine Masiello, "Latin American women actively *translate* between different registers of experience that construct, even today, alternatives to the liberal (and neo-liberal) republic" (emphasis in the original; 62). Gender negotiations around the dichotomies between male and female, centre and periphery, private and public, or power and resistance are to be found in this new wave of writing, which is characterized by its straightforward and violent language. Additionally, the recurrence of social and cultural binomials—such as the one between the good and bad mother in the Latin American imagery—creates a sense of constant anxiety that needs to be mediated through the arts.

Laurini forces the reader to enter a hostile and extremely violent place ruled by patriarchal oppression: a brothel. In an interview about her work, the author acknowledges that the main motivation that she had to write *Qué raro que me llame Guadalupe* was driven by the need to talk about what surrounds us but sometimes goes unnoticed or about what we deliberately decide to not see. She admits that the problem in Latin America is a cultural one: "we have been educated to be good housekeepers, housewives, mothers and, if we wanted to write, we were supposed to do intimate novels, romantic novels, without getting into issues that only concern men" (qtd. in Torres Pastrana). But Laurini defies this constraint through her writing, which she connects to her activism by defining her works as a weapon to fight the tragic reality around her.

The fact that this explosion of fiction made by women coincides with the consolidation of a global neoliberal economic policy is significant. A new political consciousness has emerged from the class and gender conflicts that have shaken the Latin American continent during the last few decades.[4] This change is notable in Mexico, the country where the novel is set. It is because of the importance of the previously mentioned social and cultural patterns that an interdisciplinary approach must be used when dealing with Latin American literary production. Therefore, the next pages offer a cultural and literary analysis of the text to weave a number of arguments together so as to draw a picture of the figure of the *mala madre* in contemporary literary production from an intertwined perspective.

The Triple Stigma of Mexican Symbolic Oppression

For understanding some of the general claims around the *machismo* of certain Hispanic cultures presented at the beginning of this analysis, a more specific contextualization is needed to realize how important this is for the conceptualization of the figure of the *mala madre*. In Mexico, the family is the custodian of certain values and submission to these values depends on gender-based norms, since as Adelaida Del Castillo points out, the family in Mexico is "hierarchical in structure, asymmetrical in social and gender relations, genealogical in patters of residence, and loyal to the family in its moral economy" (212). Likewise, women are often categorized by their role within society, which usually oscillates between images of good and bad mothers.

This matrifocal view of female nature poses a series of challenges to women's subjectivity, since it does not allow any female figures within this classification of the good mother other than one's own mother. Puroloco, an abuser of minors and a sexual exploiter of women, fits within this paradoxical description of a uterine son. In an argument with one of the women in *El Universo*, he says the following: "don't involve my mother in this, don't even mention her, because she was indeed a saint and she doesn't deserve to be mentioned by you, in case she gets upset in heaven when she hears you uttering her name" (16).[5]

Because of the weight of Catholic tradition, motherhood in Mexico is directly linked to both the figure of *La Virgen de Guadalupe*, the loving mother of all Mexicans, and her antagonist *Malinche*, the *chingada*.[6] Emboldened by its defeat of the Moors—the *Reconquista*—the Spanish empire moved to conquer the Americas. In order to assist the Christianization of the newly colonized territories, the Catholic Church decided to undertake a process of transculturation[7] to adapt Indigenous religions to the newly imposed cult. As a result, the deity *Tonantzín* was substituted by *La Virgen de Guadalupe*, representing the archetypal image of the sacrificial, selfless, and suffering mother as a symbol of the spiritual conquest carried out in Mexico (González 22). On the flip side of the history of colonization, there is *Malinche*, the raped mother who is regarded as a traitor and a whore. As Deborah Madsen clarifies, *Malinche*—also known as *Malintzin* in the Nahuatl language—is a historical figure who was believed to accompany Hernán Cortés as his courtesan and translator during colonization (8-9). She was actually a gift given to the Spanish conqueror to gain his favour. The conquest was an act of rape in itself, and, therefore, *Malinche* stands out in history as an allegory of this physical invasion. When discussing the scope of this dual imagery, Gloria Anzaldúa connects these two symbolic figures with the positive and negative representation of female experience in Mexico (49-56). Thus, women have been regarded by men as the incarnation of all the values represented by either *La Virgen de Guadalupe*, the Virgin Mother who never abandons her children, or *Malinche*, the raped mother of all Mexicans who was abandoned by her children.

Additionally, there is a third figure, *La Llorona*, who combines the two previous ones. In Mexican folklore, *La Llorona* is known for her symbolic ambiguity. Although she represents the weeping mother who seeks her lost children, she is also an iconographical example of the *mala madre*, since she killed her own children by drowning them in a river to punish her husband for his infidelity. She carefully hides the dead bodies of her children, but when she goes to bury them, she can no longer find them. And ever since, she has searched rivers and streams, calling out their names and weeping for them (Madsen 34). For Madsen, *La Llorona* encapsulates both the mother and the murderer, the creator and the destroyer: "The woman who is the giver of life is also the woman who condemns her children to death" (35).

Taking this into consideration, the existing parallel between Bere and both *Malinche* and *La Llorona* in *Qué raro que me llame Guadalupe* becomes obvious. As this analysis aims to show, Laurini's protagonist incarnates the figure of the *mala madre* not only through her actions but also through the social and cultural constraints that have conditioned her existence since the day she was born.

Marginal Motherhoods in Conflictive Sociocultural Contexts

For contemporary Western values "motherhood is blissful, honourable, and natural state. It is the means to wholeness.... Motherhood is the ultimate mark of a woman's success" (Shiffer 216). However, this assertion may be challenging in marginal sociocultural contexts. As Elizabeth Badinter reminds us, "Maternal love is a human feeling. And, like any feeling, it is uncertain, fragile, and imperfect. Contrary to many assumptions, it is not a deeply rooted given in women's natures" (xxiii).

What Laurini suggests with her novel is that motherhood cannot be taken for granted, since it is a social construct and, thus, subject to a series of conditions. As previously mentioned, the fluctuation between the figures of the good and bad mother represented by *La Virgen de Guadalupe* and either *Malinche* or *La Llorona* conditions female experience around motherhood in Mexico. This dichotomy deeply influences *Qué raro que me llame Guadalupe*. In the novel, Bere's maternal subjectivity is articulated in *El Universo*, the place where she started being sexually exploited as a child and through the relationship with her mother and her father, Puroloco. *El Universo*, the brother where most of the action in the novel is located, is a place in a state of exception, as Agamben would say, in which human rights are suspended in order to allow all kind of abuses. The females, children included, who inhabit this kind of limbo are marginal subjects within hegemonic systems of domination—patriarchal systems of domination—who have undergone a process of stigmatization and dehumanization.

Those who have been sexually enslaved from an early age are under the risk of becoming a mimic of their oppressors, using here Bhabha's trope of the "mimic man."[8] Accordingly, the violence that is first etched on the bodies of these subaltern female subjects may be later reproduced by them on their children. This is exactly what happens to Bere. After being arrested, she admits to her lawyer that she cannot feel sympathy: "I don't know what pity means. Nobody taught me that word, not my mother, nor the others, nor the teachers, nor the clients, nobody. Neither did I learn it by myself, so I don't know the meaning of that word and I don't care about it" (58).

Bere only realizes that she is pregnant when it is too late to have an abortion—usually performed by a midwife who helps the women working in *El Universo*. Forced to carry the pregnancy to term, she starts hating the *escuincle*[9] before he is even born because of the financial burden he will impose. Since Bere has this hatred for her forced motherhood, it is not surprising that she tries to downplay the death of her three-month-old baby: "It wasn't a big deal: *escuincle* tumbled and broke his head" (24).

It may seem from this first testimony that for Bere, maternal love has little to do with her female instinct. As Andrea O'Reilly and Silvia Caporale Bizzini highlight, maternal caring "falls within a relational context that replaces the idea of an innate female caring ability developed within the limits of a nuclear, biological and heterosexual family structure" (9). As one can imagine, Bere's dysfunctional family and abusive childhood do not fit within the previously quoted definition of maternal caring. Taking all this into consideration, *Qué raro que me llame Guadalupe* trails Laurini's attempts to denounce normalized barbarism, alluding here to González Rodríguez's eye-opening 2012 essay on the femicide machine,[10] in which the author denounces how Mexican institutions have guaranteed and even legalized impunity for the violence against women and little girls—a claim that is closely related to the motivations that Laurini had to write her novel.

QUÉ RARO QUE ME LLAME GUADALUPE AND ITS ABILITY TO RAISE AWARENESS

Chingada from an early age and led by her own mother and her own father into a sordid world of drug consumption and sexual exploitation, Bere is a contemporary *Malinche*. She also has traces of *La Llorona*, since she, too, killed her child, although contrary to the folkloric figure, she does not regret doing it. What is more, she wishes her mother had done the same to her when she was born: "when I was born, Dorys should have strangled me with a stocking and then thrown me from the table so my head would smash, crack, like when a melon falls off the table. Dorys should have placed me in a black plastic bag and left me in the garbage bin in the corner" (121).

Despite being named after *La Virgen de Guadalupe* when she was born, Bere does not represent any of the values attached to this saint. The fact that a sex worker names her daughter after a virgin is poignant, but more significant is the fact that the daughter soon forgets her real name. This is attributable to the fact that, as Bere acknowledges at the beginning of her testimony, one cannot avoid one's fate: "I have been a whore from the day I was born. Since my mother is a whore, I had no other option than becoming a whore from the first day I came to this world" (9). There is no room for saints in her life.

Thanks to the testimonial part of the novel, the reader has access to Bere's own account of both: her version of the crimes and her childhood memories in *El Universo*. Through this first-person narration, the reader can begin to feel some empathy for her unfortunate life. However, because of the different versions that she gives to her lawyer about what happened to her son, the reader soon discovers that she is an unreliable narrator. Through these testimonies, the reader knows that Bere identifies her mother as a *mala madre* for leading her into prostitution, but she refuses to identify herself as one by justifying the reasons she had to kill her baby.

Qué raro que me llame Guadalupe speaks about what hurts and shames, as it relates to the way in which women are trapped in a mayhem of violence and abuse. Beyond its literary level, the novel serves a social purpose: it reveals the unfortunate existence of subaltern women who are excluded from society and sentenced to inhabit liminal spaces. Accordingly, violence appears in its most grotesque form. By understanding Bere from the beginning of the story as both a victim and an abuser, the reader is in a dilemma: she is not a saint, but she can be regarded as a vulnerable character whose fate was damned from birth. Thus, there is nothing in her testimony that suggests that she has or is willing to show resistance. Contrary to this, she seems defeated by her fate.

Malas Madres in the Cesspool of Life

In her sociological approach to the sex industry in Latin America, Megan Rivers-Moore highlights the fact that "motherhood is central to sex workers' ability to combat stigma … by calling on discourses of survival, motherhood and consumption" (722). For Rivers-Moore women become sex workers in certain Latin American and Caribbean countries because of their need both to support their children and/or fund their addictions to such substances as drugs or alcohol. It may be true that "crucial to the narratives of several sex workers about motherhood is how sex work enables not just the survival of their children, but also ... a particular quality of mothering" (727); however, motherhood within this marginal environment is not always that clear cut. There is a backdoor to this sordid world that society usually ignores and through which, the reader has access to the ill-fated experiences of motherhood.

Bere's mother, Dorys, is a *mala madre* herself. She sentenced her daughter to a disastrous life from the day she was born. This explains why Bere hates her so much. Puroloco is also a *mal padre*, a bad father, but that does not seem to bother Bere—despite the fact "he was the master, he was the owner of the hotel, the owner of the lives of fifteen women and six little girls ... the owner of the lives of the suppliers and of all those who had any sort of link with *El Universo*" (73). This suggests that the figure of the *mal padre* does not even exist in the Latin American tradition; parenthood is not a male activity and, thus, all the responsibility for the healthy raising of children lies with mothers.

Since the novel starts *in media res*, the reader does not have access to any background information to contextualize Dorys's decision to stay in *El Universo* and consent to Puroloco abusing their daughter. The reader does know, however, that Bere is Puroloco's favourite mistress and that is why she is convinced that the rest of the women in *El Universo* are so jealous that they are conspiring to terminate that relationship. But when the *escuincle* is born and Puroloco allows Bere to keep him, the reader understands the frustration of these women when they see "flashes of surprise and fury in each other's eyes, images of lost children, abandoned, given to unknown people or to grandparents, memories of children that they could not or did not know how to raise" (76). Puroloco does not allow any of the other women to keep their children; children that could just as easily be his.

These women are deeply affected by the memory of their own children, who were taken away from them at birth. Therefore, not being able to fulfill maternal practice as "an experience that is not yet fully owned" (Caruth, 151) with their own children appears as a deeper trauma than the violence they suffer on a daily basis. The memory of their lost children stands as a memento of their past since "the wound of the mind transcends the wound of the body" (Caruth 3). It is because of the women's aborted motherhood that the *escuincle* rouses their affection to the point that they are the ones demanding Bere to fulfill her caring duties. The sex workers in *El Universo*, who have worked as secondary characters until this moment, come to light as similarly vulnerable subjects. They were not given the opportunity of becoming *buenas madres*, or even *malas madres*.

Bere's Mentorship into the Hell of the Kínder

The *Kínder* is the name given to a clandestine annexed building to *El Universo* where Puroloco hides six young girls who are abused by pedophiles. The *Kínder* is an invisible place that everyone knows about—a locus haunted by an exclusive clientele, the only ones who can afford the special rates that Puroloco has for this place. The *Kínder* is, as Paula Bianchi puts it, "a controlled zone where the bodies are regulated and submitted so that they are deprived from any kind of right" (137).

Something horrific always happens in there. The little girls that inhabit this place are described as

> little girls whose innocence and dreams were stolen from them. Bitter faces, souls unable to stop, expel and conjure up the madness that has been instilled in and rules that place. Outraged bodies, filled with desperation, sentenced to survive. Spirits, substances, energies, psyches, minds, little girls destroyed by the daily experience, those were the ones living in the *Kínder*. Girls condemned to fulfill only one role in their lives, to satisfy the perversion of the perverse ones. (87)

For the *Kínder* to work to Puroloco's standards, Bere is the one in charge of the little girls' sexual education. During the first days of their seclusion, Bere is the only female figure they see; thus, she replaces the mother from whose arms they were suddenly snatched. But Bere was also once a *Kínder* girl, and she knows beforehand that the newly arrived girls will be rebellious; they will not allow themselves to be touched, and they will fight back.

The process of breaking the girls' will is not an easy one, which is why Puroloco forces them to take all kinds of drugs. Fighting each other sometimes is the only escape valve to channel all the violence etched onto their young bodies by their abusers. When describing some of these scenes, the narrator wonders if they may just want to die in order to escape the abuse: "sentenced to madness and death, they probably just wanted to shorten the agony.... However the owner of their lives was also the one who had the last word ... and he wasn't willing to lose such a 'valuable product'" (88).

There is no doubt that these little girls, together with Bere's *escuincle*, are the most vulnerable characters in the novel. Jacqueline, for example, survived in the *Kínder* for a year before she was killed. The police actually accuse Bere of Jacqueline's murder, but it soon becomes clear that one of the *Kínder*'s clients killed the girl. Jacqueline had no way to defend herself. She was completely on her own with no one to protect her—not her parents, not the other girls, and, certainly, not Bere.

In the scenes describing the destructive dynamics that operate within the *Kínder*, the author uses a brutal hyper-realistic style to shock the reader. Rather than focusing on voyeuristic descriptions of sexual abuse, Laurini narrates the consequences of its aftermaths:

> the girl was thrown on a divan, her eyes were open and her glance was still, her mouth was closed with adhesive tape, her brown skin looked greyish, her tiny breasts were covered with thin and deep wounds, wounds made with a razor, her belly, her legs burnt with cigarettes, and blood, lots of blood, too much blood, all the blood in the world. (101)

Jacqueline is killed in the *Kínder* by an important client, who could afford to pay Puroloco for his economic loss. Nobody did anything to prevent this death. Puroloco simply made sure that her body was disposed of after it stopped being functional. Nobody mourned her death because she was just another one of the goods in a storeroom. Jacqueline's dehumanization corresponds to the lack of gender solidarity and to the impunity with which male abusers operate. After her body disappears in the desert, nobody will honour her memory.

Born to Become a Mala Madre

Bere was the daughter of a *mala madre* and a *Kínder* survivor. Instead of revolting against her fate, she simply accepts it. Through this process of acceptance, she also assumes that she can reciprocate the violence that she received. When the *escuincle* was born, he could probably sense what the future was about to bring, and the only way the baby could revolt was by crying and shouting his heart out. Aside from neglecting her baby, Bere uses him as a scapegoat for all the anger that she has been accumulating since birth: "when the tears went through my head.... I burnt him with a cigarette and he fainted, before weeping again. So I burnt him again, let's see who wins motherfucker, I used to tell him, silence for three minutes and shouting for an hour. Always the same" (106).

In *Precarious Life*, Judith Butler offers some postulations to help understand the connection between violence, vulnerability, and trauma: "vulnerability ... becomes highly exacerbated under certain social and political conditions, especially those in which violence is a way of life and the means to secure self-defence are limited" (29). The cigarette scars remain as evidence of the violence inflicted on the baby; thus, the scars speak for the baby and for the trauma penetrating his subconscious. The scars are a text to be read. They tell us what a *mala madre* can do to her baby, and they illustrate the violence that surrounds the *escuincle*. The body, therefore, becomes the social construction of violence and speaks for it, following Butler's postulations. The body of subaltern subjects, be they female or infant, turns from being something alive and autonomous to being a passive object on which social behaviour is represented through violence.

Bere makes this clear when she describes how a client hits her with his belt because he cannot perform when the baby is crying in the bedroom. The client leaves without paying after assaulting her. Immediately after that, Bere repeats this violence with the *escuincle*: "I walked toward him and I squeezed his nape with a stocking. He stopped crying and breathing. I felt relieved. I drank some tequila. I realized that I had to pretend it was an accident. I placed him over the table and I pushed him. I fell asleep for a while" (107).

Bere eventually confesses that she killed her baby and threw his dead body into a garbage bin. The reader keeps expecting some form of regret, but Bere does not seem to feel any kind of empathy for her baby. It is outside this testimony, through a third-person narration, that the reader has access to the context that frames Bere's inability to show resistance. She disposes the body in similar way to how Puroloco disposed Jacqueline's body. She dehumanizes the *escuincle* in a similar way that she was dehumanized by her own parents. Yet one small difference remains: she was commodified to be economically profitable, and baby was jeopardizing her only way of earning her living. Therefore, she was convinced that she had no other option than to kill him in order to survive.

CONCLUSION

Bere becomes a mirror for the violent figures surrounding her and, thus, adopts violence as her *modus operandi*. She is no saint, despite being named after one; nevertheless, she becomes a contemporary *Malinche*—abandoned by her mother and her father. She also possesses some traces of *La Llorona*, although she does not cry at the death of her baby. Bere actually becomes a mother, contrary to the other sex workers in *El Universo*, but she has no good maternal references from which to learn. Motherhood, as a social construct, operates on a different level than maternal practice does. Nobody taught Bere to be a *buena madre*, just to be a *mala madre*.

On the surface, Bere seems to be one of the invulnerable characters in the novel because she is violent toward the ones who cannot defend themselves, but the reader knows that she is just mirroring her own experience. Bere is still a victim of the patriarchal oppression that operates in this deeply misogynistic environment. All in all, the sordid world that surrounds both *El Universo* and the *Kínder* is nothing but the consequence of the moral corruption of a society and the result of the commodification of women as sexual objects. It is for this reason that brutal realism is the style favoured in the text. It could not be done in any other way; there is no room for magical realism to soften violence in this particular case.

Qué raro que me llame Guadalupe is a novel that raises awareness; it is a novel that enters the lives of marginal subjects thanks to a fictional character, Bere, who could perfectly represent those women who tread, with or without their children, around the edge of a world in which they are just trying to survive. Through the protagonist's own voice, the reader learns that articulating resistance under this context of extreme social and economic marginality is difficult. Mexico, seen as an example of a society in a permanent state of emergency, fits into this world of human degradation that not only suffocates the protagonists of the novel, but also the readers.

ENDNOTES

[1]All translations made from texts originally in Spanish are mine.

[2]When dealing with misogyny within a Hispanic context, it is unavoidable to make reference to the so-called *machismo*, which Jo Fisher defines as "an ideology which owes much to Spanish colonial ideas about women [,] a system of gender relations which exaggerates the differences between men and women [and which] clearly asserts the superiority of the male over the female" (3). For further references that contextualize issues of patriarchy and *machismo* in Hispanic cultures, see Anzaldúa; Marcos; Mirandé; Paz; or Fregoso and Bejarano.

[3]The expression Latin American Boom literature makes reference to the literary production of the 1960s and onwards, and is characterized by the exploitation of the postcolonial exotic. As I pointed out in a previous publication, "magical realism" and "*lo real maravilloso Americano*" are both euphemisms for violence. For further information about the connection between violence and the literature that characterizes the Latin American Boom, see the first chapter in Alonso Alonso 2015.

[4]It was after the achievements of the so-called *feminismo popular*, or grassroots feminism, that we have access to certain narratives

that put focus on some of the fundamental problems of patriarchal societies (Stephen).

[5]Subsequent references to the text under analysis are to the edition included in the bibliographical section and will be cited parenthetically by page numbers.

[6]*Chingada* is a popular Mexican word that literally means "raped" and that, as Octavio Paz explains in his widely known 1963 *El laberinto de la soledad*, is deeply rooted in Mexican history and identity.

[7]The concept "transculturation" makes reference to the process of transformation and adaptation that takes place in certain colonized territories. For Ortíz in his famous 1940 essay *Contrapunteo cubano del tabaco y el azúcar*, the term "acculturation," so often applied to processes of colonization, was not suitable for the Latin American and Caribbean experiences. The mixture of indigenous elements together with the European, African and Asian influences that had entered the continent produced, as a result, a new hybrid product in which traces of all these constituent cultures can be identified.

[8]In *The Location of Culture*, Bhabha analyzes the ambivalence of colonial discourse by making reference to the effect of mimicry over subaltern subjects during both colonial and postcolonial periods. Accordingly, the "mimic man" adopts and perpetuates the violence of the colonizer but instead of moving upward on the social scale set by the established hierarchy, the "mimic man" remains in the same subaltern position. Bhabha's conceptualization of mimicry is highly productive when applied to other situations of uneven dynamics of power such as the one under discussion.

[9]*Escuincle* is a pejorative word used in Mexico to refer to young children. Its etymology comes from the Nahuatl *itzcuintli*, which means "dog." Since Bere does not name her baby and keeps referring to him by this derogatory term, *escuincle* is the word that will appear in different parts of this analysis in order to highlight the detachment that the protagonist feels toward her own baby.

[10]González Rodríguez's brave works *Huesos en el desierto* (2002) and *The Femicide Machine* (2012) about the murder of women in Ciudad Juárez are highly recommended, since they contextualize and explain the complex network of economic interests and

sociocultural constraints that surround violence against women in Mexico and in other countries around the world.

WORKS CITED

Agamben, Giorgio. *State of Exception*. Translated by Kevin Attell. Chicago University Press, 2005.

Alonso Alonso, María. *Diasporic Marvellous Realism: History, Identity and Memory in Caribbean Fiction*. Brill, 2015.

Anzaldúa, Gloria. *Borderlands: La Frontera. The New Mestiza*. Aunt Lute, 1987.

Badinter, Elisabeth. *The Myth of Motherhood: An Historical View of the Maternal Instinct*. Translated by Roger DeGaris, Souvenir, 1981.

Bhabha, Homi K. *The Location of Culture*. 1991. Routledge Press, 1995.

Bianchi, Paula D. "Exequias Para Cuerpos Prostituidos en Dos Novelas Latinoamericanas." *Altre Modernità. Rivista di Studi Letterari e Culturali*, vol. 4, 2010, pp. 132-141.

Butler, Judith. *Precarious Life: The Power of Mourning and Violence*. Verso, 2004.

Caruth, Cathy. *Unclaimed Experience: Trauma, Narrative and History*. The John Hopkins University Press, 1996.

Del Castillo, Adelaida R. "Gender and its Discontinuities in Male/Female Domestic Relations: Mexicans in Cross-Cultural Context." *Chicanas/Chicanos at the Crossroads: Social, Economic, and Political Change*, edited by David R. Maciel and Isidro D. Ortiz, The University of Arizona Press, 1996, pp. 207-230.

Fisher, Jo. *Out of the Shadows: Women, Resistance and Politics in South America*. Latin America Bureau, 1993.

Fregoso, Rosa-Linda, and Cynthia Bejarano. *Terrorizing Women: Feminicide in the Americas*. Duke University Press, 2010.

González Rodríguez, Sergio. *Huesos en el Desierto*. Anagrama, 2002.

González Rodríguez, Sergio. *The Femicide Machine*. Translated by Michael Parker-Stainback, Semiotext(e), 2012.

González, María R. *Imagen de la Prostituta en la Novela Mexicana Contemporánea*. Pliegos, 1996.

Laurini, Myriam. *Qué Raro que me Llame Guadalupe*. 1999. Ediciones B, 2008.

Madsen, Deborah L. *Understanding Contemporary Chicana Literature*. Univeristy of South Carolina Press, 2000.

Marcos, Sylvia. "Gender, Bodies and Cosmos in Mesoamerica." *Feminist Post-Development Thought. Rethinking Modernity, Post-Colonialism and Representation*, edited by Kriemild Saunders, Zed Books, 2002, pp. 313-329.

Masiello, Francine. "Women as Double Agents in History." *Narrativa Femenina en América Latina: Prácticas y Perspectivas Teóricas*, edited by Sara Castro-Klarén, Iberoamericana, 2003, pp. 59-72.

Mirandé, Alfredo. *Hombres y Machos: Masculinity and Latino Culture*. Westview, 1997.

O'Reilly, Andrea, and Silvia Caporale Bizzini. "Introduction." *From the Personal to the Political: Toward a New Theory on Maternal Narrative*, edited by Andrea O'Reilly and Silvia Caporale Bizzini, Susquehanna University Press, 2009, pp. 9-31.

Ortíz, Fernando. *Contrapunteo Cubano del Tabaco y el Azúcar*. 1940. Cátedra, 2002.

Paz, Octavio. *El Laberinto de la Soledad*. 1963. Cátedra, 1997.

Rivers-Moore, Megan. "But the Kids Are Okay: Motherhood, Consumption and Sex Work in Neo-liberal Latin America." *The British Journal of Sociology*, vol. 61, no.4, 2010, pp. 716-736.

Shiffer, Celia. "Babies and Boundaries: Mother-Speaking in Rachel Cusk's *A Life's Work*." *From the Personal to the Political: Toward a New Theory on Maternal Narrative*, edited by Andrea O'Reilly and Silvia Caporale Bizzini, Susquehanna University Press, 2009, pp. 210-224.

Stephen, Lynn. "Rural Women's Grassroots Activism, 1980-2000: Reframing the Nation from Bellow." *Sex in Revolution: Gender, Politics, and Power in Modern Mexico*, edited by Jocelyn Olcott et al., Duke University Press, 2006, pp. 241-260.

Torres Pastrana, Sandra. "Pocas Escritoras de Género Negro Porque nos Enseñaron a 'Ser Buenas'." *Cimacnoticias: Periodismo con Perspectiva de Género*, 4 Sept. 2008, http://cimacnoticias.com.mx/node/47005. Accessed 14 Sept. 2015.

Celluloid Marys

Discovering and Listening to the Bad Mothers Behind the Criminals in Popular Crime Films

MICHELLE HUGHES MILLER, GERALDINE M. HENDRIX-SLOAN, AND M. JOAN MCDERMOTT

MOTHER BLAME, the tendency to attribute blame to mothers for the problematic conditions and behaviours of their children, is not a new phenomenon (Thurer xv; Ladd-Taylor and Umansky 3; Reimer and Sahagian). Whether conceived as part of a backlash to first- and second-wave feminist movements, as a reflection of a patriarchal society that "is structured to persecute mothers" (Reimer and Sahagian 3), or as a more enduring phenomenon that is accentuated in the current political and economic climate, blaming mothers for the problems of their children is evident in cultural discourse within the United States (US) and most of the Western world. That discourse can be extremely pejorative; as Seidel states, "Hatred of the bad mother is still politically correct"(i). Molly Ladd-Taylor and Lauri Umansky have traced developments in "the politics" of mother blame across the twentieth century in the U.S. (10-17). Between 1900 and 1950, a mother's neglect, abuse, or even coddling was viewed as the primary source of problematic behaviour in children and trouble within the family structure (Jones 105; Ladd-Taylor and Umansky 10-14). Anita Ilta Garey and Terry Arendell cite a wide range of literature documenting that bad mothers have been blamed for a variety of things, including the following: autism, schizophrenia, drug use, rebelliousness, aggressive behaviour, poor school performance, learning disabilities, and low self-esteem among their children (293-294). Mothers have also served as a scapegoat for social and economic disadvantage, which has been associated with their children's criminality (Kierkus and Hewitt 123). Our target in this chapter is an even narrower concern, where maternal action (or inaction) has been identified as a factor in child criminality (Hoeve et al. 777). For instance, when speaking about two-year old James Bulger's murder in 1993 by two ten-year olds, Maggie O'Neill notes that the blame for the actions of the boys was placed in part on their mothers, as an element of what is wrong in society (22). In such representations, mothers become both symbolic of social ills and the causes of these ills themselves. In this chapter we add to the conversation a focus on cinematic representations of mother blame in contemporary crime films to tease apart how such films contribute to and reinforce the Bad Mother trope within these theoretical arguments. Specifically, we describe constructions of bad mothering within three crime films—*Boyz-n-the-Hood* (1991), *Catch Me If You Can* (2002), and *We Need to Talk about Kevin* (2011)—identifying the actions and inactions of the mothers that are portrayed as to blame for the crimes of their children. We also review context in these films to identify maternal voices in discussions of bad mothering. Ultimately, we consider the extent to which bad mother claims exist alongside maternal resistance to or acceptance of such claims in contemporary crime films.

BACKGROUND

Problems of children are often attributed to their mothers' inadequate performance of the responsibilities of motherhood. For Sara Ruddick, the needs of protection and wellbeing (preservation), emotional and intellectual nurturance (growth), and training children so that they can "grow into people whom they themselves and those closest to them can delightedly appreciate" (social acceptability) constitute maternal practice (20-21). Within U.S. family law, Michelle Hughes Miller has argued that judges interpret these maternal responsibilities, which they then use to evaluate mothers in family courts (172). Hughes Miller describes five maternal responsibilities: physical caretaking, financial, nurturance, relational, and moral (132). For Ruddick and Hughes Miller, it is the performance of mothering across these domains or elements that is relevant to critiques about mothers—including what mothers did not do, as opposed to what mothers did (Hughes Miller 138).

Our chapter aims to further the collective understanding of how cultural reproductions of mother blame persist, in part through the representations of the Bad Mother trope in popular cinema. By focusing our attention narrowly on the mothers of criminals in crime films, we target the most heinous of outcomes for "bad mothering": the child's own involvement in criminal, and sometimes violent, behaviour. Yet we avoid standard cinematic tropes that accompany crime films regarding bad mothers by intentionally analyzing three films in which the mothers are not alleged to be abusive or criminals themselves. Rather, in each film, it is the quality of the mothers' relationship with their children, particularly their interactions, that is portrayed in the film as the source of the child's crimes. Because these films place blame for children's crimes on mothering that is not criminalized but rather is integral to everyday maternal practice, this heightens the difficulty to ascertain the parameters of bad mothering and broadens our cultural imaginings of the bad mother. Our celluloid Marys are not criminals, in the legalistic sense of that word. Rather, they are criminalized by their failures in maternal practice and, thus, are portrayed as responsible for the criminality of their children.

The critical feminist film literature on women and motherhood has grown exponentially over roughly the same time period as motherhood studies itself (1980s to the present). There remains, though, a dearth of knowledge related to the understanding of the role of bad mothers in cinema, with an exception of "the stereotyping of the monster mother ... theorized and made popular by Freudian psychology" (Podnieks 9). Scholars have addressed the portrayal of mothers in film (Bassin et al.; Fischer; Kaplan; Seidel), and race, class, and gender representations in film (hooks; Willis; Bailey; Seidel). Much of the early work on motherhood and film focuses on melodramas, rather than crime films (Fischer 6). In *Cinematernity*, Lucy Fischer enlightens the reader to the history of mothers in cinema, seeking to "confront the cultural and artistic 'amnesia' around mother that Rich, so eloquently, decries—to 'recall' the importance of the maternal register within cinematic discourse"(31). Such efforts reflect the importance of the media in defining norms about motherhood (Douglas and Michaels 7).

Few scholars, however, have explicitly considered the link between bad mothers and their children's criminality in film. Even in their well-regarded treatise on crime in the movies, Nicole Rafter and Michelle Brown only tangentially present mother blame as an explanatory element in a few films, namely *The Bad Seed* and *Capturing the Friedmans* (42, 133). Other exceptions to this pattern include Su Epstein and Fischer. Epstein describes how serial killers are repeatedly represented as the products of "evil" mothers who "might be domineering, promiscuous, indecent, abusive, or neglectful"(257). Fischer recognizes this same point in passing, pointing to the *Eyes of Laura Mars* (1978), in which a serial killer blames his abusive sex worker mother but does not examine the phenomenon in any depth (151). Fischer also considers *White Heat* (1949) and explains the criminality of the protagonist played by James Cagney in part through the lens of the mother-son relationship (106). But Fischer's analysis emphasizes Cagney's character development rather than his mother's mothering; she only notes that the film portrays his mother as "hard," "butch," and loving toward her son (96).

U.S. cinema is a rich venue from which to generate ideological assumptions about bad mothers. Media forms create, reflect, and perpetuate cultural ideas and ideals of appropriate and inappropriate behaviours, relying on ideologies and cultural motifs to provide a common sense understanding of their meaning (Yar 77). Angela McRobbie and Sarah Thornton argue the following: "Social reality is experienced through language, communication and imagery. Social meanings and social differences are inextricably tied up with representations" (570). For Majid Yar, "crime films become sites within which the meanings of crime and criminality are simultaneously articulated, explored and negotiated" (74). The meaning of film can be derived, in part, from decisions made in its production, which reminds us to pay attention to discursive elements of the film that speak to understanding or context (Humphries 7; Rafter and Brown 9). For film scholars such as Alison Young, "every cinematic image is structured around a preferred meaning"(86). Thus, while the audience interprets the film, the intention of the filmmakers can be read through their ontological positionality. In this way, popular films tell us who the filmmakers believe we are as a society, and they offer us explanations for phenomena, such as criminal behaviour (see Campbell 98).

Yet U.S. cinema remains an androcentric world, wherein primarily male protagonists are featured and women, including mothers, are viewed on the periphery, if at all. For Elizabeth Podnieks, this positioning of mothers as objects rather than subjects means that films often have other characters speaking for mothers, or about mothers, rather than incorporating maternal voices into the text (5)—what might be described as the maternal being spoken through the masculine (Arnold 72). Negating mothers' voices also may result in negating the context within which the problematized behaviours occurred, reinforcing mother blame in the process (Seidel 69-70). When mothers are allowed to speak, it opens up the possibility for resistance and redefinition of the characters and of motherhood itself (Podnieks 6). But what is more common is, in Ann Hall and Mardia Bishop's phrasing, "the mother ... appear[s] on the surface and then disappear[s]" (xii). This means that not only are the realities of mothers' lives not present in the media but their absences are not fully acknowledged (Worthington 30). Voice, then, for mothers in film—even alleged bad mothers—is resistance in the form of maternal personhood, which rejects "the ideological work of helping to maintain the status quo," as it relates to mother blame (Seidel 105).

IDENTIFYING BAD MOTHERS IN CRIME FILMS: A NOTE ON METHODOLOGY

The three films included in this analysis of bad mothers were selected through a screening process. Popular U.S. crime films from 1980 to 2015 were identified based on an initial review of their abstract on *boxofficemojo.com* using Rafter's definition of crime film as, "films that focus primarily on crime and its consequences"(5). Once identified, each of the 156 identified crime films was coded for criminal causality, with elements of mother blame identified through a close viewing and interpretation of the film. Fourteen films[1] were identified as explicitly incorporating mother blame, three of which we discuss here. The films we chose to discuss were selected[2] because each provides a richly complex visual and discursive representation of bad mothering not related to maternal criminality or abuse, and provides the opportunity for the mothers to articulate their own context and behaviours. For these three films we engaged in scenographic analysis, assessing both discursive and visual content and cinematic strategies, including lighting, camera angle, and timing (Young 87-88).

FRAMING BAD MOTHERS

Boyz-n-the-Hood (1991) is a film about a group of young men and their struggle to develop masculinity within the context of gang activity, violence, neighbourhood degradation, drugs, and victimization present in South Central, Los Angeles, in the 1980s. The audience is introduced to three young boys, Tre, Ricky, and Doughboy (Darren), and their families. Within the same crime-producing social ecology, the three friends grow up with very different outcomes, and the audience is led to believe that this is largely because of the family structure and varied parenting they receive.

Mother blame permeates this film—from the broad message of "mothers cannot teach boys how to be men" to the more specific examples of how mothers in this film fail to meet the needs of their children through abusive behaviours, neglect, or abandonment. Although other scholars have justifiably focused on the intersectionality of race and gender as it relates to the "ineffectual mothering" present in this film (Bailey 82), our analysis focuses on the relationship between Doughboy's criminality and his mother. Doughboy, unlike Tre or Ricky, develops from a juvenile delinquent to a career criminal. Doughboy and Ricky are brothers with different biological fathers and are raised by their mother, Brenda, but the audience sees that they do not receive the same treatment from their mother. From the start of the film, Doughboy endures emotional abuse by his mother. In one instance, she screams at him: "You ain't shit; you don't do shit; you just like your daddy." It is quite obvious to their friends that Ricky is the favoured child: Brenda is kind, loving, and encouraging to Ricky, and emotionally abusive to and dismissive of Doughboy. Later in the film, a college recruiter visits the house to talk with Ricky about his future playing football for USC, and his mother says, "My baby is going to university. I always knew you'd amount to something." In contrast, the audience never sees a moment when Doughboy is encouraged for his actions. Her cruel words become a self-fulfilling prophecy for Doughboy: as a boy, he is taken into custody for stealing and spends time in juvenile detention. This delinquency is followed by more arrests and prison time as an adult. Doughboy drinks, gambles, and sells drugs in his own neighbourhood.

In the dramatic climax of the film, Ricky is the victim of a drive-by shooting, and Doughboy carries Ricky back to his home, fatally injured. In this scene, Brenda is hysterical with grief and shock, but her grief quickly turns to anger, which she directs at her surviving son: "What did you do? You did this!" Doughboy's participation in gang life is why his mother blames him when Ricky is shot and killed by rival gang members. But it is important to note that even before the killers are identified, Brenda believes Doughboy is somehow to blame. For the filmmakers, though, that blame is not held by Doughboy, as this is not an anti-gang film. Rather, blame ultimately lies with the mother, as it was Brenda's verbal abuse and differential treatment of her boys that led Doughboy down the criminal path. Furthermore, the Bad Mother trope is used to explain Doughboy's criminality, which reasserts the true message of the film: mothers cannot properly raise well-adjusted sons on their own without the help of a strong male figure—a point Bailey also makes in her discussion of *Boyz* (82) and one that reflects the myth of maternal inferiority (Caplan 96). Thus, Brenda is blamed not only for her emotionally abusive behaviour but for not being able to provide Doughboy with the male guidance necessary for him to develop appropriate masculinity. Early in the film, foreshadowing the violence that is to come, Tre's father, Furious, explains that the absence of a father in Brenda's home is key: "They don't have anybody to show them how to [be responsible]. They don't. You going to see how they end up, too." His assurance that Brenda cannot serve as a responsible role model is disconcerting but emblematic of the mother blame throughout the film.

The film ends with Doughboy seeking revenge for Ricky's death—a murder that Tre chooses not to participate in because of his father's guidance. In this storyline, the viewer is reminded yet again that Doughboy has no such guidance because of the inadequacies of his mother (read: any mother). The day following the murder of Ricky's killers, Doughboy discusses with Tre how he sees his life at that moment: "I ain't got no brother. Got no mother neither. She loved that fool more than she loved me." Two weeks after Doughboy buried his brother, he himself is killed.

Brenda is vilified in the film as an emotionally abusive mother (to one of her sons), as someone who cannot provide effective guidance (because she is not a father), and as the root of the criminality that becomes Doughboy's life and results in his and Ricky's deaths. Without a father—the viewer is told—the boys are doomed. There is no attempt in the film to understand why both boys' fathers are absent. Nor is there any attempt to provide any context for Brenda's mothering. The onus, then, falls directly on Brenda—not the absent fathers or even the "Hood" itself—for Doughboy's criminal behaviour. The film shows both the blame and the solution: Brenda is a bad mother because she is not a father. A father would have prevented this tragedy.

The concept of maternal abandonment is poignantly displayed in the film *Catch Me If You Can* (2002). In this film, the criminal, Frank Jr., lives most of his tender years in a happy household. This idyllic image is shattered, however, when his father's impending bankruptcy leads to financial stress and, ultimately, to his parents' divorce. It is in the process of discovering his mother's unhappiness in her marriage that the beginning of Frank's sense of maternal abandonment emerges. In a touching scene, Frank comes home from school to discover in his parents' bedroom his dad, who is in shock, his maternal grandmother (who is packing up his mother's things while speaking French), his mother, and a lawyer who is coordinating his parents' divorce. After springing the news of the divorce on him, they tell him he must fill out a form in which he decides with whom he will live after the divorce. In presenting the divorce to Frank, Paula, his mother, says the following: "You don't have to be scared. I'm right here, Frank. I'll always be here. But there are laws. Everything in this country has to be legal. So what we need to do is make some decisions." But Frank, who appears to be in shock, is incapable of deciding with whom he will live, so he runs away. Thus begins his odyssey into criminality.

The film lays out three explanations for Frank's crimes. First, financial necessity. Frank, as a teenager, has no marketable skills to financially survive and, as Paula later explains to the police looking for him, "A seventeen-year-old boy has to eat." Yet the reason for this financial necessity is rooted in parental failures: his father's financial woes and his mother's divorcing of his father. This is the causal factor that Yar emphasizes—familial factors rooted in the failures of the family itself (78). However, we argue that since Frank does not express resentment or anger about his father's bankruptcy, film watchers are left with the presumption that Frank would not have left home or begun his life of crime had Paula not uprooted her family by seeking a divorce. His mother abandons his father; ergo, his mother abandons him. Frank's relationship with his mother is so distant after Frank runs away that Frank does not learn of Paula's remarriage or the birth of his half-sister until well after the fact.

At the end of the film, Paula's new life is seen through Frank's eyes. Frank has escaped from the police only to journey to her new home. Peering at her through a frosted window, he finds Paula happily surrounded by a new family, complete with a new husband and a young daughter. The image of his mother in this new life is compounded by the holiday festivities—a Christmas tree aglow through the window and the film soundtrack playing "The Christmas Song," with the lyrics "And every mother's child is gonna spy, to see if reindeer really know how to fly." Frank then learns, looking through the glass, that the girl in the window in his mother's house is also his mother's child. As Frank is led away from the home in handcuffs by several police officers, Paula comes to the door with her new husband and with her new daughter in her arms. The image is unmistakably complete, as all three individuals fill their Christmas-framed doorway while Frank is driven off in the back of a police car. The viewer is left with the understanding that Paula has not just abandoned Frank and his father but replaced them.

Frank's feelings are not entirely clear in the film, although he does find his abandonment difficult to discuss or even think about. The bad mother apparent in such scenes does not tend to originate, then, from Frank's discourse. His visit to his mother's new home even appears to be an effort to reclaim the relationship, which portends a lack of anger at Paula. But a cathartic exchange does not take place, and the viewer is left with the knowledge that Frank will go to jail, whereas Paula's new "duplicitous" (Åström 206) life is complete, without him. That, perhaps, is the main way that the film depicts mother blame: the absence of maternal regret or loss from Frank's running away at the beginning of the film and from him being taken away at the end. None of the emotions often construed to illustrate maternal concern are depicted by Paula in the film. The outcome is that the viewer learns in consistent, albeit largely unstated ways, to blame Paula for Frank's criminality, not just because she left but because she did not demonstrate that she cared he did also.

We Need to Talk about Kevin (2011) departs from the other cinematic forms of bad mothers previously discussed. This film illustrates emotional neglect indicative of a lack of maternal instincts and an inability to bond with one's own child as the explanation for the child's criminality. Neglect, here, is not simply the absence of care; rather, the film portrays the mother, Eva, as a bad mother because she is ambivalent and disconnected from her son, Kevin.

Kevin uses a non-linear narrative structure, heavily relying on flashbacks, to tell the story of Eva, a mother whose teenage son, Kevin, commits mass murder at his school and the killing of his sister and father at their home. In the film, Kevin as a young toddler is depicted as nonverbal and possibly autistic. Then, upon the birth of his sister, he is portrayed as selfish and manipulative. By the time Kevin becomes a teenager, the audience is given the impression that he is angry and disenfranchised. O'Neill takes some time to discuss the subjectivity of bad mothering presented in *Kevin*, but using the book from which the movie is written rather than the movie itself (35-40). Her interpretation of the allusions to Kevin as being "intentionally cruel" in the text are more apparent in the film, as various cinematic endeavours reinforce this negative image of Kevin, such as his lack of empathy for Eva's feelings and disregard for negative consequences (O'Neill 37). Whereas the text allows us to question Eva's subjectivity and Kevin's "cruelness," the film leaves no doubts—there is something different about Kevin. But this difference only complicates the complicity and/or blame on Eva. For instance, Eva is shown as disengaged from her infant son, unable to emotionally connect with what the audience presumes may be a special-needs child. What initially appear to be signs of postpartum depression develop into Eva's ambivalence toward her son. Whether her ambivalence fits Sarah LaChance Adams's definition—which is the "simultaneous desire to nurture and violently reject their children"—is not entirely clear, although there are moments in the movie, described below, where Eva appears to engage in both behaviours (4). In addition to Eva's ambivalence, the heightening of Kevin's "difference" reinforces this mother blame. O'Neill interprets both Kevin and, ultimately, his failed mother as symbolic representations of the evils in our society (40-41).

The film opens with a younger and freer Eva attending the Florentine Tomato Festival, covered in red, alluding to the violence that later occurs and providing the template for the blood-red imagery that permeates the rest of the film, presumably to give the viewer a sense that the violent incident is never far from Eva's thoughts. This first scene gives a brief glimpse of her past and demonstrates the freedom and hedonistic lifestyle that she gave up to be a mother. However, unlike many other "bad" celluloid mothers portrayed as promiscuous (Brenda), or self-involved (Paula), Eva is physically present in her son's life (although she does mention wanting to leave). Her sexuality is evident but always within the context of her relationship with her husband. Eva is not a woman who neglects her child because she strives for attention or is consumed with meeting her own needs. Rather, the audience sees a woman who tries to build a close relationship with her son but to no avail. The film gives the impression that she does not know how to nurture or build rapport with Kevin. Her frustration builds first as she deals with a crying, colicky infant and later a young boy, still in diapers, who destroys her home office space by shooting paint all over the walls she lined with maps.

In this scene, Eva is decorating the walls of her office in their new home when Kevin comes in and says, "Those are stupid." She responds by trying to explain that everyone should have a special place of their own, and she offers to help him decorate his room. The symbolism in this scene is transparent: she is literally covering the walls of her office, a prison of sorts, with maps of all the places she no longer is able to travel because of Kevin and domesticity. Then when she returns from a phone call in the other room, she finds him splattering all her maps with paint. Kevin's destructive behaviour, portrayed as gleefully confrontational in the film by the young actor, adds to Eva's growing frustration with Kevin, and the audience sees her anger boil to the surface in the "potty training" scene when Kevin purposely defecates in his diaper immediately after she has changed him. Eva's response is immediate and violent—the only time such violence from her is seen in the film. She picks him up and throws him across the room, breaking his arm. Kevin lies for her to his father, blaming his injury on a fall off the changing table. Years later, when Eva visits Kevin in prison, they are both reminded of this event by the scar on his arm. Kevin's assessment of the act and his mother is telling, as he says: "this is probably the most honest thing you've ever done." The instance of physical abuse by Eva is a sort of bonding experience in the film—rare and overshadowed by their overall relationship of tension and animosity—demonstrated when young Kevin says to his mother as they discuss the upcoming arrival of a sibling: "Just because you get used to something, doesn't mean you like it. You don't like me." Although it is unclear whether Eva does, in fact, like Kevin, it is equally unclear whether he does, in fact, like her either. The problem, then, is the shared ambivalence, which cyclically arises from the interplay of Kevin's rejection and Eva's frustration. Yet Eva's blame, rather than Kevin's, is central to the movie; although Kevin is presented as a difficult and cruel child, it is Eva who is the mother, and on whose shoulders rests the demands of social acceptability (Ruddick 21).

Throughout the film, Eva bears the brunt of her son's crimes through the blame she receives from the community—from the recurring vandalism of her house being defaced with red paint to the violence perpetrated on her by the parents of the children Kevin killed. The community blames her, and she blames herself. And it is in the latter experience that the power of the film occurs: its depiction of the depths of self-blame that Eva experiences after Kevin's violent act. Interestingly enough, why the community and the parents of the murdered children are angry with Eva (as opposed to Kevin) is not entirely clear in the film. Eva is initially a part of the group standing outside the gym, as she is worried about Kevin as they are worried about their own children. Indeed, the film jumps right into mother blame, as these parents blame Eva solely through an understanding that since Kevin killed, his mother must be somehow to blame. The same assumption occurs within the film's depiction of Eva's self-blame. Although the audience does see the history of the frustrated mother-son interactions, it is shown entirely through her eyes, in her retelling to herself of how things turned out. Indeed, in *Kevin*, the audience rarely hears others' explanations for why Eva is a bad mother, even from Kevin himself. Instead, the audience hears the maternal voice articulate, for once, her understandings of herself as a bad mother. We turn to this maternal voice and the voices of the mothers in our other films in the next section.

MATERNAL VOICE

Each of the films depicts bad mothers in distinctive ways, but in addition, despite depicting mother blame, the films vary widely in their incorporation of maternal voice in response to those claims. In *Boyz*, there is no sign of maternal reflexivity for Brenda, although early on the audience sees Doughboy taken away by the police following a shoplifting incident, and witnesses Brenda's emotional response, which can be interpreted as both angry and embarrassed. She does not get to contextualize her mothering in the film, to reject and/or accept the bad mother label, or even to talk back to Furious's presumptions about the importance of fathers. She simply exists in the film as a caricature of bad mother and gives the audience no reason to question the claims about the outcomes of her bad mothering. Though played brilliantly by Tyra Ferrell, the character of Brenda is little more than a prop in the film's design to assert the importance of African-American fathers to their families.

In contrast, Paula in *Catch Me* is allowed voice, but the film reinforces the character's abandonment of Frank through her denial of Frank's criminality. Paula responds to the police questioning by claiming, essentially, that Frank cannot be blamed for what he did—he had to eat. Negating both the crimes that Frank commits and the seriousness of those crimes to the chagrin of the authorities, Paula defends Frank as a good boy merely trying to survive: "Half the kids his age are on dope, throwing rocks at police. And they scared me to death because my son made a little mistake." This argument is instructive because in negating Frank's crimes, Paula is negating her own culpability for his engagement in criminality. In addition, she demonstrates with these few words and lack of emotional concern that she cares little about what he does, which prepares the viewer for Paula's lack of concern about Frank himself. Although Paula is faced with mother blame, she rejects it because there is no behaviour that is blame worthy.

In *Kevin*, Eva is the site of much of the mother blame, and it is her vision of her own failures that create the sterile and isolated conditions of her life. Interestingly, even though Eva is the subject of the film, she appears almost lost within her self-blame, avoiding interactions on a number of occasions with others she believes could—and sometimes do—blame her (for instance, a boy injured by Kevin during the attack). Her dreams and her flashbacks frequently speak to her understandings of her challenges while mothering Kevin, with the scenes played without sympathy or acceptance. Although the audience learns how difficult Kevin was to mother in Eva's memories and during her visits with him in prison, she is equally harsh on herself. Viewers become so immersed in Eva's self-blame and the film's depictions of others' mother blame that it is difficult to understand the violent act without invoking Eva's culpability. In this way, *Kevin* merges a maternal voice that has internalized the Bad Mother trope with visual depictions of Eva that do not depict bad mothering. The result is similar to the use of red imagery to reinforce the violence of the story: these generic mothering memories (smoothing her son's hair, asking him about his day) are painted with the aura of "not good enough." In the end, the audience accepts that Eva is a bad mother because she has told us so herself.

DISCUSSION

As our research suggests, bad mothers in popular U.S. crime films originate both in mothers' actions and in their failures to act. When mothers fail to care for their children or abandon them, as in *Boyz* or *Catch Me*, their children are depicted as rudderless, with no strong connections to home or community to prevent their involvement in criminality. *Kevin* is yet another argument; even with attention, mothers can still fail, which makes *Kevin*'s story line the most intriguing of our films. When mother blame is intimately connected to the mother's relationship to her child, in her engagement in nurturance, protection and love, we are left wondering what is to be done.

Collectively, bad mothers in these films originate from the perceived preventative power of maternal practice, which is the ultimate paradox: in valuing maternal practice, we reify its importance—our importance—in the lives of our children, creating the milieu within which the bad mother inevitably arises. Embedded in mother blame is the understanding that if the mothers had only behaved differently, their children would not have been involved in crime. Through their abandonment, inaction, or failed action, our celluloid Marys do not prevent the criminality of their children, and the films intimately and relentlessly hold them accountable for their failures. Their accountability helps to define and surveil the accountability of mothers off screen as they also engage in maternal practice.

In the instances when a mother's actions are visible or contextualized within the films, viewers can sit back and accept this as a cautionary tale in which the good celluloid Marys are mothers who nurture, protect, love, engage, and lay down their lives for their children. Bad mothers—those who allow abuse to occur, engage in abuse themselves, or neglect or abandon their children—should expect that their children will be engaged in serious or violent crime. Although this might allow for these celluloid criminals to become understandable as linear outcomes of their childhood experiences, that linearity belies the complexity of the criminals' choices. Furthermore, it ignores the context within which mothering—good, bad, and all gradients in between—occurs. In all of these films, it is not the nature of maternal action that is most represented as blame worthy but rather the nature of the mother-child relationship. As caregivers, as sources of love and attention, as culturally presumed to be their children's greatest fan, these three mothers fail. They are depicted as inattentive or calculating; they are emotionally abusive or uncaring; they are distant or repulsed. The films are purposeful in their representations of the mothers—even as they use images, music, flashbacks, and asides as evidence of maternal shortcomings. The films articulate presumptions about good mothers that further shame the characters here, even if such presumptions are impossible to envision enacting. From *Catch Me*, we learn that a good mother should not be driven by financial concerns (what mother has not?). From *Kevin* and *Boyz*, we learn that a good mother should not let any negative feelings about her children surface, which is not so far removed from endorsing the argument that all mothers should constantly wear the mask of motherhood described by Susan Maushart (2). From *Boyz*, we learn that fathers are invaluable and mothers should help their children manage and maintain such relationships, even when their fathers fail them too (*Catch Me*). These messages are in part merely visual representations of cultural demands on mothers more generally, but their power lies in that they collectively and cinematically link mother blame, for failures in maternal practice, directly to crime. Eva's heartfelt and debilitating self-blame in *Kevin* is the outcome because as an audience we believe this mother, and all mothers, should see what we see—their culpability in their child's crimes. Failure to recognize and articulate their own blame, then, further marks them as bad mothers. But at the same time, the internalization of mother blame is a never-ending regression of regret, as Eva demonstrates. If mothers are demanded to assume blame and to internalize and accept as legitimate the claims of bad mothering such as those depicted in these films, how can they resist the label of bad mother? As we demonstrate with these three films, mothers, even when given opportunities in films to respond to claims of mother blame, rarely do so by denying the blame directly. This is not surprising; the demand for maternal accountability is ubiquitous. And opportunities for mothers to assert their own subjectivities as good, or even "good enough" mothers (Silva 2), are constrained by the surveillance culture within which all mothers exist (Douglas and Michaels 6). Indeed, in interpreting maternal voice as a site of resistance in this chapter, we perhaps impose a higher standard on these films than exists within the social world, where mothers' resistance to claims of bad mothering can be easily ignored.

In the end, these three films do not articulate bad mothers as the cause of crime. Instead, they show how such an argument, conceived in academic theory and perpetuated in popular culture, can be visually made. Through imagery, dialogue, and story arcs, these films envision what we already thought we knew: bad children are raised by bad mothers. Yet it is in the actual portrayal of bad mothers that we learn the real truth: without reliance on tropes of abuse or criminal behaviour, these films problematize maternal practice in the development of criminal behaviour, at the expense of the mothers themselves.

ENDNOTES

[1]The fourteen films containing mother blame as an explanation for criminality are the following: *Agnes of God* (1985), *Nuts* (1987), *Boyz-n-the-Hood* (1991), *Final Analysis* (1992), *The Hand That Rocks the Cradle* (1992), *The Good Son* (1993), *The Outsiders* (1993), *Natural Born Killers* (1994), *Blow* (2001), *Catch Me if You Can* (2002), *Red Dragon* (2002), *The Manchurian Candidate* (2004), *We Need to Talk about Kevin* (2011), and *Only God Forgives* (2013).

[2] Of the remaining eleven films, six portray a criminal, abusive, or absent mother. Three depict similar themes or comparable elements to the films that we discuss but in much less detail. We cut analyses of *Nuts* and *Natural Born Killers* to save space in this chapter.

WORKS CITED

Adams, Sarah LaChance. *Mad Mothers, Bad Mothers and What a "Good" Mother Would Do: The Ethics of Ambivalence*. Columbia University Press, 2014.

Arnold, Sarah. *Maternal Horror Films: Melodrama and Motherhood*. Palgrave Macmillan, 2013.

Åström, Berit. "'Because My Mother Was a Liar and a Whore': Adulterous Mothers and Paternity Uncertainty in Jo NesbØ's *The Snowman*." *The Mother-Blame Game*, edited by Vanessa Reimer and Sarah Sahagain, Demeter Press, 2015, pp. 204-218.

Bailey, Frankie Y. "Screening Stereotypes: African American Women in Hollywood Films" *Women, Violence, and the Media*, edited by Drew Humphries, Northeastern University Press, 2009, pp. 75-98.

Bassin, Donna, et al. *Representations of Motherhood*. Yale University Press, 1994.

Boyz-n-the-Hood. Directed by John Singleton. Columbia Pictures, 1991.

Campbell, Alexandra. "Imaging the 'War on Terror': Fiction, Film and Framing." *Framing Crime: Cultural Criminology and the Image*, edited by Keith J. Hayward and Mike Presdee, Routledge, 2010, pp. 98-114.

Caplan, Paula J. *The New Don't Blame Mother: Mending the Mother-Daughter Relationship*. Routledge, 2000.

Catch Me If You Can. Directed by Steven Spielberg. DreamWorks Pictures, 2002.

Douglas, Susan J., and Meredith W. Michaels. *The Mommy Myth: The Idealization of Motherhood and How It Has Undermined All Women*. The Free Press, 2004.

Epstein, Su. "Mothering to Death." *"Bad" Mothers: The Politics of Blame in Twentieth Century America*, edited by Molly Ladd-Taylor and Lauri Umansky, New York University Press, 1998 pp. 257-262.

Fischer, Lucy. *Cinematernity: Film, Motherhood, Genre*. Princeton University Press, 1996.

Garey, Anita Ilta and Terry Arendell. "Children, Work, and Family: Some Thoughts on 'Mother Blame.'" *Working Families: The Transformation of the American Home*, edited by Rosanna Hertz and Nancy L. Marshall, University of California Press, 2001, pp. 293-303.

Hall, Ann C., and Mardia J. Bishop, editors. *Mommy Angst: Motherhood in American Popular Culture*. Praeger, 2009.

Hayward, Keith J., and Mike Presdee, editors. *Framing Crime: Cultural Criminology and the Image*. Routledge, 2010.

Hoeve, Machteld, et al. "A Meta-analysis of Attachment to Parents and Delinquency." *Journal of Abnormal Child Psychology*, vol. 40, no. 5, 2012, pp. 771–785.

hooks, bell. *Reel to Reel: Race, Sex and Class at the Movies*. Routledge, 2009.

Miller, Michelle Hughes. *The Criminalization of Motherhood: The Intersection of Gendered Policy and Familial Ideology*. Diss. University of Nebraska-Lincoln, 1997.

Humphries, Drew. *Women, Violence, and the Media*. Northeastern University Press, 2009.

Jones, Kathleen W. "'Mother Made Me Do It': Mother-Blaming and the Women of Child Guidance." *"Bad" Mothers: The Politics of Blame in Twentieth Century America*, edited by Molly Ladd-Taylor and Lauri Umansky, New York University Press, 1998, pp. 99-126.

Kaplan, E. Ann. *Women and Film: Both Sides of the Camera*. Methuen, 1983.

Kierkus, Christopher A., and John D. Hewitt. "The Contextual Nature of the Family Structure/ Delinquency Relationship." *Journal of Criminal Justice*, vol. 37, no. 2, March–April 2009, pp. 123-132.

Ladd-Taylor, Molly, and Lauri Umansky, editors. *"Bad" Mothers: The Politics of Blame in Twentieth Century America*. New York University Press, 1998.

Maushart, Susan. *The Mask of Motherhood: How Becoming a Mother Changes Everything and Why We Pretend It Doesn't*. The New Press, 1999.

McRobbie, Angela, and Sarah L. Thornton. "Rethinking 'Moral Panics' for Multi-mediated Social Worlds." *British Journal of Sociology*, vol. 46, no.4, 1995, pp. 559-574.

O'Neill, Maggie. *Transgressive Imaginations: Crime, Deviance and Culture*. Palgrave Macmillan, 2012.

Podnieks, Elizabeth, editor. *Mediating Moms: Mothers in Popular Culture*. McGill-Queen's University Press, 2012.

Rafter, Nicole. *Shots in the Mirror: Crime Films and Society*. Oxford University Press, 2000.

Rafter, Nicole, and Michelle Brown. *Criminology Goes to the Movies*. New York University Press, 2011.

Reimer, Vanessa, and Sarah Sahagain, editors. *The Mother-Blame Game*. Demeter Press, 2015.

Rich, Adrienne. *The Fact of a Doorframe: Poems Selected and New, 1950-1984*. W.W. Norton, 1984.

Ruddick, Sara. *Maternal Thinking: Toward a Politics of Peace*. Beacon Press, 1995.

Seidel, Linda. *Mediated Maternity: Contemporary American Portrayals of Bad Mothers in Literature and Popular Culture*. Lexington Books, 2013.

Silva, Elizabeth Bortolaia, editor. *Good Enough Mothering? Feminist Perspectives on Lone Motherhood*. Routledge, 1996.

Thurer, Shari L. *The Myths of Motherhood: How Culture Reinvents the Good Mother*. Houghton Mifflin Co, 1994.

We Need to Talk about Kevin. Directed by Lynne Ramsay. Oscilloscope, 2011.

Willis, Sharon. *High Contrast: Race and Gender in Contemporary Hollywood Films*. Duke University Press, 1997.

Worthington, Marjorie. "The Motherless "Disney Princess": Marketing Mothers Out of the Picture." *Mommy Angst: Motherhood in American Popular Culture*, edited by Ann C. Hall and Mardia J. Bishop, Praeger, 2009, pp. 29-46.

Yar, Majid. "Screening Crime: Cultural Criminology Goes to the Movies." *Framing Crime: Cultural Criminology and the Image*, edited by Keith J. Hayward and Mike Presdee, Routledge, 2010, pp. 68-82.

Young, Alison. "The Scene of the Crime: Is There Such a Thing as 'Just Looking'?" *Framing Crime: Cultural Criminology and the Image*, edited by Keith J. Hayward and Mike Presdee, Routledge, 2010, pp. 83-97.

Bad Motherhood in Contemporary Argentine Cinema

Illustrating the New Political Agenda

FERNANDO GABRIEL PAGNONI BERNS,
PATRICIA VAZQUEZ, AND JUAN JUVÉ

DURING THE last decade, Argentina has gone through a period of severe ideological crisis known within the nation as "the split," which divides those supporting the government of the Kirchners (Nestor and Cristina)[1] and those critical of it. This apparently irreconcilable split has slowly started to place politics and ideology at centre stage again, after years of political apathy.

The image of motherhood has had to face a split all of its own. During the last years, the image of motherhood has been rife with contradictions: mothers and maternity as the apex of nationhood, motherhood as choice rather than a mandate, and motherhood as just another corrupted institution within a corrupted country. One striking aspect within Argentinean culture is the elevated number of filmic mothers who are now constructed as "bad," especially in their relationship with their little children. Strongly working against the cultural landscape of the "self-sacrificing" mothers that helped build a national text in the past, these new mothers mirror the deconstructive image that mothers in contemporary Argentina project: a complicated amalgam of empowered women.

In this chapter, we will discuss some notions of motherhood within Argentina to later delineate a brief history of motherhood in national cinema. In the last section, we will examine such films as *Ciencias Naturales* or *Las Mantenidas sin Sueños* to point the ways in which Argentinean cinema illustrate the complexity of these new, so-called bad maternities that avoid been bounded within the national tradition of "all-suffering women."

MILLENNIAL ARGENTINA: FROM CRISIS OF REPRESENTATION TO THE SPLIT

This chapter can be understood as a continuation of a previous essay, "Motherhood and Identity in Contemporary Argentine Cinema," in which we articulate some ideas about filmic representations of maternity in Argentina. Our hypothesis then was that the Argentina of the new millennium lacks a concrete, univocal project of identity, giving rise to the configuration of the maternal as "singularities" (Pagnoni Berns 281).

That was the situation at the moment of writing that essay. There was not a prevalent ideology, and that lack of definition shaped, for better or for worse, social and cultural representations. The political climate was dominated by the motto "*que se vayan todos*" ("politicians, go home!"), a phrase that makes reference to the general disillusionment about politicians no matter to what party they answer (Cleary and Stokes 85). After a decade (the 1990s) dominated by savage neoliberal practices and political corruption under Carlos Saúl Menem's governance, and after the serious economic and social crisis of 2001, people began to feel cut off from political debate. The general idea was that all known politicians were corrupt and the only solution was fresh blood. In fact, when president Nestor Kirchner was elected president in 2003, he was mostly unknown for the majority of Argentineans (Skard 232), and his electoral win was due more to "the vacuum of power" than any personal characteristic (Cortés-Conde and Boxer 50).

The Argentina of the last five years, however, has strongly increased its commitment with ideology and politics. The new dominating motto is a shorter one: "*la grieta*" ("the crevice" or "the split"). For anyone who is unaware of Argentine politics, this word seems irrelevant. In turn, every Argentinean knows what is meant when someone speaks about *la grieta*.

The split refers to the fact that in popular wisdom Argentina is separated into two irreconcilable parts: one that defends the politics of *Kirchnerismo*—as is called the period of governance of Nestor Kirchner (from 2003 to 2007) and his wife Cristina Fernandez de Kirchner (from 2008 to 2015)—whereas the other part is critical of the Kirchner years of governance. The former celebrates the Kirchners' commitment to the politics of human rights and the development of the state of welfare, whereas the latter criticizes recurrent political corruption, populism, Cristina Kirchner's aggressiveness, and the attacks to independent journalism.

Obviously, thinking Argentina as divided into two parts is an oversimplification, since there are many citizens uninterested in politics or positioned within a grey area. But as mentioned, this ideal responds to popular wisdom, and not a day passes without a mention about the famous *grieta*. The Kirchners have achieved their goal of transforming Argentina's fragmented society into a nation thanks to a new narrative (Cortés-Conde and Boxer 51): now, the citizens are K (those who support *Kirchnerismo*) or Anti-K (those who are critical). Argentina has become very politicized in the last few years.

One of the social actors that most strongly supported *Kirchnerismo* is *las Abuelas y Madres de Plaza de Mayo* (Grandmothers and Mothers of Plaza de Mayo). During the late 1970s and early 1980s, the Plaza de Mayo, the main square in Buenos Aires where the presidential house sits, became a highly contested space. In defiance of the repressive military government that had taken the government through a coup d'état in 1975, the Mothers of the Plaza de Mayo protested every Thursday against the disappearances of their children. They were considered "crazy woman" through the dictatorship period (from 1975 to 1982). Only with the welcome return of democracy in 1983 did their image turn into one of brave women fighting for justice and for the recovery of their kidnapped children. Later, the Kirchners elevated the mothers to the status of national heroes. Margarite Guzman Bouvard narrates the importance of the mothers: "These women came out of the shadows, out of a cultural, historical, and social invisibility and into the center of the political arena to challenge a repressive government" (60). This image of heroism is explicitly stated when compared with other symbols of justice: "Their efforts to infuse politics with ethics and with respect for universal human rights are reminiscent of the work of Gandhi and Martin Luther King, Jr" (60).

The Grandmothers and Mothers of Plaza de Mayo uncritically sympathized with *Kirchnerismo* and its politics, and they have been heavily criticized for that. As their support increased, so did the large public transfers of money granted to the foundations of both branches of the organization—mothers and grandmothers. Soon enough, suspicion about corruption in the grandmother's branch spread through the media (Moene and Soreide 58). Because of the government's sympathies with the groups, the accusations of corruption were not investigated, which only furthered the antipathy among many Argentinians about the role of the Plaza mothers and grandmothers in politics.

The Kirchner's era has been one inextricably linked to contradictory images of motherhood and femininity. For Cristina, "being a woman makes her marginal and a victim," yet women, under her presidency, have to be "daring" and brave; Cristina Kirchner herself is considered a "male dominator" (Cortés-Conde and Boxer 57, 60). She advocates for a new woman identity that comes from individual empowerment rather than traditional roles. Cristina Fernández de Kirchner has "rarely incorporated her experience as a mother into her political campaign" (Christie 21), yet she presents herself as the mother of all the Argentineans ("Me siento").[2] On the one hand, the Grandmothers and Mothers of Plaza de Mayo were turned into symbols of national fight and identity. On the other, they were potentially corrupt women using their personal losses as excuse to become rich at the state's expenses. These contradictory notions of womanhood and mothers—all of them cohabiting in the same time and space—open the path to deconstruct motherhood for the very first time in Argentina's history.

In this complex arena, the popular image of maternity was deconstructed. The maternal figure in contemporary cinema is divided, like the country itself, into two parts: first, there are heroic mothers who fight against all odds to save, not themselves, but their children. *Leonera* tells the story off an incarcerated woman fighting to give her son a better life. *Refugiado* revolves around a mother running away from her abusive husband to protect her son from any harm, even if this means sacrificing everything. Also, the personal history of Estela de Carlotto, leader of the Mothers of Plaza de Mayo was turned into a film in 2011 (*Verdades Ver-*

daderas, La Vida de Estela). Other films, however, gives increasing presence to bad mothers who illustrate the crisis of the traditional role of women within the Kirchner era, and the way in which they contrast with the classical mother in their refusal to sacrifice themselves. They actively work against any idea of self-sacrifice and act to demystify motherhood. Thus, both the filmic heroic maternal figures sketched above and the bad mothers studied later in this chapter complement, illustrate, and legitimate the circulation of new paradigms about womanhood and motherhood proposed after 2003 in Argentina.

ARGENTINE FILM AND MOTHERHOOD: A BRIEF HISTORY

Cinema shapes discourses that create a sense of belonging. In the case of Argentine cinema, its importance in the creation of national identity is so large that according to Claudio España, "the Argentines went to the movies to learn to be Argentines" (130).

Culture was one of the most popular forms of social formation, and during its classical period (1930s to 1950s), Argentina had a dynamic film industry. The canonical film genre in Argentina's classical cinema was the melodrama, in which the expectations and anxieties of the population were deposited. The melodrama is a didactic genre, since it teaches a specific set of "civilizing" behaviours and moral rules to form a strong nation with its own identity.

Within melodrama shined a particular subgenre called the "melodrama of mothers" (Viviani). In these films, any transgression committed by the central female character is punished in the end by the extreme suffering, or even death, of the transgressors, who would then be redeemed. This mother sacrifices everything to make her child achieve an exemplary social status. The collapse of the female protagonist is presented in parallel with the achievements and the triumph of the son or daughter as redemptive arcs. The mother sacrifices everything, sometimes even her own life, to reaffirm the citizenship of her children. This discourse on motherhood complements the immigrant ideology, in which immigrants sacrifice much of their lives to work in hoping to give their children a better future in a new land.

BAD MOTHERHOOD IN CONTEMPORARY CINEMA: THE GIFT OF IDENTITY

Motherhood mostly disappeared from cinema up to the late 1990s, when a new movement called "new Argentine cinema" gradually grew in popularity. A new breed of directors emerged who "look[ed] at problems in Argentine society with a quirky, youth-oriented perspective" (Falicov 119).

Contemporary Argentine cinema, framed by the new social female role encouraged by *Kirchnerismo*, has given birth to a corpus of films that privilege the mother who deviates from the crystallized act of self-sacrifice. For example, the film *Conversaciones con Mamá* tells the story of Jaime, who is trying to save money, as he is a facing a personal financial crisis. He decides to sell the house in which his elderly mother lives and invites her to instead move in with him. For Jaime, there is no doubt that his mother will agree—he expects self-sacrificial (traditionally rooted) behaviour from his mother—but to his surprise, his mother refuses. This mother works in opposition to the classical mother and decides to think on her own rather than going along with her son's request and sacrificing her autonomy. To Jaime's consternation, his mother confesses that she is dating a homeless pensioner who now lives with her. Thus, the mother is doubly reconfigured as "bad": first, by placing her desires ahead of those of her only son, she undermines the sacrificial aspect of motherhood; and second, despite her age, her sexuality is emphasized.

Made in 2004, with Nestor Kirchner having been president for only a year, the film is a bridge between the neoliberal crisis of the first years of the new millennium and the slow deconstruction of motherhood. Both Jaime and Gregorio are victims of neoliberal practices. The mother, in turn, is the first sign of new times, preluding changes to come. She has no name; she is only "the mother," which connects her with the neoconservative gender traditionalism commonplace through the 1990s. However, this mother subverts gender expectations rather than confirms them.

Fatherhood and motherhood are understood as performative roles. In this sense, Emily Jeremiah argues that "maternity is no longer seen as a fixed, static state; rather, it is viewed as a set of ideas and behaviours that are mutable, contextual" (21). That fixed figure of the mother could be related to classic Argentine cinema. Jeremiah presents motherhood as a performative act (22)—a series of socially constructed gestures, a constant "doing" through reiterative practice (25-26).

However, in popular wisdom as in practice, motherhood is inextricably tied to other persons—children. In maternity, any gesture breaking the repeated maternal gestures that build maternity always involves another vulnerable entity, the child. In *Conversaciones con Mamá*, such a gesture of subversion can be observed in the mother's refusal to leaves the home. For an audience used to seeing Argentinean films, this may seem like a powerful act, even if both mother and son are adults. If the subversive act involves the denial of a maternal gesture toward a little child, then it becomes an ethical problem (Jeremiah 27). Thus, the subversive gesture can be criminal: neglecting of a child.

This issue is illustrated in *Las Mantenidas sin Sueños*, a film that foregrounds bad motherhood and is about the relationship between Florencia and her young daughter, Eugenia. The film opens with Florencia leaving a clinic after having an abortion—a taboo topic, even for *Kirchnerismo*. Her mother, Sara, waits in the car to take her home. However, Florencia has not gone through with the abortion. Everything has been just a subterfuge to take money from her overprotective mother. Florencia does not work, nor does she want to, even though she is the mother of a young daughter who lives with her in a shambled apartment, which does not even have electricity—cut off for lack of payment. It is Eugenia who assumes control of the house: she cooks, cleans, and takes care of general responsibilities, whereas her mother lies stretched out on the couch, asleep or waking up from the effects of cocaine consumption. "Florencia actively chooses not to care for her daughter, and thus does not occupy a maternal role" (Pagnoni Berns 292).

However, the relationship between Florencia and her daughter is certainly good: Eugenia is mother to her own mother, and Florencia treats her daughter as an adult. When Florencia tells her daughter that she is pregnant and will not abort the fetus as her mother wants her to, Eugenia asks her mother if the father of the child is her boyfriend. Florencia acknowledges that she does not know. The relationship between the two is good because both speak to one another as equals. It must be pointed that there is no doubt that Florencia does love her daughter. When the contents of a bag of cocaine vanish, Florencia fears for the health of her daughter and goes into a panic. However, despite her love, she simply declines to fulfill the role that society expects of her. Eugenia deeply loves her mother, even if Florencia inflexibly denies her maternal role.

What Florencia gives to her daughter is individuality and identity outside the mother-daughter dyad. The adolescent female begins to mature and distance herself from her mother in an attempt for individuation, and in the film, her individuality is granted from the very beginning through "alternative" mothering. In *Las Mantenidas sin Sueños*, there is no rivalry between the two women but rather a sisterhood—an "alternative to the divisive mother-daughter model" (Henry 182).

This search for identity and empowerment complements the Kirchners' project of revision of identities and nationhood. There were projects to revise history and cultural identity in Argentina linked with the bicentennial celebrations (Alberto and Elena 308). The Kirchners also gained social legitimation through a discourse based, in part, on the recovery or adopting of identity. During *Kirchnerismo*, there was an increase in the number of "*nietos recuperados*" (recovered grandchildren) and in the claims for usurped identities. Through Cristina Kirchner's term as president, the kidnapping and the changing of a child's identity practiced by Argentina's military regime between 1976 and 1983 was listed as a form of child violence, and the subject of identity is inextricably linked to *Kirchnerismo*.

Through a feminist perspective that critically examines the meanings of motherhood, both films successfully complement the social climate. These bad mothers and their refusal to self-sacrifice legitimate the new empowered woman proposed by the public agenda. Both bad mothers favour the constitution of a potential identity based in a womanhood sustained in more practices than just motherhood.

The issue of identity, politics, and motherhood is even more visible in *Ciencias Naturales*, a film that presents a brief but interesting glimpse of bad motherhood. The film encapsulates both maternal heroism and bad motherhood in the context of Argentina's politics. Lila is a young girl living and studying in a rural school in the far north of Argentina. She is adamant to meet her father, who abandoned her mother when she was pregnant. Lila's mother, Rosa, refuses to let her daughter travel to meet her father, and the only help that the girl finds is in her teacher Jimena who, risking her job, agrees to accompany the girl on her adventure.

Female teachers have been, traditionally, known in Argentina as "the second mother" (Fischman 83). Jimena is the good mother here: as she explains to Lila, she is risking her job and even can facing criminal accusations for taking the girl on a trip. She, like the classical mother, is sacrificing everything for her "daughter." Her maternal role is enhanced in the first scenes, when Jimena is the one who takes care of Lila's first menstruation rather than her real mother, who is nowhere to be seen. Furthermore, Jimena is the person in charge of giving Lila back her own identity, a topic that recalls the claims for identity of the Grandmothers and Mothers of Plaza de Mayo. In this sense, Rosa fulfills the role of the bad mother, the one who metaphorically kidnaps children and keeps them in the dark about their real identity. If Jimena is the sacrificial mother, Rosa mirrors the military dictatorship that ruled Argentina from 1976 to 1983. She denies helping her daughter and sharing any information about her father as well. She refuses to give to her daughter an identity of her own. Furthermore, Rosa treats Lila as if the little girl were just an object. To Rosa, Lila has no more identity than that of being a daughter—a possession inextricably linked to her by the ties of motherhood.

When Jimena asks Rosa for some help with Lila's identity, the mother angrily rebukes the teacher, informing her that her daughter goes to school to learn, not to have her mind "twisted" by ideas about identity. The fear of schools "twisting" the minds of young people was an excuse for military intervention and the restructuring of the education system in the 1970s, which furthers the links between bad motherhood, the denying of identity, and the military government (Manzano 222). Rosa shows up only briefly in the film but enough to establish her as an obstacle to Lila's identity. Rosa claims that what took place with Lila's father "did happen to me," putting her experience first and foremost and wiping out her daughter's rights to know her identity.

Ciencias Naturales subtly plays with the Argentinean past and social configurations about motherhood. These representations closely follow the Kirchners' purpose of elevating the Grandmothers and Mothers of Plaza de Mayo to the category of national heroines fighting for justice and identity. It must be mentioned that Paola Barrientos, the good mother of *Ciencias Naturales*, is a fervent follower of the doctrine of the Kirchners.

As it is easy to see, bad mothers work as useful tools for both the giving of identity and the denying of identity. Thus, this particular figure explicates the polyvalent character of bad motherhood as an elastic or flexible idea that allows it to critically engage not only with social traditional discourses of maternity and gender but with other cultural issues as well.

THE NEW PROGRESSIVE AGENDA

In Cristina Kirchner's second mandate as president, now as a widow after the death of Nestor in 2010, the progressive agenda and the new politics of feminism increased. The search for identity was an important political tool within the program of government, but some new items were added in the last years. First, the civil code was reformed in order to increase gender equality. For example, women were no longer obliged to use as their last name their husbands' surnames. The new code also allowed that children bear both the name of the mother and/or father, implying a greater symmetry between spouses. In addition, it became simpler to get divorced—just one party could seek divorce, providing greater gender equality between the wife and husband.

Also, laws about gender violence have been created and/or perfected to protect women from gender violence. One of the most important advances in the Kirchner years was the legislation of the figure of femicide. For the first time, gender violence was understood as related to oppression and not just physical punishment. Verbal, ideological, cultural, institutional, and psychological forms of male abuse toward women were criminally punished. This cultural and ideological climate was sometimes channeled into popular culture coded through the figure of the bad mother, obviously a useful tool to speak of women's new status.

The film *Por tu culpa* addresses the problems of social expectations and the nurturing of little children through the figure of Julieta, a middle-class, young, divorced professional. One night, as Julieta works on her computer, her youngest son gets hurt in a little accident, and she must take him to the hospital where, after attending him, the doctors denounce her for apparent mistreatment.

She is a bad mother from minute one. The film begins with Julieta playing with her two sons. However, a call from her estranged ex-husband shapes a compendium of her so-called maternal defects: he reproaches her for keeping the children awake until late hours and for her lack of control over them. This apparent lack of control is explicit throughout the film. The kids do not obey her. Also, she screams a lot at them. Julieta seems incapable of managing her roles as a modern, working woman and as a mother. Her children simply do not obey her because she is incapable of exercising authority, seemingly because she is in charge of many tasks, more than she can properly assume. Her sons even insult her—a symbol of how weak and irregularly she fulfills her maternal role.

In fact, it is actually Julieta who accidently hurts her little son when separating him from his brother during a fight. In the hospital, she is harshly judged by the (male) doctors attending her son. Julieta is at the mercy of the authoritarian and patriarchal gaze of others—doctors, cops, her ex-husband, all of whom are male—as a bad mother and referred within the film's title as a "guilty one." When her ex-husband comes to the hospital, one of his first questions is "what have you done to him?" in reference to his son.

Julieta clearly loves her sons. Even so, her actions can be judged, from the point of view of expectations, as "bad." Before the accident, Julieta only wants to momentarily forget her sons to get some respite. She turns to the old trick of putting the kids in front of a television to keep them occupied for a while. What Julieta wants is to work at the computer—in other words, she wants to privilege, at least for one hour, her job rather than her maternal duties. To do so, she uses earphones which block her sons' voices. Audiences are able to hear only what the voice in the earphones says, so the kids are effectively forgotten and turned into a blur in the background.

The guilt is inscribed in Julieta's face. The film begins with the sound of Julieta's sigh, a lamentation filled with exhaustion. The camera follows her in close shots through the whole film, as a way to imprison her within her own guilt. When her ex-husband is talking with a lawyer about the accusation made by the doctors, his image is blurred. This way, the audiences' gaze is obliged to centre on Julieta's face, which is riddled with guilt. She knows that she is a bad mother, not because she has hurt her son but because she is incapable of fulfilling the expectations that society has deposited on her.

From the perspective of the other characters, it is obvious that Julieta should know how to raise her children because of her condition as mother (as if motherhood were preprogrammed within womanhood). Thus, they treat her as an inefficient, inept mother: that is, a bad mother. Facing this situation, Julieta seems not to know how to defend herself. Her speech is unclear, imprecise, and filled with omissions. The film ends without consequences for Julieta. There is no need for that. Even if the mother is cleared of any criminal charge, the truth is that she was accused of child abuse, an accusation that reaffirms her role as a bad mother.

Por tu culpa also illustrates forms of male violence and asks about the role that men fulfill in Julieta's world. It is significant that the children stay with their mother the night of the incident because their father could not take them out, even if it had been his time with them. And, as Julieta repeats as a mantra, the kid hurts himself playing with a toy that was a gift from the father. Fathers are guilty too, but the blame falls on the mother figure, the one obliged to be perfect or face the dangers of being classified as bad. Julieta is framed as bad by her husband and by institutions, both of them asking her to fulfill a traditional role, whereas she is guilty of trying to be both mother and professional. *Por tu culpa* explores the ethical assumption of culpability as a major theme and does so in gendered terms. For example, in the first scenes, it can be argued that Julieta has forgotten that she has children, a mocking twist on the iconic position of the Grandmothers and Mothers of Plaza de Mayo.

Whereas Julieta is framed within the tensions of the new woman who steps within the public space while mothering, the main female character of the comedy *Sin Hijos* has no problems with motherhood, but she could be considered as a bad woman because of her refusal to comply with the maternal mandate. The film is an Argentinean-Spanish romantic comedy covering some new representations and conditions of motherhood in Argentina. After his separation, Gabriel Cabau, a shop owner, has been not able to establish a relationship with another woman, and he devotes himself to his daughter Sofia. One day he reconnects with Vicky, with whom he had been secretly in love since his youth and had not seen for a long time. Following a meeting with Vicky, they start dating, but soon Gabriel learns that Vicky feels a deep aversion to children. This leads Gabriel to conceal the existence of his daughter.

The film plays with the exchange of traditional roles. It is the man here who sacrifices himself for the children, whereas women privilege other concerns, such as their careers. This issue runs parallel to Argentina's return to democracy and the Kirchner years, which come with a greater symmetry between the sexes and the politicization of issues related to feminism, implying a modification of family ties. One of the most important advances in Argentina legislation during the early years of the restoration of democracy was the divorce law, becoming law in 1987. Since then, divorced parents became commonplace. As discussed earlier, during the Kirchners' government, laws were established to protect these new realities. This new social context is represented in *Sin Hijos*.

Although the women in the film move ahead in their lives, Gabriel remains stuck in the same spot. Within the film's first minutes, Gabriel chats with Vicky. He is working in his grandfather's shop, and he is three courses away from completing a degree in architecture. After a temporal lapse of nine years, Gabriel is in the same situation, but is now dedicated to his daughter and has a scant sexual life. Since sexual chastity was an experience historically associated with femininity—women as a matter of property (Harman 196)—and keeping in mind that Vicky has an interesting sexual life, it is easy to see how gender roles are mixed up. She is sexually active, and she has no desire to nurture, which is the typical representation of a bad woman. The only character that follows the rigid stereotypes of gender is Oscar, Gabriel's father, who abandoned his son when he was fourteen. Oscar answers to the old generations in which rigid roles for women and men were mutually exclusive spheres. *Sin Hijos* implies that in current Argentine society, these social constructions are in crisis and lack the strength that they had in past times.

Vicky is the exact opposite of the sacrificial woman of classical cinema. She, unlike Gabriel, has had a life in constant movement: she has toured Europe, has worked as photographer, and she speaks several languages. She works as a tourist guide, an activity linked to movement and displacement. Unlike Gabriel, she has decided not to have children. What is more important, however, is that she feels a deep contempt toward children in general. She disobeys the traditional mandate of a women being fulfilled only by nurturing. She despises kids and hates the idea of giving birth. For her, children mean the loss of freedom. This is not just a simple preference, but involves an active militancy. Whereas the classical mothers of Argentine cinema are women whose fate was sacrificed for the sake of their children, Vicky feels fulfilled only in her professional life. In contrast, Gabriel is particularly distressed by the disjunction of hiding his daughter and keeping a relationship with Vicky or, following the good mother of classical cinema, sacrificing his personal life for his daughter, in a clear reversal of traditional roles.

Here are two examples of bad women, both of whom legitimate the new cultural paradigms about motherhood and womanhood that have recently emerged in Argentina. Julieta is a woman suffering from male and institutional violence—her so-called bad mothering a device to erase male responsibility and patriarchal prejudices. She is a victim of gender violence. Meanwhile, Vicky is a modern woman of her times, an individual who feels neither anxiety nor guilt about disliking children. However, it must be pointed out that Vicky is a Spanish woman. Argentinean cinema seems incapable to engage with maternity in such a subversive way. The totally emancipated woman, free from the constraints of motherhood, is only possible when she is a foreigner, a woman from another place.

CONCLUSIONS

The contradictions in the representation of motherhood are easy to observe in contemporary Argentinean cinema. Whereas *Ciencias Naturales* resurrects the classic sacrificial mother as a path to sustain the Grandmothers and Mothers of Plaza de Mayo's fight, the other films engage with bad motherhood as a way to resist the traditional figure of the mother.

In her article, Jeremiah confirms that the subversive act of refusing to practice the gestures of motherhood involves ethical dimensions. Jimena embodies the duties and responsibilities of the traditional mother role in classical Argentine cinema, as she has sacrificed everything for Lila. Conversely, in *Las Mantenidas sin Sueños*, Florencia's attitudes about motherhood bring her close to committing acts of criminality and neglect: not only does she continue smoking during pregnancy, but she neglects her daughter's wellbeing as she grows up. Jeremiah does not explain what these subversive acts mean in terms of maternal theory; the character of Florencia, instead, produces the answer. What Florencia gains in her subversive refusal to perform maternal gestures is individuality, the uniqueness of an identity beyond the mother-daughter dyad. Similarly, the mother in *Conversaciones con Mamá* also recovers her identity by accepting a new lover and refusing her son's wishes. She is an individual woman before being a mother. But since her son is a grown man, the subversive act is, therefore, mitigated. In turn, the mother of *Por tu Culpa*, through the devices of patriarchy, has no more identity that that of mother and, as such, she struggles to fulfill that role, and is constantly failing. Through the figure of the bad mother, the film denounces male oppression and how maternity is constructed as a play of asymmetrical powers. Vicky, from *Sin Hijos*, also explicitly addresses the social dogma of traditional motherhood. Vicky constructs her identity as an opposite to Julieta: Vicky is anything but a mother. She has an active identity as a career woman, and she is fully satisfied with it, not because of the lack of children but because she feels no obligation to fulfill any expectation.

All these films in some way use the figure of the bad mother to legitimize the politics of *Kirchnerismo*. At the moment, its progressive agenda has opened a space for a new image of motherhood to emerge, which was unthinkable some years ago. With the film industry heavily controlled by official institutions during the Kirchners' years, however, little space existed for any critical engagement with any potential political corruption in the sacred figure of the mother in Argentina. Nevertheless, there is the possibility that the mothers in these films are corrupt as the Grandmothers and Mothers of Plaza de Mayo are now considered to be for many. Only time will tell if the Mothers of Plaza de Mayo have committed criminal acts -true bad mothers. But if the sacred Grandmothers and Mothers of Plaza de Mayo were "bad mommies" like the bad mothers in these films, this potentiality only furthers the deconstruction of motherhood in Argentina, a country built, in part, on the image of motherhood. However, it must be mentioned that with exception of *Sin Hijos*, all the films were huge flops in the box office.

Now, as Cristina Kirchner comes to the end of her mandate, mothers are slowly fading away from cinema, waiting, probably, for the future. As the image of the Grandmothers and Mothers of Plaza de Mayo continues to deteriorate and the progressive politics of the female subject is put on hiatus during the change of government, we await the discourses of motherhood that the new times will bring.

ENDNOTES

[1]She ended her presidential term in 2015.
[2]All Spanish-English translations are ours.

WORKS CITED

Alberto, Paulina, and Eduardo Elena. *Rethinking Race in Modern Argentina*. Cambridge University Press, 2016.

Christie, Jane. *Negotiating Gendered Discourses: Michelle Bachelet and Cristina Fernández de Kirchner*. Lexington, 2016.

Ciencias Naturales. Directed by Matías Lucchesi, performances by Paula Galinelli Hertzog, Paola Barrientos, and Alvin Astorga, Salta la Liebre and INCAA, 2014.

Cleary, Matthew, and Susan Stokes. *Democracy and the Culture of Skepticism: The Politics of Trust in Argentina and Mexico*. Russell Sage Foundation, 2006.

Conversaciones con Mamá. Directed by Santiago Carlos Oves, performances by China Zorilla and Eduardo Blanco, MR Films, 2004.

Cortés-Conde, Florencia, and Diana Boxer. "Breaking the Glass & Keeping the Ceiling: Women Presidents' Discursive Practices in Latin America." *Discourse, Politics and Women as Global Leaders*, edited by John Wilson and Diana Boxer, John Benjamins Publishing Company, 2015, pp. 43-66.

España, Claudio et al. *Cine Argentino: Industria y Clasicismo 1933/1956*. Fondo Nacional de las Artes, 2000.

Falicov, Tamara. *The Cinematic Tango: Contemporary Argentine Film*. Wallflower Press, 2007.

Fischman, Gustavo. *Imagining Teachers: Rethinking Gender Dynamics in Teacher Education*. Rowman & Littlefield, 2000.

Guzman Bouvard, Margarite. *Revolutionizing Motherhood: The Mothers of the Plaza De Mayo Latin American Silhouettes*. Scholarly Resources, Inc., 1994.

Harman, Barbara. *The Feminine Political Novel in Victorian England*. University of Virginia Press, 1998.

Henry, Astrid. *Not My Mother's Sister: Generational Conflict and Third-Wave Feminism*. Indiana University Press, 2004.

Jeremiah, Emily. "Motherhood to Mothering and Beyond: Maternity in Recent Feminist Thought." *Journal of the Motherhood Initiative for Research and Community Involvement*, vol. 8, no. 1, 2006, pp. 21-33.

Las Mantenidas sin Sueños. Directed by Martín De Salvo and Vera Fogwill, performances by Vera Foigwill, Mirta Busnelli, and Lucía Snieg, INCAA, 2005.

Leonera. Directed by Pablo Trapero, performances by Martina Gusman, Rodrigo Santoro, and Laura García, Patagonik Film Group, 2008.

Manzano, Valeria. *The Age of Youth in Argentina: Culture, Politics, and Sexuality from Perón to Videla*. University of North Carolina Press, 2014.

"Me Siento la Madre de Todos los Argentinos." *Libertaddigital*,

28 March. 2014, http://www.libertaddigital.com/internacional/latinoamerica/2014-03-28/cristina-fernandez-me-siento-la-madre-del-pais-y-de-todos-los-argentinos-1276514359/Accessed 23 Jan. 2017.

Moene, Kalle and Tina Soreide. "Good Governance Facades." *Greed, Corruption, and the Modern State: Essays in Political Economy*, edited by Susan Rose-Ackerman and Paul Lagunes, Edward Elgar Publishing, 2015, pp. 46-70.

Pagnoni Berns, Fernando Gabriel. "Motherhood and Identity in Contemporary Argentine Cinema." *Screening Motherhood in Contemporary World Cinema*, edited by Asma Sayed, Demeter Press, 2016, pp. 281-299.

Por tu culpa. Directed by Anahí Berneri, performances by Erica Rivas, Nicasio Galán, and Zenón Galán, INCAA, 2010.

Refugiado. Directed by Diego Lerman, performances by Juliata Díaz, Marta Lubos, and Sebastían Molinaro, El Campo Cine, 2014.

Sin Hijos. Directed by Ariel Winograd, performances by Diego Peretti, Horacio Fontova and Maribel Verdú, INCAA and ICAA, 2005.

Skard, Torild. *Women of Power: Half a Century of Female Presidents and Prime Ministers Worldwide*. Policy Press, 2015.

Verdades Verdaderas, La Vida de Estela. Directed by Nicolás Gil Lavedra, performances by Susú Pecoraro, and Alejandro Awada, Aleph Media, 2011.

Viviani, Christian. "Who is Without Sin? The Maternal Melodrama in American Film, 1930-1939." *Imitations of Life: A Reader on Film & Television Melodrama*, edited by Marcia Landy, Wayne State University Press, 1991, pp. 168-182.

IV.
RESISTING BAD MOTHER NARRATIVES

Image 1: "DO I FIT IN," 2005, hand knitted wool, 800 x 340mm.
Knitted for me by Freda Burgher. In Private Collection. Photo: Douglas Atfield.

Bad Mother

FREDDIE ROBINS

KNITTING HAS LONG held associations with practical function, the production of garments to keep us warm and comfortable. Like many people, I have a desire to own functional, knitted things, but I have no desire to make them. When I was pregnant, I was continually being asked what I had been knitting my baby. As I am an artist working almost exclusively with knitting, it was assumed that she would have a wonderful array of lovingly knitted items to wear, but I had knitted her nothing. Guilt got the better of me, and she received a jumper, and with postnatal depression, she received some giant pram trousers.

Image 2: "How to Make a Piece of Work When You're Too Tired to Make Decisions," 2004 machine knitted wool, dress pins. Photo: Ed Barber, courtesy of Crafts Council (UK).

Image Two: This piece of work was conceived of during the first few months of my daughter's life when I was lying in bed at night, overtired but unable to sleep. Long before I had given birth, determined not to change a thing about my life once I became a mother, I had arranged to go to Berlin on an artist's residency six months after my due date. However, now I had given birth I was unable to stop crying, let alone concentrate on making work. This was the period in which I had knitted the giant pram trousers—luckily my daughter was a late walker, or maybe hindered by my knitting, she could not walk. Anyway, I knew that when I did manage to make work again, it would no longer be possible for me to approach it in the same way that I had before. My studio practice was built on continuity of time and thought, which was no longer available to me. My work is technically challenging, and even during my pregnancy, I found it increasingly difficult to make the necessary decisions, let alone do the required mathematical equations. My work had also been increasing in scale, and I wanted this to continue. With much less time available to me, the only way that this was possible was to make smaller components, which when placed together, would

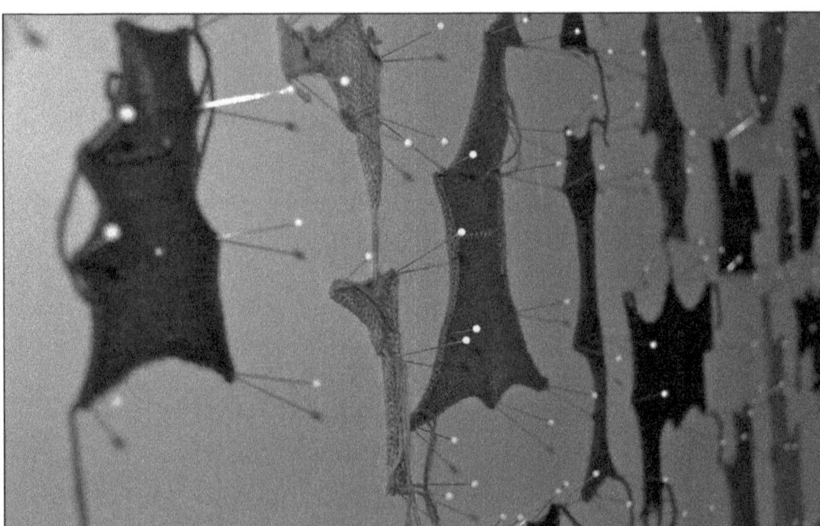

Image 3: "How to Make a Piece of Work When You're Too Tired to Make Decisions" (detail), 2004, machine knitted wool, dress pins. Photo: Ed Barber, courtesy of Crafts Council (UK).

form a large work. This piece aimed to address all of the above. It took the decision making away from me and let it rest on the throw of a dice. It also enabled me to make work in short periods of time where continuity of time or thought was not necessary. I could make work when I was tired, or I could even give the dice and instructions to someone else, and they could make it for me, no pattern necessary.

Image Three: I used three dice: one to decide the colour of the yarns that I would use; one to give me numbers for stitches and rows; and the other to decide the actions, such as "hook up side of knitting," "turn knitting," or "decrease one stitch fully fashioned at the beginning of each row." Each individual piece was made using ten actions. The instructions, numbers dice, and actions dice were modified after several experiments to give more consistently successful results. The finished piece is ongoing. The arrangement of individual pieces can be changed, and it can be added to at any time. The instructions and dice are open to modification should it become necessary or should I feel like it.

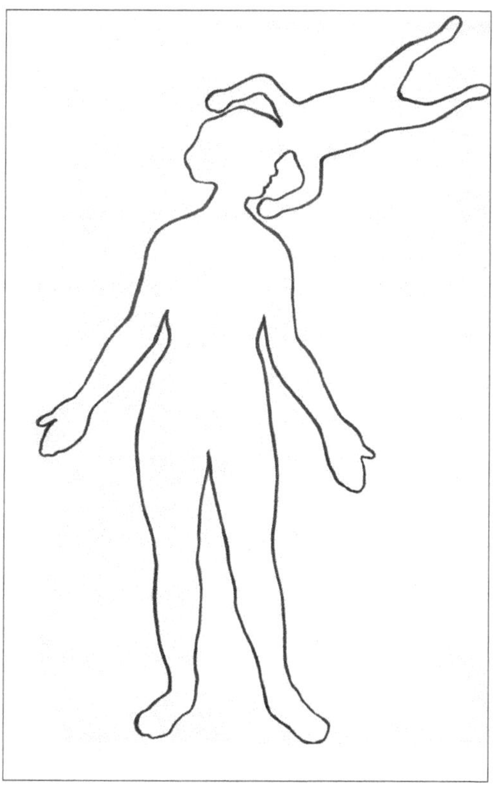

Image 4: "Untitled 1," 2006, ink on paper, 296 x 199 mm..

Image Four: When I managed to get some reliable childcare in place, I returned to the studio. I produced a series of untitled ink drawings communicating the intense emotional and physical relationship that I was having with my baby daughter. She completely consumed me, filling all my thoughts. I couldn't concentrate on anything

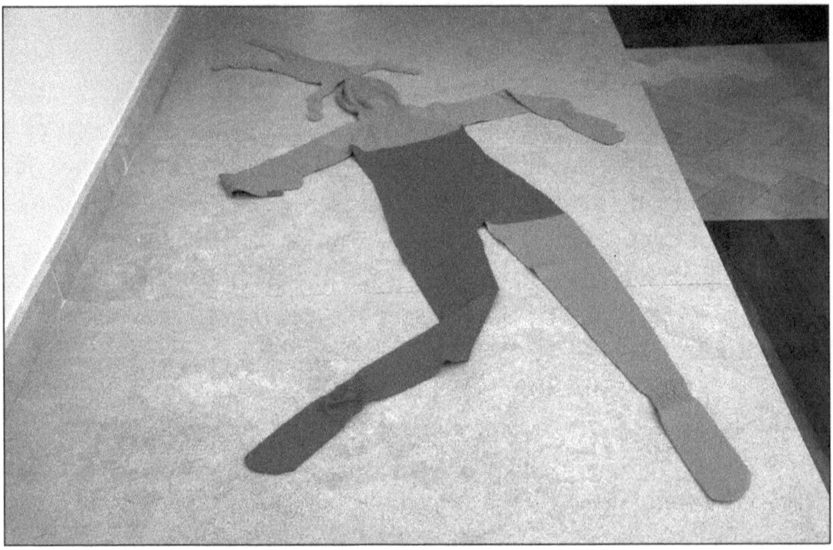

Image 5: Installation shot of "Mad Mother," 2015, machine and hand knitted wool, 2300 x 1520 x 20 mm), in "Liberties," Collyer Bristow Gallery, London, UK. Photo: Stephanie Rushton.

but the most banal of tasks if she was anywhere near me. She completely filled my head.

Image Five: Nearly ten years later, I translated the ink drawing into a material work—taking one of my industrially knitted bodies and hand knitting my baby from the top of the head, with the baby's head filling the mother's. This work was exhibited in *Liberties*, an exhibition of contemporary women's art reflecting the changes in art practice within the context of sexual and gender equality since the introduction of the *Sex Discrimination Act* (1975) in the UK. *Liberties* was curated by the curatorial partnership, Day + Gluckman, for the Collyer Bristow Gallery, London, UK. And nearly ten years later, I can still only concentrate fully in my studio, which is now at home, if my daughter is not home or is fast asleep. She still controls my head and my heart.

Image Six: In *IT SUCKS*, I subverted the traditional hand knitted Shetland Lace christening shawl to communicate the very mixed feelings, not all together positive, that I had upon the birth of my daughter and becoming a new mother. Knitting has been a source of income for women in Shetland for many years and continues to be so for some today. In the past, when

Image 6: "IT SUCKS," 2005, hand knitted 2-ply Shetland Lace Yarn, 1000 x 1000mm. Knitted for me by Audrey Yates. Photo: Colin Guilemet.

the men were at sea, it was up to the women to run the croft. Women spent their days growing crops, caring for the animals, carrying peat from the hills for the fire, and gathering winter fodder. Any free time was spent in knitting. The items made, most commonly elaborately patterned jumpers or lace shawls, were either used as essential clothing for the family or sold as a way of boosting the meagre family income. The recent renewed interest in knitting has not come from financial necessity and is associated with relaxation and fun. Having to knit for a living is not relaxing or fun. Like my experience of new motherhood and my new baby, it sucks.

Image Seven: In 2011, I was invited to take part in an exhibition—*Fifties, Fashion, and Emerging Feminism (a Contemporary*

Image 7: Installation shot of "Untitled 3" and "He's Behind You" in "Fifties, Fashion, and Emerging Feminism (a Contemporary Response)," Collyer Bristow Gallery, London, UK, 2011.

Response)—at Collyer Bristow Gallery, London, UK, by the curatorial partnership Day + Gluckman. The stereotypical image of the fifties is of a modern, clean world where glamorous women flit around homes filled with contemporary, colourful design by the likes of Lucienne Day. The truth for most women was quite different. The shadow of the war still loomed, with rationing for textiles and clothing only ending in 1949. After the war, women had reembraced the domestic roles of wife and motherhood with surprising fervour. Sex and childbirth outside of wedlock were still unacceptable—"nice girls didn't" do that. Although the contraceptive pill first came into existence in 1951, it did not go on sale in the UK until ten years later. The Abortion Act was not in place until 1967. Children born outside of wedlock, if "backstreet" abortions were not sought, were raised by other married family members, put up for adoption, or raised within institutions. I am saddened by discoveries of such situations in my own family. More haunting are the stories of the remains of babies found among the possessions of deceased elderly women. Whether these babies had died naturally is often undeterminable, but the woman's need and determination to keep her reputation intact is without doubt.

Image 8: "He's Behind You" (detail), 2011, machine knitted yarn, coat-hanger, found wardrobe, 900 x 600 x 1640 mm.

Image Eight: My sculpture, *He's Behind You*, is a reflection on these facts. A small, fragile, slightly distorted, knitted "skin" hangs inside a small, miserable, broken, dark wood wardrobe. Knitting has connotations of warmth and comfort. It has stereotypical associations with people at both ends of life, elderly women knitting

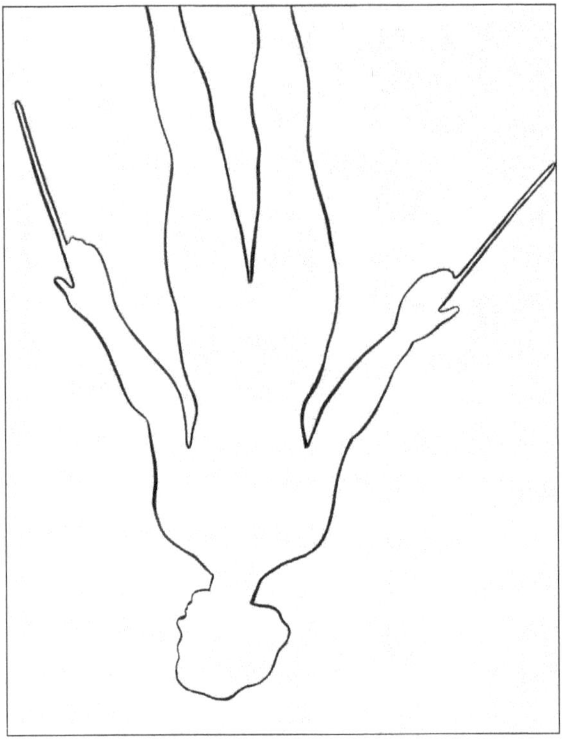

Image 9. "Untitled 2," 2011, ink on paper, 296 x 199 mm.

for newborns. More sinisterly, knitting needles were often used in self and "backstreet" abortions.

Image Ten: This problem of motherhood, or rather the problem that I have with motherhood, is revisited in this work. I have severed an arm from one of my industrially knitted bodies, filled it with builder's expanding foam, pushed a bunch of broken and bent knitting needles into the end, voodoo style, and embellished it with red lurex tubular knitting spelling out the words "bad mother." The "o" of "mother" has been turned into a sequined eye crying crystal tears. The phrase "bad mother" came from something that was said to me at Christmas. One of my daughter's school classroom assistants loves to knit. One December, she said that she had knitted my daughter a cardigan as she knew that I would never get around to it. On Christmas Eve, her husband brought it over. As he handed me the package, he said two words, not "Happy Christmas" but "bad mother." When exhibiting it through the Crafts Council's exhibition, COLLECT, (Saatchi Gallery, London, UK), six months later, a man congratulated me on what he saw as a "very honest admission."

Image 10: "Bad Mother," 2013, machine knitted wool, machine knitted lurex, expanding foam, broken knitting needles, glass beads, sequins, dress pins, crystal beads on an oak and maple wood shelf, 780 x 160 x 160 mm. In Private Collection. Photo: Douglas Atfield.

Image 11: "I'M SO ANGRY, 2005, hand knitted wool, 960 x 340 mm. Knitted for me by Jean Arkell. In the collection of KODE—Kunstmuseene i Bergen, Norway. Photo: Douglas Atfield.

Underneath Broadmoor

TAMAR HAGER

I'M PRETTY SURE she was a prostitute, and I'm pretty sure she got pregnant over and over again because in those days there were no easily accessible contraceptives. I mean, based on what you've been saying, that's the most reasonable hypothesis. How many children did you say she had? I mean, how many children do you know of? That she gave up? Because in principle, she might have had others that she gave up without any records or documentation. From what I've read of them, the postwar years in England weren't easy. True, the welfare state was already in place. Still, a lot of women lived in abject poverty and some of them were compelled to use their bodies in order to feed themselves. London looked like a moonscape. I've seen it in films, full of craters gouged out by the Germans' rockets. Food was rationed; children worked, and women tried to lead respectable lives among the ruins and the destitute neglect. But your parents lived through it all, so I'm sure you know much more about it than I do. You must have heard stories. You can read about it if you'd like to. There are lots of descriptions in history books. It was no picnic. I think that Louisa, was that her name? I think it was definitely no picnic for her. And you know how it is once you've gotten yourself into trouble for the first time. It's so hard to get yourself out. That is, if that's what you want to do. Maybe she had one illegitimate child and still thought she could find a man. And then she did find one, and she was lonely and needy and cold, body and soul, and it happened all over again, maybe in a corner of one of the craters or in the stark room she lived in with her son, while he was sleeping, and then there she was, pregnant again and what did you expect her to do? She could kill it—him or her—just like her grandmother Margaret who stood trial for it and got sent to a criminal lunatic asylum as it was called back then. She didn't. And she didn't go back to her parents in Bristol that is, assuming they weren't killed by a rocket or a bomb. I've read that thirteen hundred people living or workings in Bristol were killed in the blitz and that one hundred thousand homes were destroyed. They probably wouldn't have had enough of an income to support her and her children. When the possibility came up during one of her visits there, and those were rare because she usually couldn't make the train fare, her mother probably asked her several times whether she really thought she would be able to find work in Bristol, since times were so hard and most everyone around was on the dole. They were hard up themselves and on top of it all, they still had Toby at home. So do you actually think she could have raised them on her own? How? She did try. At first, she worked in a shop and then in small clothing factory, and then it shut down, and she started waitressing in a pub. But she never had enough to feed the three of them. Still, she didn't hand them over to the orphanage. And the shop owner offered her a raise for sex. She was pretty. And she had two children to feed. And she got pregnant again.

I didn't actually voice this monologue, but it was there, in my head, all the while that Helen was talking and especially every time she hissed something, in disdain or anger, about her grandmother Louisa or Lizzie, as she called her. My mother used Lizzie the first time she told me the story, she explained. I think I was fifteen. I listened to her disdain or anger thinking that they were probably bequeathed, mother to daughter. Helen said that her mother, Mary, had been Lizzie's third pregnancy. I thought maybe she was the reason why Louisa gave up trying. But maybe it was the other way around. Mary's arrival into the world helped Louisa understand that the children should be given a chance, a possible way out of the cycle of destitution and violence. Because how much patience can a mother have—coming home after a night of work, especially after having someone abuse her body and maybe masking it all behind alcohol or drugs. Coming home to children who want food or attention. How much attention can this woman offer anyone? I'm not saying there aren't any amazing women who are able, even in circumstances like that, to love and embrace. But to tell the truth, I don't understand how it works. I didn't say any of this to Helen, though. I just listened curious, despairing, pitying.

Helen said all the children were handed over to the orphanage down the street, one after the other. Most were sent to foster families later on. A few were adopted. Mary was adopted by a family from London that moved to Cardiff. Hard people, Helen said. Mary left home at seventeen and moved to Reading and never visited Cardiff again and just exchanges polite cards every Christmas. Still, today, Helen said. She's never met the family herself. When I asked what she meant by "hard people," she said she didn't really know because her mother had refused to talk about what actually went on there. In the research process she's started, recently, about her family, she asked about it several times. Her last attempt made her mother ask her angrily to stop. Remembering hurts. Helen decided not to ask again. I didn't ask Helen whether or not she had imagined or visualized any of what went on there between her mother and her adoptive parents. I had. I saw Mary locked up in her room for hours after her adoptive father had forced her in: How dare you talk back like that to the parents who rescued you. And her adoptive mother standing there in silence. Physical and verbal abuse. That was what I imagined. Because otherwise, how do you never go back to a family that freely chose to adopt and raise you?

We were sitting in The Prince, a pub in Crowthorne, on High street. On the table between us, Helen placed a fat red folder full of documents she had brought along. Somewhere above us were the huge, red-brick buildings of Broadmoor Hospital, one of the most heavily guarded psychiatric hospital-prisons in England, where the majority of the inmates are mentally ill and many have committed very serious crimes—although some of these have not stood trial due to their mental incapacity. The two of us had arrived there two hours earlier by train, she from her home in Reading and I from London. Margaret, a relative of Helen's, was one of the penniless mothers whose stories I had reconstructed in the course of a study I wrote on women who had killed their children in the nineteenth century and had been hospitalized and incarcerated in

Broadmoor on orders from the courts. Helen had read the papers in which I discussed my findings on Margaret and wrote me one day saying that she was fairly certain that Margaret was her relative, a grandmother of her grandmother Louisa, to be precise.

I stopped breathing when I read her email after it dropped into my inbox one morning just over a year ago. I hadn't believed such a thing possible. It wasn't that I hadn't tried to locate descendants. But given that any trace of most of the women I had studied disappeared after their release from Broadmoor—some of them probably changed their names in an attempt to start new lives, some of them must have died—my chances were slim. And against the odds someone had found me. Helen promised to tell me the rest of Margaret's story if I wished, of course, if it was of interest. It was of great interest. Margaret had been one of the central subjects of my study, and she had preoccupied me intermittently for all of ten years. Reading the first, then the second, third, and fourth emails, my curiosity about Helen and her family grew steadily. I wanted to meet her and hear the stories in person. I thought that seeing her might teach me something of what Margaret had looked like, even though I knew how groundless that was. Five generations and over 150 years of gene mixing with an array of other ancestors make a huge difference. And there were moments when I didn't want to know what Margaret had looked like because I'd imagined her as a beautiful woman and what if Helen wasn't?

When I decided to go to London to continue my research, I emailed Helen and asked if we could meet, if she felt it would suit her. She wrote back that it would, that she would be glad to meet and asked whether I had any ideas as to where we could meet. She would come to London if I wished. I didn't. I wanted to meet her at some site that was relevant to the story. I suggested the village of Crowthorne, where Broadmoor was situated, because Margaret had been sentenced to hospitalization there. The first of Broadmoor's inmates, in 1863, was a woman who had killed her daughter, I wrote Helen trying to convey the symbolism of the location, and that was before the hospital-prison even opened its gates to the criminally insane in 1868. In 1902, Dr. John D. Baker, the deputy superintendent, had written that most of the women who were sent to Broadmoor were mothers who had murdered their children, like Margaret, and you might be interested to hear that Dr. Baker was fully aware that some of these women weren't in the least bit insane. They were sent there, I wrote her, because judges, counsels for the prosecution and for the defense, as well as the juries and the rest of the judiciary, felt sorry for these destitute women, each of whom had committed a terrible deed thought to be against her maternal nature. They assumed, and rightly so, that these women had killed their children in circumstances of extreme and hopeless poverty and violence and that some of them had done so in a moment of madness brought on by despair. Like Margaret, Helen had written back.

Reading the emails on the computer screens, both of us remembered the beatings that Margaret had gotten when her husband found out she was pregnant and before then too. Something of that had leaked into the depositions of her sister, Sarah, who had lived with them for a while and said, "At times I could hear her cries from the next room. Her husband was a hard man. I feared him." Having a child meant staying with him, living under the reign of his violence which would doubtless extend to the child, too. Or leaving him and rearing the child on her own. And how should I support both of us? Her husband hadn't been at home when she gave birth aided by the village midwife. And when her sister, who according to the depositions, was no longer living with them at the time, arrived to see how she was a few hours after the midwife had left, she found Margaret asleep beside the dead body of an infant. The doctor recorded the cause of death as unknown, and the infant was buried. Then, a few days later, Margaret insisted on going to the police and confessing that she had strangled the baby. She told the policeman that she hadn't wanted an unbearable life, like hers was, for her son. The policeman noted that she had cried and said she regretted her deed, that it was a terrible one for which she should be punished. In view of her strange confession and her living conditions—which the judge, the counsels, and the jury all believed to have dragged her into insanity—the court sent her to a prison for criminal lunatics rather than the gallows. She was acquitted on grounds of insanity unanimously, without a physician's expert opinion. Margaret was conditionally discharged from Broadmoor four years later. Sarah, who by then was already a married mother, had pledged to care for her and to notify the hospital of any deterioration in her condition. Margaret's medical file contained no sign of any correspondence between Broadmoor and Sarah or her husband. The national census, conducted two years after her release, recorded Margaret in service as a maid in London and a decade later, by the time of the next census, she had disappeared.

I looked hopefully at Helen's red folder. Her email had promised me more information on Margaret's history. I asked if she'd like something to eat or drink and suggested we order now, before we started our conversation. While waiting for our two salads, I asked her how her journey had been (smooth and quick; the train arrived punctually and getting from the station to the pub had been easy and what luck it was that you had Google maps these days and you could plan your route; and how was your journey, she asked), how many children she had (two daughters and a son; Sandra had just started college this year. And your daughter is how old now? You have just one don't you? You mentioned it in your paper), and what line of work she was in, which I understood from her emails, she did part time (an educational counsellor at a school but she was considering going back to school to get a degree, perhaps in computer science).

Helen said that getting on the train, she thought that if she had told any of her friends she was going to the village where Broadmoor prison was located (everyone knew it as a prison, not as a hospital), they would have given her suspicious looks, just like her husband's when he asked whether it wouldn't be better for the two of us to meet somewhere else. She said she understood why I chose this place. She thought it was an interesting symbolic choice. But didn't I think there was some kind of curse on this place? She told me she had shivered when she got off the train.

I laughed and said I considered that an urban myth. Possibly, I said, this alleged curse she's referred to is rooted in a tale I read yesterday when I looked the place up. In 1952, a Broadmoor inmate escaped and murdered a village child before he was caught. Ever since, for sixty years, every Monday at 10:00 a.m., a siren is sounded in the village and in the surrounding villages to make sure the alarm system is in order in case of another escape. School children from the area are taught to find shelter and stay put as soon as the siren goes off. How horrible, Helen said, and cringed. Who raises children in such conditions? But where is this prison then?

Eight years earlier, in the course of my research, Yehuda and I had looked for the prison-hospital with our daughter Yael, who cried for ice cream in the backseat for the whole first hour. We drove around the village for two hours and found no one who could tell us how to get to Broadmoor. The whole time it was above us, towering up on the hill, massively paralyzing, surrounded by a high impenetrable fence. We happened onto it.

After a two hour conversation, Helen and I sat there exhausted and nibbled at our respective salads. Till just moments earlier, Helen had spoken nonstop, and I had listened. I already knew parts of the story from our email correspondence over the past few months, but it all sounded totally new. The details I knew before now transformed into part of a broader family story that included Helen's parents, her brother, and especially Margaret's granddaughter, Louisa, who had handed over all her children to the orphanage. According to Helen's story, Margaret left the service to live with a man. She hadn't been able to locate a marriage license. She said she supposed that Margaret took his surname without marrying him, as did many other women of her class and status. Divorce was expensive and nearly impossible. They moved to Bristol, where he had been born and raised. And since the city was new to her and since she used his surname and since she was already pregnant, people simply assumed they were married. They told his parents that they had had a small, quick wedding in London due to the pregnancy. They had three children, one of whom was Molly, Louisa's mother.

Every time I wonder how she could have done it, I think to myself that perhaps she was insane. Perhaps that's the explanation. Otherwise I just can't understand it. Who was insane, Margaret or Louisa? I asked her, still amazed by the fact that Margaret had started a new life in a new city with a man and with children. How do you go, just like that, from insane asylum to normative life? I wondered whether she had told her new partner that she had murdered an infant and had been incarcerated. I suppose not. I wouldn't have. I would be too afraid that he would leave. Most probably he would. But maybe the story got out, maybe someone who arrived in Bristol from London or from her village had told her husband, at some point, but in the end, they all just ignored the story because they had already been living their new lives uneventfully for some time now. Maybe she herself chose to tell her husband, eventually? Or to tell one of her daughters?

Helen looked at me surprised, unaware of my thoughts. Lizzie, she said and pulled several birth certificates out of her red folder. I found all of these at the national archive in London; she handed all of them over to the orphanage. Would you believe it? And that whole time she lived there beside them, you see? How can a mother abandon her children and never even come to visit if she's not out of her mind? That's just our hypothesis, I said. Maybe she did visit them? Maybe she stood there every day outside the fence and watched them playing in the yard? Maybe she handed them over because she thought that they'd at least get fed there and she wasn't sure she would be able to feed them? Maybe she did the best she was capable of doing as a mother, trying to secure their wellbeing by making sure that someone would meet their needs?

A few days earlier, I had left Yael with her father. She had scowled beside me in the car, all the way there and when I stopped outside his place, she didn't move or say a word. When I noted that we were there, she opened the car door, got out, took her suitcase off the back seat and marched toward the door in total silence. Just for a week. My pleas bounced back off the pub walls ringing in my ears. Sweetie, I have to go for work. Our income depends on it. I didn't say it, but I thought that at age fourteen, she may start to catch onto the fact that I didn't go away just because I enjoyed it, that I went because I had to. That's my job, that's how I make our living. Her father was paying very little alimony. But at the very same time, I knew I was lying a little too. I loved these trips among other things because they freed me of demanding maternal work and let me pass it on to Yehuda, who was a dedicated father even if he didn't pay enough child support. And just make sure she does her homework and takes a shower every day and try to steer her away from a fight with Sigal, and Anat's mom asked if she could spend the night at their place on Thursday, so don't forget, and here are some new clothes, don't let her wear the same outfit all week and try to see that she doesn't go to sleep too late because she gets unbearable in the morning and her teacher complains and.... I knew that Yehuda wasn't really listening and I knew, from our shared history, that he'd do as he pleased. But I couldn't help myself just as I hadn't been able to help myself while we were married, and I recited the list of instructions that hadn't changed much over the years and left.

But I can't stand his new girlfriend, Yael had said this time. She hissed "his new" in fury. Please let me stay at home. I'll bring friends over. You can talk to the neighbours. I'll be really responsible. And when I insisted that she couldn't stay at home even part of the time and that being the case, she would have to stay with her father, she teared up and cried. Mom I really feel bad there, she's totally not nice to me. Can't you take me along? I won't bother you, please, please mom? Later, lying in bed sleepless, I imagined the two of us walking down a London street, wrapped in coats and scarves. Yael stopped short all of a sudden and announced she was freezing and please could we go into this shop or that café so she could warm up. I saw myself standing helplessly in a department store watching her try on outfit after outfit. Isn't this pretty mom? Yuck this one is hideous. Look. Can I have this shirt too? In a daze I stared at the check served us by a waitress at a Regent Street restaurant where we'd landed when I didn't have the strength to walk any further after a day of shopping. From here on, we'll have sandwiches for every meal till we get home I muttered through clenched teeth an hour later, exhausted, when I'd done the mental arithmetic of how much was left in my account while we queued for tickets to the musical that Yael wanted to see so badly and I didn't want her to miss because it was part of her education. I imagined myself succumbing to temptation and buying tickets to two plays and then fuming all the way through the crowded theatres and the loud singing and the overacted facial gestures and the rising and falling stage sets.

What was the point? I'm sure Yael and I would have had some good times. We have quite a few of those when we travel together—heart-to-heart conversations, long strolls through streets and parks, beautiful plays, and fascinating art exhibits. I couldn't imagine these as I hesitated whether to take her along this time.

It'll cost a fortune, and I won't be able to work and where will she stay while I'm meeting Helen?

I wanted to meet Helen because I thought it might be a key to the next phase of my research or at least a basis for one of the papers I had to write if I were to get promoted and tenured and to achieve job security. Just a little push and you'll be there the dean had told me a month ago. His voice was matter of fact, business-like. On my way out of his office, I felt enormously tired, and I crumpled onto a couch in the waiting room. One of his assistants asked me whether I'd like a glass of water. No, I'll just close my eyes for a moment I said, and when I did, I could see huge armies of journals marching into a laptop screen and merging with drafts full of red-lined markups all erasing and rewriting themselves. I found myself counting: one, two, three, four, but only high-impact journals—high impact, one, two, three, four, five, six. We won't be able to promote you; we simply won't, if they're not high impact. I opened my eyes. The assistant stood above me with a glass of water. Won't you take a sip? You look pale.

Maybe Louisa, Margaret's granddaughter, will turn into my next research project? Young women after the war, poverty, loneliness, so much loneliness. How can you raise eight children on your own? Orphanages and their social function, foster families, adoption. I might call it "the tale of a family," and it would question family as a viable structure in conditions of destitution. I would ask whether, under such conditions, motherhood turns into a different role. Would a responsible mother be the one who hands her children over to the care of others, who doesn't insist on keeping them and on raising them herself? I had thought of it on the plane, as I reread my email correspondence with Helen. One of her letters had said that she had renewed contact with Lizzie and met her twice but that she didn't dare ask her anything about the past because she was afraid of destroying the magic of their meetings and their surprising closeness. She's really nice, Helen wrote me, and she loves to talk about the war years, but for now, she hasn't said a word about her children. She hasn't even mentioned my mother, although she knows who I am.

I asked her to ask Louisa about Grandmother Margaret. If she could, that is. It seems safer to me because it doesn't concern the children she gave away. I'll be happy to hear anything she can tell you about Margaret. It would be interesting to hear what she remembers of her. How she looked, for example; what colour hair and eyes she had. Whether she was slim or heavy. I imagined her slim. And whether she had any idea at all that her grandmother had murdered an infant she gave birth to and was committed to an insane asylum. And if she did, what she thought of it. I came close to writing her that my livelihood depended on her willingness to do this, and I thought about the compelling article I'd write following Margaret's voice, possibly traceable in the voice of her granddaughter, Louisa, and in Louisa's granddaughter Helen, telling me these stories in her own words. Duplications, reflections, diffractions. A beautiful paper in a high-impact journal.

At some point in the course of our meeting in the pub, Helen told me that Margaret's act, which she had read of in my publications—she articulated this softly, and I had to bend close to hear it—and grandmother Lizzie's abandonment of her children had made her think that maybe the family had some genetic defect. She said that had put her on guard and she had started following her girls closely for fear of it. Every argument with them had turned into a potential threat. At some point later, I thought I'd been infected by Margaret and Lizzie and that I was going crazy. My daughters' looks at me and the way my husband's eyes followed me at home were signs that I was losing it and that I had to pull myself together or they'd have to do something about it. One day they sat me down in the parlor and suggested I get some counselling, psychotherapy, just a few sessions. I refused. I knew I was fine. It was just my fear of what I'd read about the family. But it did make me see, all at once, how easy it is to go insane or to be labelled insane.

I asked Helen whether she'd like a drink. She said no. I ordered a glass of wine. She apologized that she had to phone her husband. She had totally forgotten that she'd promised a neighbour she would water her plants while she was abroad. It had to be done today because it hadn't rained all week. Maybe her husband could do it.

I thanked the waiter who stood my wine glass on the table. Helen moved away to make her phone call. And suddenly I remembered I'd forgotten to call Yehuda. When I'd refused to let Yael stay home alone, with or without friends, I promised I would talk to her father and tell him how she felt about his new girlfriend. She had said it was useless and wouldn't help, and I insisted that it might. But the days leading up to my trip had been so packed that I had forgotten and then, after I left, I had forgotten that I'd forgotten. Now I remembered. My heart stopped for a split second. What kind of mother am I? How could I forget? But Yael hadn't mentioned it at all during yesterday night's phone conversation. After we'd parted without a word, she actually sounded happy and talkative and told me in detail how she and one of her friends had been convulsed with laughter at something that this friend had said during one of their classes and the literature teacher had sent them out of the classroom. Five minutes into the details of what the friend had said and what she had said and what the teacher had said, I lost patience and found myself scolding her, feeling it misplaced yet unable to stop myself, you're sent out of class too often Yael. I hope you're doing your homework and that your father doesn't need to lecture you. Given our talk on the telephone, I thought things might be working out. Maybe that woman had stopped picking on my daughter or maybe Yehuda had gotten it together and told her off. Maybe Yael broke down in tears, and he hugged her and threw the woman out for good. I laughed at the scene of the banished girlfriend. Why do I still care at all after seven years?

Helen came back and sat down beside me. She said she couldn't remember whether she'd already had a chance to tell me that Lizzie had died without her finding out why she decided to hand her children over to the orphanage. She's so sorry but she hadn't had a chance to ask about Margaret. Actually, there had been a few opportunities but she hadn't dared because she hadn't known how Lizzie might be affected by that piece of information, which may well have been new— that is, about the murder of an infant. Now, she thinks that maybe someday she'll write the family story, after her mother dies. Along with my daughter, she said, we'll conduct research like you did. We'll interview the other seven children and write a book about it. How wonderful, I said politely, feeling a tinge of anger and disappointment, as I suddenly realized that I was losing my chance to tell a family story centred on Louisa's wrenching tale. I wondered whether Margaret was still mine to study and write. And what about her new children? Or had Helen appropriated her in the very act of giving me new information about her life? All these questions stayed unasked, and the words stuck in my throat. How wonderful that you'll write about it all, I said, I'm sure it will be fascinating. Helen stood up, and I stood up in response. I must go, she said. She explained that her husband hadn't been home, and she had to water the neighbour's garden. She smiled. It was really interesting to meet you, she said. I'm glad you suggested it, and I hope we'll find other opportunities to meet. We hugged.

I stared at her back as she walked away and then at my glass of wine and I thought of Louisa. What had I been thinking? Writing a quick and easy paper about her? I would need another ten years of exhaustive research. What did I know about her and her contemporaries? Nothing at all save what Helen had told me now and what little I had read in the months leading up to our meeting. A meeting for purposes of research, this was how I had justified the trip to London filling the funding forms. This was what I had called it to myself too, every time I thought of it. Over the past year, without realizing, I had turned Helen into my research project. But this research project was an actual living breathing woman. Not even a dead one like her great great grandmother, whose story I had studied. How dare I think I could decipher anything at all in a two-hour conversation.

I mused over Helen's anger at Louisa. I thought about how she had tagged her insane at every point in our conversation or our emails where she showed any empathy toward her grandmother. She could only forgive a mentally ill woman these deeds. Faced with this, I hadn't dared to share my historically viable hypothesis that she had been a prostitute. I hadn't dared tell her that in a reality where contraceptives weren't an option and abortions were illegal, Louisa was sufficiently sane and responsible not to insist on raising the children she had borne and to commit them, instead, to the care of others giving them a chance of normative life. How close can I really come to telling Louisa's story? How close can Helen come? Which standpoint allows a telling of this complex tale? Looking into the last of the wine in my glass, I wondered if there is some vantage point from which to tell a reality with both deep emotional familiarity and reflective distance while avoiding the temptation to judge. What courage one may need to be able to say that my great grandmother was a murderess and my grandmother was a prostitute and they did what they did within and due to unjust social structures and generations of women's oppression. Better to explain their conduct as insanity, as singular cases of emotional breakdown. In face of Helen's insistence on not seeing the social realities, how could I tell the story as I saw it? That is, if she allowed me to in the first place? And if she didn't, did I wish to fight her and claim ownership assuming that I understood Louisa's motives better than she did or because my training as a feminist historian gave me a better grasp of systems of oppression? Or because I felt political responsibility to give voice to the oppressed women I met along my way? Or just because I was a researcher, and I wanted to tell this story, which was, I thought, relatively easy to reconstruct, and I had a little girl to feed?

I got up. My train back to London would be leaving in an hour, and I had a twenty-five minute walk to the station. I walked into the cold air. I was so glad I hadn't brought Yael along into this cold, into this vortex of sad stories of mothers and daughters. I walked quickly staying close to the walls along the way, trying to escape the cold. No signs anywhere indicated the way to Broadmoor. But the air was soaked with its threatening presence.

Feminism, Infanticide, and Intersectionality in Victorian America

KEIRA V. WILLIAMS

IN THE UNITED STATES, when a woman kills her own children, the crime is legally defined as homicide, like any other intentional murder. Yet in American culture, infanticide is depicted as a different kind of crime from the killings that daily populate the big screen, primetime television dramas, and the twenty-four hour news. The media and the general public resort to traditional stereotypes of woman and motherhood when they attempt to understand infanticide, and they divide violent mothers into two groups: the "mad" women who must have been driven insane by their postpartum hormones or the "bad" ones who rid themselves of their children for selfish, sexual reasons, also known as the "nuts or sluts" argument (Shrier 17). "Bad motherhood" is a category that has historically been defined by race and class in American culture and history; if "good mothers" are portrayed as white and middle class, then women who do not fit these categories—minority and working-class mothers, for instance—are often represented as *a priori* unfit or, at least, dysfunctional mothers (Douglas and Michaels 141; Eyer 17). In cases of maternal infanticide, then, mothers who are perceived as bad—a category that is, to be sure, defined by demographics as much as behaviour—receive harsher legal punishments (Oberman 711; Williams 167).

Despite these simplistic stereotypes, there is a developing consensus among medical scholars and experts that maternal infanticide is heavily correlated with postpartum mental illnesses, which are, in turn, heavily correlated with specific socioeconomic factors. Poverty, a lack of social or community support, and intimate partner violence, for example, are all linked to both postpartum depression and maternal violence, including infanticide. Yet these three discourses—the legal, in which maternal infanticide is seen as the same as other homicides; the cultural, in which the crime is seen as incomprehensible, evil, and/or insane; and the medical, in which this kind of violence is understood within both psychological and socioeconomic contexts—are disparate and disconnected. They have yet to be linked in any kind of coherent legal analysis, prevention methods, or treatment programs. Making this connection could help to shift understandings of maternal violence as *a priori* evidence of "bad motherhood" to a contextualized response that takes into account the constraints upon and experiences of American mothers.

In this chapter, I examine two key cases from the nineteenth century—the cases of Margaret Garner in 1856 and Hester Vaughan in 1868—to illustrate that there is a discernible history of feminist analyses of maternal infanticide that bridge these discourses by incorporating the concept of intersectionality. "Intersectionality" is a term coined by black feminist legal scholar Kimberlé Crenshaw in an attempt to theorize the experience of living within multiple, simultaneous forms of oppression (Crenshaw 139). Although there is some confusion over the term and much debate over its uses, many researchers outside of feminist theory employ what is known as the "unitary" or "additive" model of intersectionality, in which it is assumed that each demographic variable, such as race, class, or gender, has an additive effect to an individual or group's experience of discrimination or oppression. In this view, for instance, a poor, African-American woman would be "seen as a sum of the effects of these three demographic variables" (Dubrow 89). A problem with this approach, as some feminist scholars have pointed out, is that it tends to focus on the "experiential" level of analysis, ignoring, in particular, the structural level (Yuval-Davis 197).

Perhaps a more useful way to apply an intersectional analysis to case studies of maternal infanticide would be to employ the "multiplicative" or "categorical" approach to intersectionality, in which one's experiences of oppression are more than the simple sum of various demographic factors. Rather, "the influence of demographics on a social outcome is conditional on the intersection of the demographic categories" (Dubrow 89). In other words, gender, race, ethnicity, class, nationality, age, and other categories are intertwined axes of identity, but "they are also intrinsically different" and thus entail different constraints, experiences, and outcomes (Huijg 7). The significance of this approach is that it provides a more complex account of experiences and offers multiple levels of analysis, from the individual, to the familial, to the community, to the structural.

Although intersectionality is a relatively recent feminist theory—the term was coined in the late 1980s—at key moments in the history of American feminism, activists have deployed this concept, firmly connecting the personal and the political through analyses of maternal infanticide. A kind of intersectionality, in fact, defined the feminist approach to two major cases in the mid-nineteenth century, which is, perhaps, a surprising source of intersectional feminism. During the second half of the nineteenth century, organized feminism progressively moved toward a singularly minded focus on white female suffrage—a goal that reflected race-based, and generally racist, political expediency—by the end of the century, when Jim Crow began to take firm root in the South (Newman 8). Moreover, feminists such as Susan B. Anthony, Elizabeth Cady Stanton, and Lucy Stone—white women who were educated, socioeconomically comfortable, and well travelled by virtue of their roles as public speakers in the suffrage movement—failed to recognize their own structural privileges and, thus, their distinct social advantages of race and class, even as they argued for an intersectional approach to infanticide. But to dismiss the entire feminist movement of the Victorian era as racist or classist would be to overlook key historical analyses of the structural connections between motherhood, race, class, and violence in the United States.

Because infanticidal mothers, if only due to the nature of their crimes, are some of the most marginal women in American society, an intersectional analysis of their stories can make plain the complex intersections of gender, race, class, violence, and the law at both the experiential and the structural levels. And despite the virtual feminist silence on infanticide in recent decades, there is a long, if forgotten, American tradition of examining cases of maternal infanticide according to the tenets of intersectionality.

In the second half of the nineteenth century, white, middle-class feminists took up the causes of two prominent murdering mothers, Margaret Garner and Hester Vaughan, in ways that can help to contextualize twenty-first-century questions about intersectionality and infanticide.

"A SISTER AND A PERSON": THE CASE OF MARGARET GARNER

In January 1856, Margaret Garner, a slave, took advantage of frigid weather by running across the frozen Ohio River with seven enslaved family members, crossing from Kentucky into the free state of Ohio. Federal marshals, along with Garner's owner, set off in pursuit of the escapees, and they quickly located the runaways in a cabin on the north side of the river. As the white men approached, Levi Coffin, the famous abolitionist affiliated with the Underground Railroad, reported that the "fugitives were determined to fight, and to die, rather than to be taken back to slavery" (559). Garner made a fateful decision as her pursuers surrounded the cabin: rather than see her children returned to slavery, she would kill them, and then kill herself (Coffin).

In an act that got much press attention and that was later immortalized in Toni Morrison's prizewinning novel *Beloved* (1987), Garner managed to slay her two-and-a-half-year-old daughter and to wound her other children before the white men broke in and forcibly subdued the runaways (Weisenburger 73). In keeping with the racism of the day, a Cincinnati newspaper reporter interviewed a Kentucky man who described Garner as "common and cross-tempered" and as a "flat-nosed, thick-lipped Negro woman," who was destined through her own racial biology to commit the heinous crime (Reinhardt 32).

The Garner case clearly hinged on issues of race and slavery, but to some observers, this was also a case about gender. News reports described three of Garner's children as "bright," "mulatto," and "almost white," obvious indications that Garner was the victim of sexual abuse by the white men on the Kentucky plantation, almost assuredly her owner and/or his adult sons (Mitchell 16; Weisenburger 48). Levi Coffin, in his account, singled out Mary, Garner's slain daughter, as "practically white" (563). One historian who closely examined the plantation records determined that Garner gave birth to each of her children roughly five to six months after the white mistress on her plantation delivered each of her own, indicating that Garner's owner used her as his sexual outlet during his wife's pregnancies (Weisenburger 8), a not uncommon occurrence in the racialized slave system that prominently featured widespread sexual abuse (Jacobs; McLaurin; Lerner 46). To antislavery observers, Garner's owner's inconsolable sobs over the body of her two-year-old daughter served as further circumstantial evidence that he was the father of some of Garner's children. In her resistance to slavery, they argued, Garner had destroyed her master's "property" and his "progeny" (Weisenburger 77-78).

Abolitionists took up the case immediately, and members of the women's rights movement quickly realized their common ground. The organized feminist movement was primarily made up of white, middle-class women from the northeastern United States. Although racial privilege was their means of access to a public platform, and it is of course problematic to argue that they "spoke" for Margaret Garner, who, as a female slave, literally had no legal voice—in most slave states, slaves could not testify against white men (McLaurin 90)—the activists nevertheless provided a nuanced reading of the Garner case as one that revealed the traumatic intersections of sex, race, and class, or what scholars have deemed the "triple jeopardy" of the female slave experience (Keetley and Pettegrew xviii). Recognizing the opportunity to advance the two causes with which she was most commonly associated, and which provided her a measure of power and access in this case, Lucy Stone, the famous abolitionist and women's rights advocate, managed to visit Garner in her cell just before the end of the trial. "It was no wild desperation that impelled her," Stone proclaimed of the imprisoned mother, "but a calm determination that if she could not find freedom here, she would get it with the angels" (qtd. in Blackwell 184).

As rumours circulated that Stone's intention had been to procure for Garner a knife with which to commit suicide, the final day of the trial began with an argument over the legality of this visit. Prosecutors accused Stone of smuggling a weapon, and she asked to respond to the accusation by addressing the courtroom after they adjourned. Her request was granted, another marker of her racial and class privilege in this case and an indication that the equation that white Victorian feminists often made between female oppression and racial slavery in the United States was misguided. Garner, the accused, by law had to remain mute during the proceedings, whereas Stone, an activist bystander, was allowed to command the attention of the entire courtroom. At the end of the day, Stone "supplanted" the judge on the bench and put forth an impassioned defense of Garner. She argued for Garner's humanity "as a sister and a person," and she condemned both the racial system of slavery and the sexual politics that undergirded the abominable institution. Garner's owner, Stone told the packed courtroom, was a rapist, and Garner had reacted against this sexual violence with a crime of her own, the only agency she had as a woman in bondage. Garner was no monster; she had acted, Stone concluded, on the basis of deep maternal instinct: "The faded faces of the Negro children tell too plainly to what degradation the female slaves submit. Rather than give her daughter to that life, she killed it. If in her deep maternal love she felt the impulse to send her child back to God, to save it from coming woe, who shall say she had no right not to do so?" (qtd. in Reinhardt 40). In other words, infanticide, in this case, was an act of desperation committed by a powerless woman, terrorized by the various intersections of racial and sexual politics within the mutually oppressive systems of slavery and patriarchy.

Although much of the contemporary white media saw only an incomprehensibly evil slave woman, Stone and her feminist cohort indicted the systemic oppression that created this murdering mother. Stone's defense of Garner, and her charges of sexual assault against the slave owner, did not save Garner; she and her remaining family members returned to slavery one month after the murder, based on tenets of the federal Fugitive Slave Act of 1850. But abolitionist and feminist publications widely reported that Garner's owner was visibly uncomfortable, "perspiring with anguish and shame"—an admission of guilt, in their estimation (qtd. in Kerr 92).

Stone's fiery courtroom challenge represented an articulation, for the first time, of an explicit, intersectional analysis of maternal infanticide by the organized American feminist movement. She located the roots of this crime not in the allegedly deranged, degenerate mind of the slave woman but rather in the socioeconomic institutions that worked together to thoroughly oppress Garner to the point that she had no other option as a mother. Garner, through her actions, and Stone, in her legal defense, demonstrated that the precipitating context was the destructive effects of structural oppression, not individual deviance—a charge that suffragists would take up again a dozen years later in defense of another headline-making mother.

"A CHILD OF OUR SOCIETY": THE CASE OF HESTER VAUGHAN

In February 1868, Hester Vaughan, a teenage English immigrant, was arrested in Philadelphia for the murder of her newborn. Vaughan had been in the United States for less than two years; she ventured over from England in 1866 with a man whom she believed to be her husband, until he abandoned her when she discovered that he had another wife and children. Following this abrupt desertion, Vaughan sought employment as a maid in a wealthy household. Although some details are in dispute, it is clear that Vaughan and her employer, or someone in his household, had a sexual relationship. Some observers assumed "seduction," a common sexual trope of the era, in which a wily man sexually compromises a naïve young woman. However, the relationship was possibly a more violent one that included repeated sexual assault enabled by extreme coercion and even outright physical force. Dr. Clemence Lozier, a female gynecologist, later deemed Vaughan "a victim—not of seduction or misplaced affection—but of *rape*, by a brute" ("The Administration of Justice—Hester Vaughan's Case").

The pregnancy ended Vaughan's employment in the wealthy household, for she was immediately fired once she informed her employer of her status. Alone and pregnant in a foreign country, Vaughan rented a room and did odd jobs for the remainder of her pregnancy. The details of her childbirth are a bit unclear. Some reports state that Vaughan, "malnourished and living alone in an unheated room at 703 Girard Avenue," gave birth in her own rented space. Other reports state that Vaughan was homeless; wandering the streets in labour during the "winter storms," she sought shelter in an abandoned garret to deliver her child. Weakened and delirious from labor, Vaughan apparently asked a neighbour for a "box in which to place a dead baby." The neighbor notified the police, who shortly thereafter arrested Vaughan for murder. The coroner ruled that the infant had been smothered ("The Case of Hester Vaughan"). Vaughan was jailed and went to trial the following summer. At issue was whether she intentionally suffocated her baby or whether she accidentally rolled on top of the child after she gave birth, an act that her defenders attributed to "puerperal fever" following childbirth (Rakow and Kramarae 73-75).

Like the case of Margaret Garner a dozen years earlier, Vaughan's trial caught the attention of prominent activists within the movement for women's rights, particularly Susan B. Anthony and Elizabeth Cady Stanton, who covered the case for close to a year in their journal, *The Revolution*. According to the journal, Vaughan was "prosecuted by a male district attorney, defended by a male attorney, found guilty by an all-male jury and sentenced to death by a male judge," which feminists found indefensible in a system in which citizens had a right to be judged by their peers (qtd. in Cullen-Dupont 214). Stanton contended that Vaughan was bamboozled by her defense attorney, who pocketed her few remaining dollars, met with her once, and then did not see her again until the trial. Despite inadequate counsel, Vaughan did have some vocal and relatively powerful defenders outside of the courtroom. Dr. Susan A. Smith, one of the first female MDs, wrote to the governor of Pennsylvania on Vaughan's behalf, explaining:

> [When] her child was born, she told me she was nearly frozen and fainted or went to sleep for a long time. You will please remember, sir, throughout this period of agony she was alone, without nourishment or fire, with her door unfastened. My professional opinion in Hester Vaughan's case is that cold and want of attention produced painful and protracted labor—that the mother, in endeavoring to assist herself, injured the head of her child in its birth—that she either fainted or had a convulsion, and was insensible for a long time. (qtd. in Cullen-Dupont 214-215)

The lack of response from the governor to this expert opinion prompted Vaughan's supporters to contact Stanton and Anthony.

Sensing an opportunity to advance their case against the patriarchal legal system, the incensed feminists organized a protest and sent the following resolution to the governor as well as to several major media outlets:

> Whereas, The right of trial by a jury of one's peers is recognized by the governments of all civilized nations as the great palladium of rights, of justice, and equality to the citizen: therefore, Resolved, That this [Working Women's National] Association demand that in all civil and criminal cases, woman shall be tried by a jury of her peers; shall have a voice in making the law, in electing the judge who pronounces her sentence, and the sheriff who, in case of execution, performs for her that last dread act. (Cullen-Dupont 215)

But the protests failed to persuade those in power. The judge argued that "some women must be made an example of," and Vaughan was convicted and sent to prison to await her execution (qtd. in Dubois 145).

Vaughan's supporters did not give up; rather, they intensified their efforts as Stanton and Anthony cried inadequate counsel and insufficient evidence. On the lecture circuit and in the pages of *The Revolution* for the better part of a year, they excoriated the patriarchal society that would so persecute a helpless servant girl. For the suffragists, Vaughan's was a paradigmatic case that represented many things: the discriminatory legal system that both judged and silenced women; the economic vulnerability and class inequality of working women; and the sexual double standard that placed Vaughan in the predicament of giving birth to a "bastard" with no support from the father. Still smarting from the recent ratification of the Fourteenth Amendment and Fifteenth Amendments, which included the word "male" in the extension of citizenship and voting rights to African Americans, the suffragists folded Vaughan's case into their larger struggle (Dubois 76; Baer 282). Some observers, including Horace Greeley, the editor of the *New York Times*, argued that the feminists were getting off-message and forgetting the true nature of the trial, "complicating the case of this poor woman by ... abstract notions not connected with it" (Farless).

It is true that the women of *The Revolution,* at times, veered into advocacy for female legal representation or suffrage in articles that were ostensibly devoted to the Hester Vaughan case, and this rhetoric can certainly be seen as hijacking Vaughan's case to suit their political agenda. However, their logic is useful, as these activists insisted on the clear links between legal, marital, medical, economic, and political systems of oppression in the case of maternal infanticide. In the nineteenth century, infanticide was widely viewed as a "serious social problem," and feminists provided a broad analysis that eschewed the assumption that women who killed their infants were simple deviants who refused to conform to the prescribed maternal role. Like abortion and prostitution, the feminists argued, maternal murders of children "were not women's crimes but the results of men's crimes against women" (qtd. in Rakow and Kramarae 73).

Structural inequality thus determined the constraints on maternal behaviour. This systemic reading of infanticide as a wild act by women made desperate by patriarchy, the sexual double standard, and class hierarchy was novel for its time, although the depictions of Vaughan in the pages of *The Revolution* often featured familiar female stereotypes of the era. In these accounts, Vaughan was invariably virtuous, a pure-hearted young immigrant who had been doubly duped by her two-timing husband and her rapist employer (Farless). Yet even as they represented Vaughan as manipulated and helpless, the feminists only proclaimed her innocence in one issue of *The Revolution*, in which Dr. Lozier suggested that there was no evidence that the baby had been delivered alive. Otherwise, they generally acknowledged her guilt, which they framed as a pathetic, desperate kind of maternal agency within the limiting and destructive contexts of patriarchy and poverty ("The Case of Hester Vaughan" 357-358; "Hester Vaughan," November 1868, 8).

In the pages of *The Revolution*, Vaughan became a symbol of all women, not just as a victim of seduction, but at the same time, the writers depicted Vaughan as a specifically vulnerable woman of the working class. Their intersectional analysis, however, was tempered, as they negotiated the specifics of Vaughan's situation with their own universalizing calls for gendered justice. Stanton and Anthony wielded their racial and class privilege openly, appealing to their upper-class readers as "moral housekeepers," depicting Vaughan as a naïve girl in a fatal situation over which she had no control (Spencer-Wood, 202). Yet they generalized Vaughan's experiences when they asked the mothers among their readers to consider their own experiences. The core problem, they explained, was the perversion of the institution of motherhood under patriarchy, which resulted in both a sexist and classist system: "So long as by law and public sentiment maternity is made a disgrace and a degradation, the young and inexperienced of the poorer classes are driven to open violence, while money affords the rich the means of fraud, protection, and concealment" (qtd. in Rakow and Kramarae 77). This system, which kept women "dependent on man," resulted in resentment of men by women, so much so that the "children of such unions must needs be unloved and deserted" ("Infanticide" 74). The crimes in this case were multiple and ongoing: Vaughan was seduced and exploited by both her employer and the legal system, and the death of her child would be compounded by her own death sentence. The writers of *The Revolution* concluded: "if that poor child of sorrow is hung, it will be deliberate, downright murder." The month after Vaughan's sentencing, they lamented, "Her death will be a far more horrible *infanticide* than was the killing of her child" ("Hester Vaughan," November 1868, 8).

Despite the unpopularity of this rhetoric, which sounded to opponents like an overblown defense of child murder, *The Revolution*'s postconviction campaign actually worked. The governor of Pennsylvania pardoned Vaughan in the summer of 1869 on the condition that Vaughan return to her home country immediately. Stanton and Anthony raised the funds and paid Vaughan's passage. The last word on Vaughan from nineteenth-century feminists was her simple letter of gratitude, published in *The Revolution* in August of 1869 (Cullen-Dupont 215).

Certainly, the governor did not pardon Vaughan because of his suffragist tendencies; indeed, he was more likely swayed by the deliberate depiction of Vaughan as a classic Victorian "fallen woman" and a tragic victim, which relied on popular stereotypes of feminine weakness. And to be sure, twenty-first-century feminists should be careful when analyzing the intersectionality of nineteenth-century activists, as is it not especially nuanced and often somewhat elementary. Just as Anthony and Stanton's whiteness and class status enabled their activism, not to mention their publications, Vaughan's whiteness most certainly played a large role in her popularity with *Revolution* readers and in her subsequent release, a fact unacknowledged by the activists. Moreover, in other cases, these white, middle-class activists employed explicit classism and racism in their pursuit of suffrage; indeed, a "white saviour" complex pervaded much of their political ideology and strategy, particularly by the end of the century (Newman 7). Nevertheless, this nineteenth-century defense of maternal infanticide is instructive. Stone, Stanton, and Anthony based their protests on the theory, famously advocated by a later generation of American feminists, that the "personal is political": maternal infanticide was a seemingly private act that occurred within the context of a patriarchal sexual, social, and legal system that created conditions that forced some women to murder.

CONCLUSION

Victorian feminists thus relied heavily on a sort of crude form of intersectional analysis in their impassioned defenses of Margaret Garner and Hester Vaughan. Intersectionality, as an accounting of human experiences, often involves more than two variables (Dubrow 85), as was the case with both Margaret Garner and Hester Vaughan. Garner experienced more than the historical "double bonds of race and sex" (Gunderson) of all African-American women; she was a bound labourer, human property, a forced mother, and homeless, without community beyond the few family members in the cabin at the time of the crime, as she had just escaped slavery. The complex interactions of these categories, rather than their simple sum, determined her experiences, as Lucy Stone argued on her behalf. This kind of deployment of multiplicative intersectionality is admirable, but for one thing: the seeming invisibility of white, middle-class status, the very intersection of which allowed Lucy Stone to position herself as the major female voice in this case.

Likewise, in Vaughan's case, the enormous privilege of being native-born white women, in addition to the socioeconomic privilege that enabled Anthony and Stanton to publish *The Revolution*, remained unacknowledged. In short, Stone, Anthony, Stanton, and their cohort, even as they struggled against patriarchy, benefited from their racial and class positions within the hierarchical social system. As Dieuwertje Dyi Huijg argues about other case studies of this same problem, these white women had insider-outsider status within the white patriarchal system: "even if they do not individually oppress (in potency), they do … 'represent the oppressor'" (5). Victorian feminists failed to recognize how their feminist activism was informed by racial and class privilege, thus limiting the uses of multiplicative intersectionality in their quest for feminist goals beyond these infanticide cases. And it should be reiterated that this was not simply an unintentional blind spot on their part; in their pursuit of suffrage, many of these women were actively racist and classist, as many scholars have shown (Davis 70-87; Newman 4-8).

The feminist analysis of maternal infanticide in the late nineteenth century is nonetheless historically informative, even if it is not "perfect" from a twenty-first century, intersectional feminist perspective. When white and middle-class feminists of the Women's Liberation Movement of the 1960s to 1970s made claims to a "Global Sisterhood" (Huijg 5-6; 9), they replicated the privileged mistakes of Victorian feminists who claimed sameness with slave women or with impoverished immigrant women. This privileged mistake, however, was productive, as it helped to spawn black feminism and, indeed, the theory of intersectionality (Crenshaw).

This repeated historical misstep is germane to the study and treatment of maternal infanticide because it illuminates the failure to connect the various discourses through which society tries to make sense of violent mothers. In the past generation, feminist criminologists have corrected the so-called stag effect in that field by focusing on female offenders (Chesney-Lind 2; Jones; Wilczynski), and these case studies and theories have begun to combine with recent research on postpartum psychological disorders, as medical experts now recognize the sociocultural dimensions of experiences of motherhood. In addition, a flurry of feminist research at the turn of the twenty-first century has challenged the overwhelming idealization of white, middle-class, American motherhood, arguing that it is not just unrealistic, it is also actually destructive, particularly in the lives of those mothers who are defined as "bad" due to such demographic factors as race, class, marital status, and ethnicity (Douglas and Michaels 141; Eyer 17; Ladd-Taylor and Umansky).

There is now an emerging, multidimensional perspective that has the potential to account for these various discourses as well as for the multiple factors that contribute to incidents of maternal infanticide. Traditionally, medical research has focused on types of inequality, such as those of gender and race, as separate causal factors. This "unidimensional" approach "assume[s] that gender inequality is monolithic across racial/ethnic lines and that racial stratification is similar for women and men, respectively" (Brown and Hargrove 181). Recent studies, however, have quantified the multiplicative effects of gender, race, ethnicity, and class on health disparities in the United States (Brown and Hargrove; Kelly). More specifically, both psychological and legal studies have begun to focus on experiences of race, ethnicity, and socioeconomic factors in cases of postpartum depression (Butterfield; Hagen; March; McIntyre et al.; Schernitzski; Segre et al.; Zittel-Palamara et al.). These scholars—who span the fields of criminology, jurisprudence, medicine, nursing, psychology, and sociology—generally do not explicitly cite the feminist theory of intersectionality. Likewise, current feminist theory generally does not engage with this medical and legal research. Despite the scholarly research on maternal violence in the early 1990s (Ashe and Cahn; Dougherty; Stark and Flitcraft) and a more recent critique of the destructive discourse of ideal motherhood, the current feminist movement offers little to no analysis of maternal violence broadly or infanticide specifically (Williams 188).

Thus, these feminist, historical, medical, and legal discourses are disparate, and this disconnect has very real consequences for infanticidal women. Intersectionality is, perhaps, the key to making this connection. A twenty-first-century discourse of maternal infanticide may do well to learn from the past successes and missteps of the activists examined herein, who advocated on the behalf of violent mothers by arguing that political and social constructs—race, slavery, class, poverty, motherhood—intersected in tangled, and sometimes violent, ways in the experiences of marginalized women. By making the very personal experiences of violence and motherhood political, these carefully crafted responses to news-making infanticide cases connected these violent women's biopsychological symptoms to the socioeconomic traumas of motherhood within contemporary racist, classist, and sexist society, even as the activists failed to comprehend their racialized and class-based roles as agents within the systems of oppression. These analyses, flaws and all, are instructive, as they potentially provide the groundwork for a twenty-first-century feminist analysis that reconceptualizes and links the legal, cultural, and medical discourses of maternal infanticide. The concept of multiplicative intersectionality can serve as the theoretical bridge between these various discourses, thus providing a means to integrate feminist theories of motherhood with the legal, cultural, and medical treatment of infanticidal mothers in the twenty-first century.

WORKS CITED

"The Administration of Justice--Hester Vaughan's Case." *New York Times*, 4 December 1868, p.4, query.nytimes.com/mem/archive-free/pdf?res=9800E6DF1E3AEF34BC4C53DFB4678383679F-DE. Accessed 9 May 2016.

Ashe, Marie, and Naomi R. Cahn. "Child Abuse: A Problem for Feminist Theory." *The Public Nature of Private Violence*, edited by Martha A. Fineman and Roxanne Mykitiuk, Routledge, 1994, pp. 303-305.

Baer, Judith A. *Women in American Law: Vol. I, From Colonial Times to the New Deal.* Holmes & Meier, 1985.

Blackwell, Alice Stone. *Lucy Stone: Pioneer of Women's Rights.* Little, Brown and Company, 1930.

Brown, Tyson H., and Taylor W. Hargrove. "Multidimensional Approaches to Examining Gender and Racial/Ethnic Stratification in Health." *Women, Gender, and Families of Color*, vol. 1, no. 2, 2013, pp. 180-206, muse.jhu.edu/article/524011. Accessed 9 May 2016.

Butterfield, Jessica. "Blue Mourning: Postpartum Psychosis and

the Criminal Insanity Defense,
Waking to the Reality of Women Who Kill Their Children." *John Marshall Law Review*, vol. 39, no. 2, 2006, pp. 515-538.

"The Case of Hester Vaughan." *The Revolution*, vol. 2, no. 23. 10 December 1868, pp.357-358.

Chesney-Lind, Meda and Lisa J. Pasko. *The Female Offender: Girls, Women, and Crime*. SAGE Publications, 2003.

Coffin, Levi. *Reminiscences*. Friends United Press, 1861.

Crenshaw, Kimberlé. "Demarginalizing the Intersection of Race and Sex: A Black Feminist Critique of Antidiscrimination Doctrine, Feminist Theory and Antiracist Politics." *The University of Chicago Legal Forum*, vol. 140, 1989, pp. 139-167.

Cullen-Dupont, Kathryn. "Hester Vaughan." *The Encyclopedia of Women's History in America*, edited by Kathryn Cullen-Dupont, DaCapo Press, 1998, 259-260.

Davis, Angela. *Women, Race, and Class*. Random House, 1981.

Dougherty, J. "Women's Violence Against Their Children: A Feminist Perspective." *Women and Criminal Justice*, vol. 4, no. 2, 1993, pp. 91-114.

Douglas, Susan, and Meredith Michaels. *The Mommy Myth: The Idealization of Motherhood and How It Has Undermined All Women*. Free Press, 2004.

Dubois, Ellen. *Woman Suffrage and Women's Rights*. New York University Press, 1998.

Dubrow, Joshua Kjerulf. "How Can We Account for Intersectionality in Quantitative Analysis of Survey Data? Empirical Illustration of Central and Eastern Europe." *ASK: Society, Research, Methods, vol.* 17, 2008, pp. 85-102.

Eyer, Diane. *Motherguilt: How Our Culture Blames Mothers for What's Wrong with Society.* Times Books, 1996.

Farless, Patricia. "Hester Vaughan: Infanticide, Women's Rights, and Melodrama." Florida Conference of Historians Annual Meeting, March 2004, http://fch.fiu.edu/FCH-2005/Farless-Hester%20Vaughan.htm. Accessed 9 May 2016.

Gunderson, Joan. "The Double Bonds of Race and Sex: Black and White Women in a Colonial Virginia Parish." *Journal of Southern History*, vol. 52, no. 3, August 1986, pp. 351-372. *JSTOR*, www.jstor.org/stable/2209567?seq=1#page_scan_tab_contents.

Accessed 9 May 2016.

Hagen, Edward H. "The Functions of Postpartum Depression." *Evolution and Human Behavior*, vol. 20, no. 5, 1999, pp. 325-359, http://dx.doi.org/10.1016/S1090-5138(99)00016-1. Accessed 9 May 2016.

Hayes, Sharon. *The Cultural Contradictions of Motherhood*. Yale University Press, 1996.

"Hester Vaughan." *The Revolution*, vol. 2, no. 5, 10 December 1868, p. 360.

"Hester Vaughan." *The Revolution*, vol. 2, no. 20, 19 November 1868, p.8.

Huijg, Dieuwertje Dyi. "Tension in Intersectional Agency: A Theoretical Discussion of the Interior Conflict of White, Feminist Activists' Intersectional Location." *Journal of International Women's Studies,* vol. 13, no. 2, March 2012, pp. 3-18.

"Infanticide." *The Revolution*, vol. 1, no. 4, 6 August 1868, p.74.

Jacobs, Harriet. *Incidents in the Life of a Slave Girl, 1860*. Boston, 1861, http://docsouth.unc.edu/fpn/jacobs/jacobs.html. Accessed 9 May 2016.

Jones, Ann. *Women Who Kill*. The Feminist Press at City University of New York, 1996.

Keetley, Dawn, and Pettegrew, John, editors. *Public Women, Public Words: A Documentary History of American Feminism*. Madison House, 1997.

Kelly, U.A. "Integrating Intersectionality and Biomedicine in Health Disparities Research." *Advances in Nursing Science*, vol. 32, no. 2, 2009, pp. E42-E56. *NCBI*, doi: 10.1097/ANS.0b013e3181a3b-3fc. Accessed 9 May 2016.

Kerr, Andrea Moore. *Lucy Stone: Speaking Out for Equality*. Rutgers University Press, 1992.

King, D.K. "Multiple Jeopardy, Multiple Consciousness: The Context of a Black Feminist Ideology." *Signs*, vol. 14, no. 1, 1988, pp. 42-72, cleisabeni.com/uploads/6/0/4/7/60470251/multiplejeopardymultipleconsciousness.pdf. Accessed 9 May 2016.

Ladd-Taylor, Molly, and Lauri Umansky. *"Bad Mothers": The Politics of Blame in Twentieth-Century America*. New York University Press, 1998.

Lerner, Gerda, editor. *Black Women in White America: A Docu-*

mentary History. Vintage, 1992.

March, Christie L. "The Conflicted Treatment of Postpartum Depression under Criminal Law." *William Mitchell Law Review*, vol. 32, no. 5, 2005, pp. 244-263, http://open.mitchellhamline.edu/cgi/viewcontent.cgi?article=1099&context=wmlr. Accessed 9 May 2016.

McIntyre, Lynn, et al. "The Felt Experience of Low-Income Mothers." *Affilia*, vol. 18, no. 3, August 2003, pp. 316-331.

McLaurin, Melton. *Celia, A Slave.* University of Georgia Press, 1991.

Mitchell, Sarah. "Mother, Murderess, or Martyr? Press Coverage of the Margaret Garner Story." *Seeking a Voice: Images of Race and Gender in the Nineteenth Century Press*, edited by David B. Sachsman et al., Purdue University Press, 2009, pp. 13-26.

Morrison, Toni. *Beloved.* Vintage, 1987.

Newman, Louise. *White Women's Rights: The Racial Origins of Feminism in the United States.* Oxford University Press, 1999.

Oberman, Michelle. "Understanding Infanticide in Context: Mothers Who Kill, 1870-1930 and Today." *The Journal of Criminal Law and Criminology*, vol. 92, no. 3-4, Spring-Summer 2002, pp. 707-738. *JSTOR*, doi: 10.2307/1144241. Accessed 9 May 2016.

Rakow, Lana F., and Cheris Kramarae. *The Revolution in Words.* Routledge, 1990.

Reinhardt, Mark. *Who Speaks for Margaret Garner? The True Story that Inspired Toni Morrison's* Beloved. University of Minnesota Press, 2010.

Schernitzski, Rebecca Ann. "What Kind of Mother Are You? The Relationship Between Motherhood, Battered Woman Syndrome, and Missouri Law." *Journal of the Missouri Bar*, vol. 56, no. 1, January-February 2000, pp. 50-57.

Segre, Lisa, et al. "The Prevalence of Postpartum Depression: The Relative Significance of Three Social Status Indices." *Social Psychiatry and Psychiatric Epidemiology*, vol. 42, no. 4, 2007, pp. 316-321. *Iowa Research Online*, doi: 10.1007/s00127-007-0168-1. Accessed 9 May 2016.

Shrier, D, editor. *Sexual Harassment in the Workplace and Academia: Psychiatric Issues.* America Psychiatric Press, 2009.

Spencer-Wood, Suzanne M. "Western Gender Transformations

from the Eighteenth Century to the Early Twentieth Century: Combining the Domestic and Public Spheres." *Historical and Archaeological Perspectives on Gender Transformations,* edited by Suzanne M. Spencer-Wood, Springer Press, 2013, pp. 173-214.

Stark, E., and E. H. Flitcraft. "Women and Children at Risk: A Feminist Perspective on Child Abuse." *International Journal of Health Services*, vol. 18, no. 1, 1988, pp. 97-118, http://journals.sagepub.com/doi/abs/10.2190/3K8F-KDWD-QYXK-2AX5. Accessed 9 May 2016.

Weisenburger, Steven. *Modern Medea: A Family Story of Slavery and Child Murder from Old South.* Hill and Wang, 1999.

Wilczynski, Ania. *Child Homicide.* Greenwich Medical Media, Ltd, 1997.

Williams, Keira V. *Gendered Politics in the New South: The Susan Smith Case and the Rise of a New Sexism.* Louisiana University Press, 2012.

Yuval-Davis, Nira. "Intersectionality and Feminist Politics." *European Journal of Women's Studies*, vol. 13, no. 3, 2006, pp. 193-209, http://journals.sagepub.com/doi/abs/10.1177/1350506806065752. Accessed 9 May 2016.

Zittel-Palamara, K., et al. "Desired Assistance versus Care Received for Postpartum Depression: Access to Care Differences By Race." *Archives of Women's Mental Health*, vol. 11, 2008, pp. 81-92. Accessed 9 May 2016.

Fixed or Shifting Notions of "Bad Mother"?

Considering Past and Future Australian Adoption Practice

SUSAN GAIR

ADOPTION, as it was commonly understood by the mid-twentieth century in Australia, had an established order and a set of formal and informal rules and regulations that prescribed how adoptions should be conducted. The practice of adoption was widely assumed to be benevolent, right, proper, and beyond dispute. The major characteristics of nonrelative adoption in Australia by that time were severance of family ties, legal and otherwise, between the adopted child and the birth parents; the establishment of a legal relationship between the adoptive parents and adopted child as though the child had been born to the adoptive family; and the maintenance of a "closed" legal adoption bound by confidentiality and secrecy. Adoption was seen as a solution for both the stigma of illegitimacy and the problem of infertility, and it remained relatively unchallenged until the late 1970s by which time the numbers of children available for domestic adoption began to slump (Healey; O'Neill et al.).

Between 1968 and1994, Australia-wide, over ninety-seven thousand adoption orders were made. In 1971 and 1972 alone, there were almost ten thousand adoption orders, and by 2012, this number had reduced to 333 (Healey 1; O'Neill et al. 28). White children under the age of one year adopted by nonrelatives represented the majority of all adoptions during this time. Decreasing numbers of adoptions have been attributed to many factors—including financial support for single mothers more widely available from 1973, the destigmatizing of illegitimacy, some recognition of the rights of the child, and the acknowledgment of the rights and responsibilities of mothers and fathers. Although each Australian state had slightly different child adoption legislation, national legislation also affected adoption practice. Contributing legislation included the *Family Law Act* (1975), the Levine Judgment (1971), which permitted abortion under certain conditions, the Child Care Act (1972), the Children Equality of Status (1976), the Status of Children Act (1978), and Australia's ratification of the United Nations Convention on the Rights of the Child (1989) (Healey). Until the introduction of the *Children Equality of Status Act* 1976, children of unmarried parents were illegitimate and in law considered to be "*fillius nullius*"—the child of no one (Inglis 1).

For Australian Aboriginal mothers and their children, the illegitimacy stigma did not appear to apply, and nonrelative adoption was understood to be alien to Aboriginal family structure (Healey). Nevertheless, many Aboriginal children were removed from their families and communities for perceived neglect. Torres Strait Islander people, Australia's second Indigenous group, practised a form of unique, "customary" adoption (Healey 11). Subsequently, significant emerging evidence identified that where social policies result in severed cultural ties, the consequences can include fractured cultural identities that, in turn, can trigger mental health issues and intergenerational trauma (Human Rights and Equal Opportunity Commission). By the 1990s the rights of mothers to keep their babies and the rights of children to know their genetic and cultural heritage had been embraced, although intercountry adoptions appeared to be treated differently (Healey). Although white families adopting or even fostering Aboriginal children in Australia is viewed as mostly unacceptable, adoption of foreign-born children has continued to be viewed as acceptable and necessary for humanitarian reasons, with mothers' rights or cultural ties rarely highlighted (Human Rights and Equal Opportunity Commission).

More recently, the human costs and harm of past adoptions have entered the social story of adoption, and society's unquestioned collusion with the myth of adoption as the "perfect answer" has been challenged (Watson and Granvold, 111). Contemporary adoptions commonly are understood to be acceptable because no other solution for the child's care is available. In this chapter, the Australian adoption story is explored in a quest to illuminate both shifting and prevailing notions of "bad" and good mothers, whereas Judith Butler's notion of performativity may help provide conceptual space for a healing way forward.

ADOPTION—A STORY OF TWO BAD MOTHERS MADE GOOD

In Australia, with similarities to some other Western countries, from the late nineteenth to mid-twentieth century, adoption became a closed legal process that extinguished past parental ties and authorized new (adoptive) parents to rear the child (O'Halloran 25-26). Legally, adoption was a confidential, irrevocable state-based child welfare process in which babies deemed to be unwanted were placed predominantly but not exclusively with childless couples; the state was relieved of any burden of care, and women raised the children as if they were born to them (O'Neill et al.). Routinely, unmarried mothers bearing illegitimate babies were deemed to be wayward, undeserving, unfit to mother, bad, and even mad, and they were strongly encouraged by professionals and their own families to abandon their baby to the state to preserve social and moral values (Marshall and McDonald; Matthews; Bernoth). Religious and welfare bodies upheld the notion that for single mothers who had violated patriarchal ideals of family life, the solution was adoption of their illegitimate babies by good hearted, deserving, married women who had sound health and morals and who were, therefore, deemed to be fit and ready to mother (O'Halloran 31; Wegar 78). The idea that systemic class and gender expectations, poverty, and patriarchal ideals of womanhood underpinned the supply and the demand of babies for adoption—and not individual failings—was an uncommon analysis (Wegar).

As noted, the closed adoption solution can be understood as a reconstruction of two deviant and stigmatized mother groups in crisis (Abrams; Healey; Solomon). Although some (bad) single mothers did keep their babies, many babies were relinquished for adoption. Later, many mothers—who might have comforted themselves that they had made a good decision for their baby's future by giving them up for adoption—were paradoxically condemned in relation to the same social taboo that they were coerced to breach. A pregnant woman who did not raise the child she birthed was seen to embody the "archetype" of bad mother for abandoning her child (Abrams 179). In line with accepted societal gender stereotypes, a good woman was a married woman who produced and raised children after marriage (Solomon). Therefore, married women who did not give birth to children transgressed social expectations of womanhood and were also seen as deviant.

According to Katarina Wegar, although the social construction of bad, single pregnant women is well known, the social construction of adoptive motherhood has remained a comparatively neglected research topic. Although some women might have perceived the normative expectation of motherhood as an unwanted "calling" (Rich 43), many adoptive mothers would have considered adoption as a desirable solution because of the great social pressure to have children (Solomon). Childless women had to meet various criteria—age, economic, health (no unresolved infertility issues), and traditional family values (stay-at-home mother)—in order to be eligible to perform the mothering role through adoption (Wegar). The accepted adoption narrative helped transform deviant, infertile women into "good" mothers. A simple code switch enacted the perfect solution. A married woman with no child was transformed into a mother. Correspondingly, with her consent, a single mother was transported back to her pre-pregnant self, and her mother status and her child were rendered invisible (Healey; Wegar).

However, from the 1970s, women whose children were lost to them through closed adoptions began recounting traumatic stories of being coerced to sign forms by professionals or family members (The Senate Community Affairs References Committee). Many others maintained that they did not ever sign the required paperwork. Most recently, it has been established that a culture of forced adoption prevailed in Australia, with associated stigma and stereotypes that silenced mothers for decades (The Senate Community Affairs References Committee). Although Bettina Arndt has argued that the realities for single mothers have been minimized by "revisionist thinking" (19-22), many mothers have, nevertheless, spoken out about being stigmatized and excluded and about feeling grief over their missing baby.

Mothers reported feeling unable to speak publicly at the time about their hidden pregnancies, their traumatic birth experiences, and the coercion to sign the adoption consent (Bernoth). Many mothers felt silenced about being permanently separated from their babies because women who relinquished their children commonly understood that they were agreeing to perform the accepted social script to remain "anonymous and untraceable" (Inglis 11). Often young, in personal crisis and vulnerable, many mothers reported not being informed of their legal rights to keep their babies. Rather, they were made to feel immoral, unworthy, selfish, and a bad parent if they did not give their children a better opportunity in life by consenting to adoption (Robinson). In some cases, single mothers were deliberately denied access to counselling prior to giving consent (Australian Association of Social Workers).

EXCLUDED STORIES

Various authors have identified the rejection of some subjective accounts for a variety of reasons. For example, Judith Krulewitz found that empathy for the stories of some rape victims was constrained by social norms and value judgments (qtd. in Duan and Hill 265). Equally, James Baldwin has revealed how many publishers rejected his writings about racism to render racial discrimination invisible. For whatever reasons, it seems that some accounts of events are considered outside what is an acceptable account. In theorizing this notion, both Ellen Swartz and Christine Stanley have identified a master narrative as a script that specifies and controls how social processes are carried out, whereas stories running opposite or counter to the presumed order can be named counter-narratives. Other authors similarly have written about metanarratives that exclude and stereotype individuals whose experiences or reality falls outside the prescribed social norms (Meininger 196). Metanarratives often are imbued with elements of dominance and subordination. James Scott uses the terms "public," "hidden," and "backstage" transcripts to describe what may be understood as allowable and unspeakable stories (202).

The case of past adoption can be considered through such a lens of public and backstage stories. The dominant, promoted, and accepted public adoption transcript labelled single mothers as bad and constructed adoptive mothers as good mothers (after the adoption of an unwanted baby), whereas counter-adoption stories of wanted babies and coerced and forced adoptions remained hidden and "unspeakable" (Gair and Moloney 49). In recognition of the power of dominant public narratives to subjugate, control, and render outcaste, Herman Meininger has urged reflection that enables a "better story" to emerge—one more inclusive and socially just because the "unacceptable" has been shifted from its place of rejection (197).

In Australia, there also appear to be legitimate, public stories and less legitimate, backstage stories of missing children. When children are lost or missing, including runaways or parent abduction, public empathy is high. Yet other Australian missing children have not been seen in the same empathic light. Examples include a "Stolen Generation" of Aboriginal children, British child migrants transported to Australia, forgotten Australians (Australian children in long-term state care), and past forced and closed adoptions (Humphreys; Human Rights and Equal Opportunity Commission). These children went missing from the everyday lives of their mothers and families, sometimes without a trace, yet public empathy for these missing children was minimal. Such examples share some key similarities, including a neglectful, undeserving bad mother or parent, and a feel good storyline featuring rescued children. This narrative seems so evident that it may even remain engrained and unquestioned in the psyche of ongoing generations of Australians.

BREAKING THE SILENCE

In Australia, the enormous human toll of coerced and forced adoption for many mothers began to be revealed during the 1980s when mothers broke their silence about their involuntary separation from their children. Emerging research identified that many mothers did not put the experience behind them; rather, they suffered grief that increased rather than decreased over time, sometimes resulting in lifelong trauma (Cole; Wells; Winkler and Van Keppel).

The accepted adoption narrative contained an array of powerful assumptions and social prescriptions that served to disenfranchise, exclude, and render birth mothers bad, invisible, and silent. For example, unmarried mothers were labelled immoral, the child was labelled illegitimate (Inglis), and the stated need for secrecy was so that the child (and the mother) did not carry the illegitimacy stigma. Furthermore, it was proclaimed to be in the best interests of mothers and babies that contact be permanently severed immediately after the birth, before any mother-child bond had developed. In more recent times, it has been hypothesized that the mother-child bond begins in the womb (Moloney and Gair).

It was assumed that birth mothers might grieve for a short time, but then they would get on with their lives. However Michael De Simone has found that some mothers' grief was severe and prolonged. There was an absence of any social recognition of the complexity of loss for parties to adoption or the power of social expectations. Although it has been reported that many adoptees had positive family relationships with their adoptive families (Marshall and McDonald), mental health issues have been extensively documented for both adoptees and birth mothers, often attributed to issues of grief and loss of mother-child relationships. A socially constructed bad mother stigma, a social expectation that a mother would not abandon her baby, and an associated, psychological attachment and separation anxiety over the severed mother-child bond—all could have affected and shaped women's ongoing emotional adjustment (Abrams; Condon; Gair, "The Psychic Equilibrium"). By the late 1990s, after relentless lobbying by birth mothers, an inquiry in New South Wales into past adoptions heard stories of coercive and forced adoption practices in that state. Most recently, as noted, a commonwealth adoption inquiry found that forced adoptions were common across most Australian states.

A PERSISTENT BUT DYNAMIC MORAL NARRATIVE

It could be assumed that moral judgments associated with past adoptions have shifted and hidden backstage stories have been heard. Yet recent research findings may challenge that assumption. In a recent study focusing on felt empathy for stigmatized groups, social work students' lack of empathy for birth parents may help highlight the persistence of the immoral, single mother narrative (Gair, "Social Work Students" 45). In classroom-based research, second year students were asked to define empathy, articulate their empathy for four real life vignettes, and reflect on how they made sense of their own responses. One vignette featured a mother's story of coerced relinquishment of her baby. In my study, I had speculated, incorrectly as it transpired, that the adoption narrative might evoke a high empathetic response given the changes in public sentiment concerning forced adoptions. Yet in some students' own reasoning about their minimal empathy response, they made moral inferences about the mother's behaviour and her decision making at the time of the adoption, even though it was clearly identified that it was a case of coerced adoption. For example, this student noted: "I feel she made a bad choice at the time." Another student explained: "Although I would like to try to understand, and I could inadvertently put myself in her shoes... I have no experience with this, in fact the opposite—perhaps empathy in this case would take me longer" (Gair, "Social Work Students" 45).

The findings from that study suggest that the past stigma of single mothers as bad, though discredited, may have prevailed. A similar study reported findings of minimal empathy expressed by some professional helpers for young, single mothers who did not fit their construction of "deserving" (Rutman et al.). It seems that only a mixed acceptance exists, even after the emergence of a revised adoption story, amended policies, and some public empathy over the past treatment of single mothers.

Of interest, with reference to the bad label in adoption, Nancy Verrier has inferred that a "bad guy" label existed and could shift between players in the adoption reunion narrative (153). According to Verrier, sometimes the bad person may be the adoptee, viewed as "ungrateful" for wanting to search for the mother, whereas the birth mother attracts condemnation and the bad label for searching for her child because she "made her choice and should stick to it" (155). Equally, adoptive mothers are not immune to having the bad mother label assigned to them for being infertile and for raising the child of another mother. This shifting label seemed evident in an earlier adoption study on the experiences of adoptive mothers raising adopted children (Gair, *Adoption: A Different Road* 401). Some adoptive mothers expressed feeling at the mercy of changing social policy and social sentiment, and they felt that they had "fallen from grace" as quotes from these three adoptive mothers illuminate:

> Years ago I think people thought relinquishing mothers were bad and adoptive mothers were good.
>
> Attitudes have changed towards adoptive parents, like towards birth parents.
>
> Years ago, where would the babies have gone? Adoptive parents were encouraged to adopt. The feeling now is that we "took" the babies. (Gair, *Adoption: A Different Road* 401)

The findings of these studies may contribute to supporting a notion that a good mother, bad mother dichotomy may be an enduring moral discourse in Australian society, and that although at times the bad mother label may be perceived to shift and change, it may, nevertheless, remain a fixed feature in the adoption story.

INTERCOUNTRY ADOPTION—A PREVAILING TALE OF GOOD AND BAD MOTHERS

Although intercountry adoption appears to be distinctly different to past closed and forced adoptions in Australia, the underpinning moral narrative may still be evident. The 1993 Hague Convention on Protection of Children and Co-operation in Respect of International Adoption establishes international standards and cooperative measures to safeguard the interests of children, and Australia ratified the Convention in 1998. According to Peter Selman, nearly one million children were adopted internationally by Western families, including many Australian families, between the end of the Second World War and 2008 (324). Of interest, the growth of intercountry adoption in Australia has increased as the availability of domestic babies for adoption declined significantly (O'Neill et al.).

Intercountry adoption in Australia has been considered to be a sanctioned, legitimate, and humanitarian way to build a family.

Factors cited as contributing to the need for humanitarian intervention for overseas-born children have included one-child policies, poverty, little available social welfare support, limited availability of contraception, and cultural rejection of children born outside of traditional family formation (Selman). Yet Patricia Fronek and Denise Cuthbert have identified that intercountry adoption practices may reflect some of the discredited and unethical practices and breached human rights evident in past Australian domestic adoptions, including coerced and forced adoptions. According to Siobhan Clair, Australia has been implicated in cases where children have been stolen off the streets in Ethiopia and India, and these children, victims of child traffickers, have been adopted into Australian families (5).

This scenario may provide evidence of an enduring and alluring adoption narrative of bad mothers and abandoned children, for whom good mothers can provide homes. It seems, at least for some of Australia's intercountry-adopted children, that they were not abandoned or unwanted by mothers who were unable to care for them (Clair). Equally, a different backstage narrative remains unspoken. Many adoptive families may embrace the narrative of families formed because mothers from developing nations had to abandon their children and that humanitarian intervention was necessary. Yet as evidenced by Alexandra Young, the primary reason Australian parents pursued intercountry adoption was infertility and yearning to be a parent (131-135). Again, an analysis that systemic, class and gender inequalities and poverty contribute to the supply of overseas-born babies—or that patriarchal ideals of womanhood continue to fuel the demand for babies for adoption—appears uncommon. Narratives of humanitarian rescue and parental deficits also prevail because structural solutions may render intercountry adoption programs unnecessary, which closes this pathway to motherhood.

PERFORMANCE OF THE ADOPTION STORY

Katrina Jaworski has discussed Butler's notion of performativity as a practice that is continually remade through repetition, by which "discourse produces the effect that it names" (140).

Drawing on Butler's work, Jaworski explains that performativity can undermine the emotional correspondence between a person's emotional interior and exterior, but that there may be no choice because the practice has a historical or ritualized existence in the society. That is, performers either unknowingly or powerlessly play their part, perpetuating the public, social narrative through their actions, even to the betrayal of their inner self. The usefulness of Butler's notion, according to Jaworski, lies in its ability to offer conceptual space to dismantle discourses that are manufactured to appear as the natural order of things. In reading adoption through the lens of Butler's notion of performativity, it could be seen that birth mothers and adopted mothers perform the prescribed public adoption transcript in both past and current adoptions. Adoptive mothers take up the mothering role and become known as the mother, acting as if she gave birth to the child even when the child knows they are adopted; the family's everyday life includes members claiming familial relationships that are not biologically based (mother, sister, father, grandmother) and all enact that script. To complete the picture, the adoptive mother commonly is named on the birth certificate as the mother. Equally, the birth mother speaks of subsequent children because she has been silenced as mother of the relinquished child and denied the language or legitimacy to speak her reality because her mother label had been transferred to another woman (Meggitt). Certainly, this is evident in the case of past coerced adoptions. In the case of intercountry adoption, which has been the only real option for adoption in Australia in the last two decades, adoptive mothers have continued to access motherhood through this sanctioned process and perform their prescribed role.

In summary, by the mid-twentieth century in Australia, adoption was constructed in a way that sacrificed some mothers and their babies while new mothers were legitimized. Birth mothers, adoptive mothers, and children all were co-opted to perform the approved adoption story. The good-bad mother ideology of the past, dominant adoption narrative may also be evident in current intercountry adoptions, in which patriarchal gender norms and mothering expectations are identifiable. A better story and a healing way forward may rest in recognizing structural inequalities affecting some women's lives, respecting all women's capacities and strengths, and honouring transparent and authentic relations for all mothers and children through open adoptions.

CONCLUSION: OPEN ADOPTION AS A WAY FORWARD

The idea of open communication in adoption has been gaining support worldwide since the 1960s (Sykes; Gritter). Open domestic adoption legislation, policies, processes, and practices have been endorsed in many countries as a key strategy to counter separation grief and to avoid unethical practice. In Australia, states and territories have begun to move away from closed domestic adoption from the late 1970s, and in most states, some form of contact, usually information exchange, is practised to varying degrees (O'Halloran). Some authors have argued that open adoption brings risks of ongoing interference and fears of delayed development of the new adoptive mother-child relationships. Conversely, it may be the case that judgmental labelling and severed birth bonds are based on a perception that only "monodimensional" parent-child relationships are possible rather than faith and investment in "multidimensional" parenting possibilities available through open adoption (Sykes 21, citing Pennie and Best). In particular, open intercountry adoption has attracted very minimal attention and this may be an area for future research-informed policy development (Scherman and Hawke).

Past Australian child adoption was portrayed in "win-win" terms, in which children who were unwanted or abandoned by their bad mothers were saved by good mothers, and all players performed their roles. A critical lens, however, reveals cracks in this rosy veneer; a moral adoption narrative has prevailed and may still underpin current Australian adoption policies. Equally, it seems that although adoption may need to remain one option in a continuum of care for children in need, a new adoption script is necessary. Even though varying degrees of openness in adoption have been implemented, policies are not uniform; for example, open intercountry adoption appears to have attracted very minimal attention or research. Likewise, negotiated open adoption for eligible children in state care appears uncommon. Yet literature suggests that wherever possible, preserving biological links may be paramount for many mothers and children to avoid unnecessary grief over children missing through adoption. Open adoption processes can enable adoptive mothers to transparently raise children and openly perform her unique role within the reality of the situation. Open adoption need not depend on creating moral unworthiness in one mother and a worthy rescuer in the other. Future domestic and intercountry adoptions, and adoptions of children from state care, could promote much more open and transparent processes in which multiple mothers (and fathers) are not routinely and forcibly excluded but are included, to whatever extent is possible, in the care of children. This recommended action may help contribute to the demise of the prevailing good-bad mother dichotomy and introduce a new, socially just adoption script.

WORKS CITED

Abrams, Paula. "The Bad Mother: Stigma, Abortion and Surrogacy." *Journal of Law, Medicine and Ethics*, vol. 43, no. 2, 2015, pp. 179-191.

Arndt, Bettina. "Giving up Baby." *Adoption. Issues in Society*, edited by Justin Healey, The Spinney Press, 1999, pp. 19-22.

Australian Association of Social Workers (AASW). "Report to the Senate Community Affairs References Committee Inquiry into the Commonwealth Contribution to Forced Adoptions Policies and Practices," Oct. 2011, www.aasw.asn.au/document/item/2270. Accessed 24 Jan. 2017.

Baldwin, James. *Collected Essays*. Library of America, 1998.

Bernoth, Ardyn. "Mothers Win Inquiry into Forced Adoption." *Adoption. Issues in Society*, edited by Justin Healey, The Spinney Press, 1999, pp. 23.

Clair, Siobhan. "Child Trafficking and Australia's Intercountry Adoption System. Research Paper" University of Queensland, January 2012.

Cole, Christine. "The Hidden Tragedy of the White Stolen Generation and its Consequences: Perspectives on Adoption in Australia from a Mother of the Stolen White Generation." *Other People's Children*, edited by Ceridwin Spark and Denise Cuthbert, Australian Scholarly Publishing, 2009, pp. 110-126.

Condon, John. "Psychological Disability in Women Who Relinquish a Baby for Adoption." *The Medical Journal of Australia*, vol. 144, no.3, 1986, pp. 117-119.

De Simone, Michael. "Birth Mother Loss: Contributing Factors to Unresolved Grief." *Clinical Social Work Journal*, vol. 24, no. 1, 1996, pp. 65-76.

Duan, Changming, and Clara Hill. "The State of Empathy Research." *Journal of Counseling Psychology*, vol. 43, no. 3, 1996, pp. 261-274.

Fronek, Patricia, and Denise Cuthbert. "Apologies for Forced Adoption Processes: Implications for Contemporary Intercountry Adoption." *Australian Social Work*, vol. 66, no. 3, 2013, pp. 402-414.

Gair, Susan. "Social Work Students' Thoughts on Their (in)Ability to Empathise with a Birth Mother's Story." *Adoption and Fostering*, vol. 34, no. 4, 2010, pp. 39-49.

Gair, Susan. "The Psychic Disequilibrium of Adoption: Stories Exploring Links Between Adoption and Suicidal Thoughts and Actions." *Australian e-Journal for the Advancement of Mental Health*, vol. 7, no. 3, 2008, www.tandfonline.com/doi/abs/10.5172/jamh.7.3.207. Accessed 10 Oct. 2014.

Gair, Susan. *Adoption: A Different Road to Mothering. Adoptive Mothers' Experiences of Negotiating and Maintaining the Mothering Role at Significant Points Across the Adoption Lifecycle.* Dissertation, James Cook University, Townsville Australia, 1997.

Gair, Susan, and Sharon Moloney. "Unspeakable Stories: When Counter Narratives are Deemed Unacceptable". *Qualitative Research Journal*, vol. 13, no. 1, 2013, pp. 49-61.

Gritter, James. *Life Givers. Framing the Birth Parent Experience in Open Adoption.* CWLA Press, 2000.

Healey, Justin. *Adoption. Issues in Society*. The Spinney Press, 1999.

Human Rights and Equal Opportunity Commission (HREOC). *Bringing Them Home: Report of the National Inquiry into the Separation of Aboriginal and Torres Strait Islander Children From Their Families.* HREOC, 1997, www.humanrights.gov.au/publications/bringing-them-home-report-1997. Accessed 24 Jan. 2017.

Humphreys, Margaret. *Empty Cradles*. Corgi Books, 1995.
Inglis, Kate. *Living Mistakes*. Allen and Unwin, 1984.
Jaworski, Katrina. "Suicide and Gender: Reading Suicide Through Butlers's Notion of Performativity." *Journal of Australian Studies*, vol. 27, no. 76, 2003, pp. 137-151.
Marshall, Audrey, and Margaret McDonald. *The Many-sided Triangle*. University Press, 2001.
Matthews, Jill. *Good and Mad Women*. Allen and Unwin, 1984. Print.
Meggitt, Marie. "To Know One's Child. The Relinquishing Mother's Dilemma." *To Search for Self*, edited by Phillip Swain and Shurlee Swain, The Federation Press, 1992, pp. 48-57.
Meininger, Herman. Connecting Stories: A Narrative Approach of Social Inclusion of Persons with Intellectual Disability. *ALTER, European Journal of Disability Research*, vol. 4, 2010, pp. 190-202.
Moloney, Sharon, and Gair, Susan. "Empathy and Spiritual Care in Midwifery Practice: Contributing to Women's Enhanced Birth Experiences." *Women and Birth*, vol. 28, no. 4, pp. 323-328. *NCBI*, doi: 10.1016/j.wombi.2015.04.009. Accessed 24 Jan. 2017.
O' Halloran, Kerry. *The Politics of Adoption*. Netherlands: Springer, 2006.
O' Neill, Cas, et al. "The Changing Context of Adoption." *Social Work In the Shadow of the Law*, edited by Simon Rice and Andrew Day, Federation Press, 2014, pp. 26-46.
Rich, Adrienne. *Of Women Born*. London: Virago, 1977.
Robinson, Evelyn. *Adoption and Loss: The Hidden Grief*. Clova Publications, 2000.
Rutman, Deborah, et al. "'Undeserving' Mothers? Practitioners' Experiences Working with Young Mothers in/from Care." *Child and Family Social Work*, vol. 7, no. 3, 2002, pp. 149-159.
Scott, James. *Domination and the Arts of Resistance*. Yale University Press, 1990.
Selman, Peter. "Intercountry Adoption of Children from Asia in the 21st Century." *Children's Geographies*, vol. 13, no.3, 2015, pp. 312-327.
Senate Community Affairs References Committee. *Commonwealth Contribution to Former Forced Adoption Policies and Practices.*

Commonwealth of Australia, 2012.
Scherman, Rhoda., and Wendy Hawke. "Openness and Intercountry Adoption in New Zealand." 3rd International Conference on Adoption Research, 2010, Leiden, The Netherlands. Lecture.
Solomon, Alison. "Infertility as Crisis: Coping, Surviving- and Thriving." *Infertility. Women Speak Out*, edited by Renata Klein, Pandora Press, 1989, pp. 169-187.
Stanley, Christine. "When Counter Narratives Meet Master Narratives in the Journal Editorial-Review Process". *Educational Researcher*, vol. 36, no.1, 2007, pp. 14-24.
Swartz, Ellen. "Emancipating Narratives: Rewriting the Master Scripts in the School Curriculum." *Journal of Negro Education*, vol. 61, no. 3, 1992, pp. 341-355.
Sykes, Margaret. "Adoption with Contact: A Study of Adoptive parents and the Impact of Continuing Contact with Families of Origin." *Adoption and Fostering*, vol. 24, no. 2, 2000, pp. 20-32.
Verrier, Nancy. *The Primal Wound*. Gateway Press, 1993.
Watson, Larry, and Donald Granvold. "Whose Baby is it? Modern Influence in Adoption Practices in the United States." *Personal Construct Theory and Practice*, vol. 5, 2008, 111-118.
Wegar, Katarina. "In Search of Bad Mothers: Social Constructions of Birth and Adoptive Mothers". *Women's Studies International Forum*, vol. 20, no. 1, 1997, pp. 77-86.
Wells, Sue. "Post-Traumatic Stress Disorder in Birthmothers." *Adoption and Fostering*, vol. 17, no. 1, 1993, pp. 30-32.
Winkler, Robyn, and Margaret Van Keppel. *Relinquishing Mothers in Adoption: Their Long-Term Adjustment*. Melbourne Institute of Family Studies, Monograph no. 3. 1984.
Young, Alexandra. *Families of Choice: A Qualitative Study of Australian Families Formed Through Intercountry Adoption*. Dissertation, The University of Sydney, 2009.

Refusing to Obey

Bad Mothers in the Israeli Culture

OMRI HERZOG AND TAMAR HAGER

MOTHERHOOD is a sacred institution in every militaristic society. Within this social context, the good mother's role is composed of two facets that seem contradictory. A good mother is protective of her children, cares for their wellbeing, and unconditionally provides love and attention. At the same time, she must be patriotic—that is, to educate her children to sacrifice and to be heroic. And when the time comes, she must deliver her children to the nation by supporting their enlistment to the army, even while knowing that military service could be life threatening.

The civil pact of militaristic society reconciles these two roles by compensating the mother who loses her child in battle if she follows and obeys her predetermined role. She must mourn in the private sphere and, simultaneously, publicly express feelings of pride, heroism, and elation, which are rooted in the valuable contribution to the state. She must convey good faith in the governing and military systems to which she has sacrificed her child. If she fills this set cultural script, she earns her public symbolic capital as a civil heroine.

Nevertheless, sometimes the son's individual story is not that of death in battle but a different story altogether—more complex and less heroic—and this fact challenges the normative maternal role. Our chapter investigates these deviating stories and focuses on two famous "bad" mothers in Israeli culture: Shula Mellet, whose son was killed in an army training accident, and Aviva Shalit, a mother of a kidnapped soldier. These two mothers faced ongoing media exposure. Although they at first acquired public admiration and respect, these mothers eventually became targets of public criticism, anger, and even contempt; they were represented as bad mothers, as each of them, in her way, had not fulfilled her scripted national maternal role.

The first part of the article surveys some theoretical concepts relating to motherhood in militarist societies. Employing these concepts, the chapter analyzes the stories of the two mothers as they were represented by several national newspapers. We argue that their cultural representations as bad mothers derived from their subversive, even rebellious, behaviour and responses, which challenge the Israeli image of the patriotic mother. Refusing to obey a publicly accepted militaristic role, each of them was judged and paid a heavy public price, which echoed their sons' tragic stories.

BETWEEN A GOOD MOTHER AND A PATRIOTIC MOTHER

In practice and as a cultural role, motherhood is a complex, historical social construct. It defines which overt and covert cultural and ideological mechanisms determine the positions, behaviours, and identities of good and bad mothering by employing social, legal, and psychological systems of reward and punishment.

Western culture usually presents mothers as caretakers and caregivers, who affirm life values and, as such, contribute to a politics of peace (Ruddick, "Preservative Love"). Miranda Alison, who studied female peace activists, argues that many of them present a "maternalist" or "motherist" position (94). In other words, they attribute their activism to their maternal instinct. Scholars such as Sara Ruddick argue that women tend to oppose war and militarism because of their socialization as potential or actual mothers who concern themselves with the children of the world.

Notwithstanding, at times of war and political crisis, the maternal role "allow[s] women to readily surrender their sons … to war, violence and death" (Scheper-Hughes, "Maternal Thinking" 353). In militaristic societies, mothers educate their children according to military values, which convey to the son or daughter that they must be ready to sacrifice their lives for the nation. Even mothers who pay the price of losing a child seem to "cling in most cases to the meaning, significance and social status entailed by a view of the death or injury in question as important, useful and non-arbitrary" (Mazali 298).

Preparing their sons for service to the nation and going to war can function for mothers as way out of the private, family, and home space—the space perceived as "natural" to them—and into the national-public space (Berkowitz). The act of enlisting and sacrificing their sons allows women a political voice that approves and legitimizes military tactics and government decisions (Enloe; Levi; Alison).

Militaristic motherhood starts from the perception of the womb as an enlistment station (Enloe). Government offices that adopt pronatalist policies use government resources to pressure women (especially those of the correct ethnic and national background) to give birth to more children (Alison). Cynthia Enloe highlights the fact that more often than not these policies are presented in militaristic terminology, (i.e., a woman that gives birth to more children—preferably male children—is perceived as a more substantial contributor to national security). Consequently, women are expected to encourage their children to enlist into the army for the sake of the motherland and its security.

In a social reality in which mothers undergo a process of militarization, two sets of expectations, based on contradicting social archetypes, are forced to coexist: the good-private mother and the patriotic mother (Slattery and Garner). Aminata Forna presents the good-private mother in Western society as the following: she is "completely devoted not just to her children, but to her role. She must be the mother who understands her children, who is all-loving and, even more importantly, all-giving. She must be capable of enormous sacrifice" (3). Sara Ruddick emphasizes that motherwork includes investment in the physical, emotional, cognitive, and spiritual care of children, and involves preparing them for the social reality driven by an urge to protect the children at any cost ("Maternal Thinking" 98).

The patriotic mother is also described as a good and caring mother; however, her cultural worth is measured "by her own willingness to accept potential injury or death of her child for the sake of the nation's war effort" (Garner and Slattery 90). The willingness to accept the sacrifice of children as inherent in their education for collective militaristic values and the act of sending them off to war stands in complete contradiction to the cultural expectations from the archetypical good-private mother, who is supposed to care for her children and protect them from pain and damage. The good mother is supposed to guard the life and wellbeing of her children at any price, whereas the patriotic mother is expected to encourage her children to participate in activity that may harm them or even lead to their death (Berkowitz; Garner and Slattery).

But what happens when a mother, who is demanded to obey the patriotic code, refuses to do so, and criticizes the conduct of the military establishment in regard to her son and refuses to be silent about the harm done to him? The image of such a mother is directly associated with the perception of a bad mother.

In Western societies bad mothers harm, abandon, and neglect their children, and even murder them (Ladd Taylor and Imansky; Rich; Forna; Douglas and Michaels; Hager and Herzog). Women who are labelled as bad mothers have demographic characteristics. There is an implied assumption that a good mother is white, able bodied, of middle or high socioeconomic status, married, and heterosexual (Chase and Rogers); as a result, anyone who does not match these parameters is suspect. The accusation of being a bad mother is a threat to any woman who deviates from social expectations in different ways: a mother whose identity does not match the hegemonic preference, whose actions and statements contradict sound and proper social-national conduct, almost automatically becomes suspect because her motherhood is problematic and even endangers her children.

In this manner, mothers who turn to political activism, for example, and come out against the establishment in public spaces risk their social and political status and are often presented as endangering good motherhood (Burwell; Capdevila; Knudson; Mazali, "Home Archeology"; Scheper-Hughes, *Death without Weeping*). Laura Knudson shows for example how American media accused Cindy Sheehan—who turned to antiwar activism after her son was killed in the Iraq war—of neglecting her housework duties and even abandoning her other children.

This chapter examines two case studies in Israeli culture, centring on mothers who were trapped between the contradicting roles of the good mother in a militaristic society—the mother who acts to protect her children and the mother who relinquishes them to the nation. Through them, we attempt to present the complexity of the maternal role in cases that are not anchored in the protocol of standard national mothering. We argue that the complexity creates a web of impossible expectations and behavioural norms, accompanied by public condemnation of the mother's behaviour: media representations depict her as a so-called bad mother, and her punishment echoes her son's story.

FROM A TRAGIC FIGURE TO AN ABUSIVE MOTHER: THE STORY OF SHULA MELLET

Amir Mellet was a young Israeli who was inducted into the Israeli air force as a flight supervisor. At the *Hatzerim* army base, where he was assigned for the first part of his military service and where the cadets were professionally trained, a tradition of tests testing the courage of the young soldiers functioned as hazing ceremonies. The role of these tests or games was twofold: to establish manhood, courage, and a willingness to take risks as a milestone toward active military service, and to reinforce a hierarchy between the young cadets who take part in the games and the veteran soldiers who facilitate them. On 21 July, 1992, Amir participated, along with fellow cadets, in a game called "net roulette." He lay on the ground on his back, holding a safety net used to stop landing aircraft. When released, this net shoots into the air at great speed. Amir held on to the net as it repeatedly thrust up and down. After several thrusts, Amir lost his grip and fell onto the landing runway. After five days, he died of his injuries. The Israel Defense Force's (IDF) version of events, as given to the press, was as follows: "A soldier was fatally wounded by an aircraft breaking cables during a training course in the facility, due to the negligence of officers at the site" (Levin 2).[1] Following the tragedy, three low-level officers were prosecuted. One was acquitted, and the two others were convicted, received suspended sentences and were stripped of their ranks.

This is a shocking and painful story of an unjust death. Such instances unfortunately occur in every conscription cycle; they are usually labelled as "training accidents," and a wall of silence surrounds them. In many of these cases, the army will treat them, after the fact, as a heroic and necessary death, sanctified by the ethos of sacrifice for one's country. Amir Mellet was named a casualty of war by the Department of Soldier Memorialization, who "died in the line of active duty" (Levin 2). However, in the Israeli collective consciousness, the heroes of this story were not Amir or the officers who supervised the game; the heroine was Amir's mother, Shula Mellet.

Shula Mellet did not accept the army's version, according to which the death happened during training. She did not match the normative standards of the bereaved mother who mourns her son privately in the family circle, but her mourning was reflected in the public sphere as a civil representation of courage and willingness to sacrifice. Mellet took her struggle against the army to the public sphere in a way that emphasized the mundane, arbitrary, and nonheroic aspects of her son's death (Rosental). She demanded that the commanders be brought to justice. And to ensure that similar accidents were not repeated in the future, she demanded the establishment of a strict policy of zero tolerance for hazing games. In an interview she was quoted saying: "The practice of blaming the [lowest ranking soldier] must stop. We must say NO to the cover-ups. I and other parents go to the military courts and witness how justice isn't being done. The absence of representation in the military courts for the boys, the bereavement and the loss, is a travesty of justice" (qtd. in Kizel 8).

When Shula Mellet's private mourning was translated into organized activism against military authorities, she was portrayed as the leader of a hostile organization, comprised of bereaved mothers (Rosental). She and other parents whose sons and daughters were injured or killed in training accidents were present at all hearings in the military courts that dealt with training accidents, often disrupting the procedures. They published press releases in which they protested the injustice of what they perceived as cover-ups of these accidents. They became familiar characters in the courts: "I have to be at the trials. I have to write everything,' Shula said. 'They, the military establishment, just aren't trustworthy'" (Levin 3).

Shula Mellet's representations in the public space focused on judgmental coverage of her confrontation with the military authorities. These representations were exacerbated after her suicide, two years after her son's death. The media was quick to paint the retrospective portrait of a crazy delusional woman in the public consciousness—vengeful and obsessive, dark and rigid—who wrecked her family and neglected her other children: "a tormented woman, complex.... All her time was devoted to the obsessive fight against IDF authorities.... She slowly lost her mind" (Cohen 4-5). In an interview three months before she committed suicide, Mellet recognized the compounding moves to silence her and present her as crazy. She said the following: "I'm screaming in pain and the world ignores me. I want to tell you that a bereaved parent who dares to cry out in this country is automatically thought of as insane. We're presented as a bunch of lunatics" (qtd. in Kizel 10).

The subversion of Shula Mellet's legitimacy was directly connected to her status as a mother and the way she betrayed her national-motherly duties. Her public image was detached from the fact that she was a bereaved mother because she failed to fulfil the role allotted to her as a mother withdrawing into her grief. The image was constructed to signify the woman who fought the IDF authorities as an unfit wife and mother. In this manner, Mellet was turned into a bad mother. Her punishment symbolically reenacted her son's death. Like her son, who was repeatedly flung into the air, Shula Mellet was described as detached and lacking any grasp of reality. She was repeatedly flung by the media to the depths of neglect and insanity, which led to her death.

Indeed, in an ironic reenactment of the crime that brought about the death of her son, the mother had become the neglector and abuser. "Meanwhile, the family split in all directions, each one and their own pain," claims one of the articles published after her death (Cohen 4). Mellet was blamed for failing to hold the family together after her son's death, but the media did not present the tragedy that had befallen her and the subsequent army cover up as the reason for the neglect of her motherly duties but rather posed her deficient motherhood in an essentialist paradigm in a way that covertly exempted the army from responsibility. Her husband was quoted as saying: "All her life, Shula was demanding of herself, of me, of the kids. She didn't make our lives easy." And when the interviewer asked if she had also shown warmth towards her children, he replied: "Her motherly warmth had been extinguished within her" (qtd. in Brenner 12). Her bad mothering was implied in her son's death as well as in her daughter's miserable life. The media focused on the suffering of her daughter, who "lived in a dark hovel of an apartment. By choice, and perhaps as a result of her mother's extremist upbringing, she still breastfeeds her two-and-a-half-year-old son" (Cohen 4). The daughter then related the following: "Mom had a rough side to her. She was very critical. She would make a big deal out of everything. I know that she often hated me; not like she told me when I was little, that a mother never hates her children. She could yell at us, curse, swear, humiliate, and bring us to such desperation that we'd get sick of life" (qtd. in Cohen 4).

Can a bereaved mother be a bad mother? Mellet did not suffer her bereavement with private grief and public pride, as she should have done according to militant mother norms. The media's predominant explanation for this was her insanity. She was described as "a particularly stubborn woman, very determined, maybe neurotic, shocked by grief and collapsing in frustration" (Lipkin-Shahak 9). Her anarchic insanity explains the struggle against the IDF authorities, which was described as "vitriolic," and motivated by a "messianic zeal, with which she poured her wrath on the judges" (Cohen 4). The extremist anarchist was also documented by her husband who said: "Everything was black and white to her; it was in her nature. Everything she did was done in an extreme way. So when she fought the IDF, she did it in an extreme way" (qtd. in Brenner 13).

In the public eye, the extremist anarchism was not turned only against IDF authorities but against all soldiers. That's how Mellet became an enemy of the nation after her death: the journalist Tali Lipkin-Shahak wrote following Mellet's suicide: "Parents whose children are at age of conscription must believe in the military establishment for the sake of their sanity and for their sense of security.... Let us not be blinded and disrupt our judgment by the shock at Shula Mellet's self-initiated death, the deep regret over the progression of events in her particular case" (Lipkin-Shahak

9). A woman who does not cooperate with the national role of the grieving mother and does not carry her grief as a badge of honour that serves the values of national sacrifice is denounced by the collective and is represented as insane and/or deceitful.

FROM A SELF-SACRIFICING MOTHER TO A SELF-CONCERNED MOTHER: AVIVA SHALIT'S STORY

Nineteen-year-old Gilad Shalit was abducted by Palestinians who entered Israel from the Gaza Strip, on Sunday, 25 June 2006. Following the abduction, the IDF conducted an operation that continued intermittently for five months, during which 394 Palestinians were killed. At the same time, international officials, particularly in Egypt, led diplomatic efforts to obtain Shalit's release. At the beginning of July, Israel rejected the abductors' demand to release a thousand Palestinian prisoners, in exchange for Shalit, and declared that it would not negotiate with terrorists. On 2 October 2009, Israel released twenty Palestinian women prisoners and received a video in which Shalit asked Israel to finalize the deal and reminisced about his family. Only in October 2011, five years and four months after he had been taken into captivity, was a deal obtained between Israel and the Hamas organization, in which Shalit was discharged in exchange for the release of 1,027 Palestinian prisoners.

The issue of Shalit's release was controversial because of the necessity of releasing Palestinian prisoners, some of whom had planned terror attacks. Those who opposed the deal warned that releasing Palestinians may cause the death of many Israelis in the future and would strengthen Palestinian organizations' motivation to abduct soldiers. The voice of Shalit's parents and a large group of activists was clear: Release Gilad at any cost. This unequivocal message was especially voiced by his mother, Aviva Shalit.

As the mother of a captive soldier, Aviva Shalit was represented in the daily press in a complex manner. The image that was constructed for her was usually that of the good mother who devoted "every single bit of ... emotional, mental and psychic energy" (Douglas and Michael 6) to her missing child and did not spare efforts and sacrifices to bring him back home. Shalit was described as someone who slept only fitfully: "And then the bad thoughts begin. All the time, endlessly: What's he going through? What is he eating? Does he drink at all? Who takes care of him? Does he speak with anybody? It's endless" (qtd. in Paltar 7). Her appeal to Sarah Netanyahu, the prime minister's wife, a year later, was an appeal from one mother to another: "You're in the headlines for your genuine concern for the children of the immigrant workers. But allow me to remind you of a boy, who's already a young man, who has been captive in a hole in Gaza for over four years. From the near-far Gaza, his cry arrives at your door. Don't lock it" (qtd. in Levi 4; see also Hason 3).

In accordance with the motherhood myth that ties the mother to the private space, Aviva Shalit was presented as a private woman who had difficulty appearing on the public stage. In 2007, when she had appeared at a vigil, in *Gan Ha-em* (Mother's Garden) in Haifa, the newspaper described her appearance as a rare one (Khuri 4). In an interview for the important daily newspaper *Yediot Aharonot* in 2009, her three sisters emphasized that they were educated to avoid public exposure: "From this anonymity, that Aviva has considered holy, her face is recognized in each and every Israeli household. This is hugely difficult for her," said one of them (qtd. in Meidan and Paltar 10).

As the agreement was delayed, the Shalit family erected a protest tent in front of the prime minister's home and Shalit's parents moved in. Moving to Jerusalem represented a constant presence in the public sphere and was accompanied by Aviva quitting her job. The move and the resignation were presented in the media as her increasing devotion to her maternal role: "What are our options, to continue sitting at home?" She was quoted saying the following by one of the papers: "Our goal is that the Prime Minister will see us in the morning and see us in the evening" (qtd in. Kotes-Bar 20; see also Hason 3). During her stay in the tent she was quoted as saying the following: "For almost a thousand days I have been half a human being, even less. Because my son, my Gilad, isn't with me. Almost a thousand days, and every hour and every minute and second is like eternity" (qtd. in Kotes-Bar 21). Hence, the disappearance of her son obligated Shalit to demonstrate an absolute motherhood.

However, the sorrow and the longing were supposed to remain in the framework of the national discourse. The expectation was that Aviva Shalit would continue to affirm the belief that the leaders cared about the last of the troops, that her lost son was just as much their lost son, and as such, that they would do what was necessary to bring him home; she was obligated to accept the notion that the delay in negotiations stemmed from noble reasons. A good Israeli mother should continue fulfilling her duty as a national womb under any circumstances.

Aviva Shalit refused to identify with national interests and with the considerations of the leadership. She remained loyal to the private motherhood discourse and refused to surrender to the national ethos, which would have forced her cooperation with the public discourse and its national values. The more she adhered to the private motherhood ethos at the expense of the patriotic motherhood norms and externalized this in the public sphere, the more her statements were politically exacerbated. When the foreign minister, Tzipi Livny, said in December 2008 that "we can't always bring everyone home," she responded by saying "A very miserable statement" (qtd. in Paltar, 8). In an August 2010 article, titled "Aviva Shalit Takes Off Her Gloves," she describes the Prime Minister Benjamin Netanyahu's promises to release her son: "It's all just empty words that make one nauseous. It's impossible to listen to them anymore" (qtd. in Barak and Khuri 22).

When a mother's private pain turns into a public political statement, clashing with government policy, the distinction between the private and the public spheres seems to collapse. Moreover, the displacement of the private space into the patriotic-public space is an analogy of what happened to her son: his abduction led to her "abduction." She was removed from a stable and solid home to a heterotopic space, to a public tent; from there, she continued to vocalize and publicize her private mother's pain. She didn't comply with the discourse dealing with general peace and security questions; rather she persisted to always be Gilad Shalit's private mother, ignoring her role as a national mother who considers the needs of the collective and displays loyalty to the leaders who represent it.

The fact that Shalit adhered to her private motherhood, even in public spaces, and avoided adopting a wider political agenda, turned her into the object of criticism. Betraying her patriotic maternal duties, she became a bad mother. During her son's captivity, her consistent critique of the government created an image of a bitter woman, who meddles in affairs that are outside her authority. Her unwillingness to acknowledge the security-related price of her son's release was viewed as the representation of a selfish woman who refuses to sacrifice her son on the altar of security yet is willing to sacrifice other people's sons instead. Shalit failed to fulfill her patriotic duties, and, consequently, the quality of her private motherhood was also doubted. There were those who expected her to start a hunger strike by reminding her " audaciously and brutally of Gilad's loneliness," and those who anticipated that she would cry more in front of the cameras (Makover-Blikov 8).

Media representations, therefore, presented a character full of contradictions: too critical but too trusting, too reserved but too emotional, selflessly sacrificing but also selfish. Whatever Aviva Shalit had done, the shadow of a bad mother would always have followed.

DISCUSSION: MOTHERS' PUNISHMENT

Shula Mellet and Aviva Shalit are both mothers who became publicly visible in a militaristic society: Not because their sons died a heroic death in battle but because the dramatic script that was posed in their military service exceeded the political and aesthetic ethos, which draws a well-defined and apparent framework in Israeli culture. The mother whose son has fallen in battle can and should simultaneously fulfill the role of the private and patriotic good mother. Her duty as a good mother is to raise her son in the private sphere, care for him, and love him unconditionally; at the same time, she must prepare him for his national obligations. Losing him in battle, she will go out into the public space and be represented as someone who has sacrificed her most precious possession for the benefit of the extended family—the nation. Attesting publicly to her loyalty to the motherland, and her cooperation, obedience and internalization of national priorities, she is rewarded by embedding her representation within the value system of heroism and sacrifice alongside her dead son.

There are, however, deviations from the heroic story: soldiers die in training accidents, death without reason; soldiers are abducted by the enemy. In such cases, the role of the mother remains the same in the cultural imagination. Despite the deviation, she must cooperate with the heroic narrative, leaving her with a double-bind order: devotion to private mourning and demonstration of loyalty, heroism, and sacrifice in the public sphere. She is expected to continue being the good-private and patriotic mother.

Yet the deviations in the script make it hard to fulfill the expected motherly role. Both Mellet and Shalit were forced to formulate coping tactics that were not dictated in advance by the narrative of mourning and sacrifice. These tactics are necessarily more flexible and unscripted. Mellet and Shalit did not give in to the sacrificial ethos and did not accept the symbolic offer of compensation made by the nation. For this, they stood on public trial, addressing their competence as mothers—of their own private children and of the nation as a whole—which is expected to happen to mothers who expose the disruptions in the heroic narrative (abduction by enemy forces, death by "courage" games). They are themselves perceived as disrupting the existing military order and the ethos that frames it in the collective consciousness. With the challenge they pose to the patriotic motherhood model, they turn into signifiers of the crack or wound on the surface of the ethos of heroism, and as such, they breach its clean and healthy cultural pose.

Furthermore, the culture copes with such violations by symbolically returning the mothers to the site of the "original sin," (i.e., the drama of deviation from the ethos of heroism and of the disruption of the existing order); they are punished for the "sins" of their sons.

The symbolic return to the site of deviation (death of the son in an accident or his abduction), is expressed as media representations, unconsciously reenacting, replicating and dramatizing the story of the son. The mothers' public performances—anger, bitterness, rebellion, political recruitment, or struggle against governmental authorities—again denote the failure, the divergence, the national trauma, which are all embodied in the accident and/or abduction event. Like a distorted and deceptive return to the scene of the disaster, the mothers are also thrown into the transgressive narrative of their sons. Thus, the representations of both mothers reproduce symbolic versions of their sons' tragedies. Shula Mellet's son died during a game of "net roulette" after he was thrown onto the landing runway. Shula Mellet refused to accept the heroic whitewashing of his death and turned to the IDF and state authorities, demanding an investigation and indictment of the responsible parties. She was rejected again and again. She herself went through a symbolic "net roulette." The legal and public net flung her into the air, detaching her from the concreteness of her claim, uprooting her; thus, she lost her hold on reality. The symbolic process of detaching and flinging brought her to her death: she committed suicide by shooting herself.

Aviva Shalit's son, Gilad, was abducted by Hamas during a routine military operation in the occupied territories. Israeli public opinion, which adopted Gilad as "the son of all of us," turned its back on him when the price of his release was revealed: the release of murderers and the weakening of state security. Consequently, doubt was cast on the legitimacy of his release, creating a stormy and dichotomous discourse in Israeli culture.

Gilad's mother, Aviva, initiated a public struggle to advance his release. She did so tirelessly, confronting security bodies, government institutions, and the media. Her narrative also reproduced her son's story. Her private motherhood was "seized" by the media and was covered as a collective motherhood: if Gilad is the son of all of us, then Aviva is the mother of all of us. Gradually, however, Aviva stopped being the patriotic collective mother. She criticized the authoritarian mechanisms of the army and the government, turning into a political entity—disconcerting, challenging, defying—and the antithesis of the patriotic mother. Therefore, just like her son, who turned into the enemy against his will, so she became an object of delegitimatization. Releasing her of her collective patriotic role created doubts as to her maternal and national competence.

CONCLUSION

The tension between the roles of the private and patriotic mother is well embedded in stories of heroic death on the battlefield. In more complex stories, however, such as those outlined in this chapter, the collective militaristic maternal role is occasionally challenged and undermined as result of the mothers' reactions that divert from the accepted cultural script. As our analysis shows, when this script is undermined, the mother turns into a deviant from the given social order, sometimes against her will, and is suspected of being a bad mother to her dead or abducted child, to her other children and to the children of the nation. Subsequently, the media punishes her for breaching her duties by questioning her prescribed role but also for being a mother to a son whose life and/or death disrupted the desirable collective story. This negative public response to what is perceived as a disruption of the preferred militaristic version of the dead son and his mourning sacrificing mother carries a symbolic meaning. Instead of the statement in Ezekiel (Chapter 18:2) that "The fathers have eaten sour grapes and the children's teeth are set on edge" —that is, the next generation pays for its ancestors' sins—the public narrative turned into "Sons have eaten sour grape, and the mothers' teeth are set on edge."

ENDNOTE

[1]We examine the representations of Shula Mellet and Aviva Shalit in the Israeli (Hebrew) press. All translations of press's quotations from Hebrew to English are our own.

WORKS CITED

Alison, Miranda. *Women and Political Violence: Female Combatants in Ethno-National Conflict*. Routledge. 2007.

Berkowitz, Nitza. "'Women of Valor': Women and Citizenship in Israel." *Israeli Sociology,* vol. 2, no. 1, 1999, pp. 277-318 (In Hebrew).

Brenner, Dani. "Shula Mellet, Mother of the Soldier Who Died in the Net Roulette, Committed Suicide Yesterday." *Ma'ariv*, 8 Feb., 1994, pp. 12-13 (In Hebrew)

Burwell, Dollie. "Sometimes the Road Gets Lonely." *Politics of Activist Voices from Left to Right*, edited by Diana Taylor, et al., University Press of New England, 1997, pp. 62-69.

Capdevila, Rose. "Lysistratus, Lysistrata, Lysistratum: Constructing the Identities of Mother and Activist." *Psychology of Women Quarterly*, vol. 34, 2010, pp. 530-537.

Chase, Susan. E., and Mary F. Rogers. *Mothers & Children: Feminist Analyses and Personal Narratives*. Rutgers University Press, 2001.

Cohen, Tzahi. "To the Desert: This Week, an Hour Ago, Shula Mellet Reached the End of Her Tether, Mother of Amir (RIP), Who Died in the Net Roulette, Shot Herself." *Yedi'ot Aharonot*, 1 Feb., 1995, pp. 4-5 (In Hebrew)

Douglas, Susan. J., and Meredith W. Michaels. *The Mommy Myth: The Idealization of Motherhood and How It Has Undermined Women*. Free Press, 2004.

Enloe, Cynthia. *Maneuvers: The International Politics of Militarizing Women's Lives*. California University Press, 2000.

Forna, Aminata. *Mother of All Myths: How Society Molds and Constrains Mothers*. HarperCollins, 1999.

Hager, Tamar, and Omri Herzog. "The Battle of Bad Mothers: The Film *Mama* as a Commentary on the Judgment of Solomon and on Contemporary Motherhood." *Journal of the Motherhood Initiative for Research and Community Involvement,* vol. 6, no.1, 2015, pp. 121-133.

Hason, Nir. "Aviva Shalit to Sarah Netanyahu: You Were Concerned About The Children of Migrant Workers,Help Us: Fifth Birthday in Hamas Captivity." *Ha'aretz,* 29 Aug., 2010, p.3 (In Hebrew)

Khuri, Jackie. "Gilad Shalit's Mother: We Will Not Be Silent, Not Another Year Without You: First Commemoration of the Second Lebanon War—Vigil to Release the Abducted with Aviva Shalit, Micky Goldvasser." *Ha'aretz*, 13 July, 2007, p.4. (In Hebrew)

Kizel, Arieh. "I Cry Out From My Bleeding Heart, the Last Interview with Shula Mellet Before Her Suicide: A Bereaved Mother Talks About The Death of Her Son Amir Who Died in a Game of 'Net Roulette.'" *Yedi'ot Aharonot*, 8 Feb., pp. 8-11. (In Hebrew)

Knudson, Laura. "Cindy Sheehan and the Rhetoric of Motherhood: A Textual Analysis." *Peace & Change*, vol. 34, 2009, pp.164-181.

Kotes-Bar, Chen. "The Five Bad Years: 'The Son of All of Us Finally Returns to Be My Son': Aviva Shalit's Struggle Ends This Week, After 1941 Days." *Ma'ariv's Weekend*, 21 Oct., 2011, pp.16-18 and 20-22. (In Hebrew)

Levi, Eli. "From a Mother to a Mother: Aviva Shalit Takes Off the Gloves." *Ma'ariv*, 2 Aug., 2010, p.13. (In Hebrew)

Levi, Yagil. "How Military Recruitment Affects Collective Action and Its Outcomes." *International Studies Quarterly*, vol. 57, 2013, pp. 28–40.

Levin, Ron. "Shula Mellet Tragedy of a Mother—On the IDF Disaster Affair." *Ma'ariv*, 8 Feb., 1994, pp. 2-3. (In Hebrew)

Lipkin-Shahak, Tali, "Let Every Hebrew Mother Know." *Davar*, 9 Feb., 1994, p. 9. (In Hebrew).

Mazali, Rela. "Ethnically Constructed Guns and Feminist Anti-Militarism in Israel." *Interventions,* vo.9, no.2, 2007, pp. 289-308.

Mazali, Rela. *Home Archaeology*. Hakkibuz Hameuchad Publishing, 2011. (In Hebrew)

Meidan, Anat, and Nurit Paltar. "Sisters in Pain: They Don't Bother Her With Questions and Don't Advise, They Only Support—Gilad's Mother, Aviva Shalit's Three Sisters." *Yedi'ot Aharonot Sabath Supplement*, 20 Mar., 2009, p.10. (In Hebrew)

Paltar, Nurit. "I Know the Boy I Sent, I Don't Know Who I'll Get Back: An Interview with Gilad Shalit's Mother, Aviva Shalit, Following Operation Cast Lead in Gaza." *Yedi'ot Aharonot Sabath Supplement*, 9 Oct., 2009, pp. 8-6. (In Hebrew)

Barak, Ravid, and Jackie Khuri. "Minister of Foreign Affairs, Livni, on Gilad Shalit: We Can't Always Return All the Soldiers Home." *Ha'aretz*, 11 Dec., 2008, pp. 22-23.

Rich, Adrienne. *Of Woman Born: Motherhood as Experience and Institution*. Virago, 1986

Rosental Reuven. *Is Bereavement Dead?* Keter. 2001. (In Hebrew).

Ruddick, Sara. "Maternal Thinking." *Maternal Theory: Essential Readings*, edited by Andrea O'Reilly, Demeter Press, 2007, pp. 96-113.

Ruddick, Sara, "Preservative Love and Military Destruction: Some Reflections on Mothering and Peace." *Maternal Theory: Essential Readings*, edited by Andrea O'Reilly, Demeter Press, 2007, pp.114-144. (Original work published 1984).

Scheper-Hughes, Nancy. *Death without Weeping: The Violence of Everyday Life in Brazil*. University of California Press, 1992.

Scheper-Hughes, Nancy. "Maternal Thinking and the Politics of War." *Peace Review: A Journal of Social Justice,* vol.8 no.3, 1996, pp. 353-358.

Slattery Karen and Ana C. Garner. "Mother as Mother and Mother as Citizen: Mothers of Combat Soldiers on National Network News." *Journalism*, vol.13, no.1, 2011, pp. 87-102.

V.
WHERE DO WE GO FROM HERE?

Heather Munro, "Wings and Roots," 2006, ink on paper, 5 x 7 inches.

FurryLove

LIAT ELKAYAM

The mother laid the baby on the bed.

*

Another wonderful product from BabyBot Industries!

Stressed? Strained? Burdened with care?
Finding it hard to meet your daily quota for The Mechanism AND take care of your new baby?
Realizing it's both risky and pricey to hire a human nanny?
Rest assured, your worrying days are over. We, here at BabyBot, have nothing but you and your best interests in mind.
Welcome to our ever growing, one billion FurryLove users community!

Instruction manual, FurryLove, model TB, serial number RU-R2D2/2043
Keep these instructions for future reference, as they contain important information.

BabyBot TB models: White Polar Bear, Winnie the Pooh™ (WarnerBros-Disney-Rosom Universal), Pink Goldilocks Bear.
Upper half: 100% cotton.
Bottom half: 90% polyester, 10% cotton.
This robot is surface washable only. Do not immerse. Wash surface part in low heat, no wring cycle. Do not use in drier. Detach

surface by unzipping the back.

For use with infants from 3 kg weight and 55 cm length.
Recommended use with infants up to 12 kg weight.
Never use with infants over 14 kg weight. Exceeding this weight causes the robot to automatically lock and shut down.
Overriding the lock may endanger your child.

*

The baby was lying in his bed, sleeping peacefully. Boom boom boom. Light beatings spread through his limbs in a circular motion. In his dream, he floated through a watery liquid, completely cradled and held.

*The dream ended, and the baby awoke. His eyes opened wide. The surroundings were satisfactory. They were familiar. He stretched a small hand to pet the soft dwelling place. He pulled over the pink furry creature to his right, crushing the tag at its bottom. The tag read in round, glowing, pink letters: MyMiniFurryLove, model pink/*TB.

The baby clutched the pink teddy bear close to him. His warm body wriggled indulgently against the soft fur, both swaying lightly to the beat of the pulsations. Boom boom boom ba-boom. The baby began to fuss.

*

Battery replacement:
Requires four AA **alkaline exium** batteries (included).
Only adults should replace batteries.
Required tool: Philips screwdriver (not included).
To avoid battery leakage:

- Remove batteries during long periods of nonuse.
- Do not mix old and new batteries.
- Use only batteries of the same or equivalent type, as instructed. Standard alkaline or rechargeable batteries are not suitable for this product.

If the BabyBot begins to operate erratically after battery replacement, you may need to reset the electronics. Slide the power/volume switch off and then back on.

Accessories:

BabyBot comes with a partially perishable accessory package required for its operation.

The accessory package includes the following:

- Electrode diapers.
- Klandopine diapering cream.
- Wet wipes.
- One pack of Maternex,™ the only food that builds your baby's immune system!
- Six BinkyWinky™ one-piece pacifiers.
- Four BabyBot FurryLove bottles (please note: the feeding function cannot be used with any other kind of bottle. FurryLove bottles can also be used for preserving breastmilk).
- Three Basic FurryLove toys (noisemaker, chewing ring, and small-scale BabyBot Pink Goldilocks Bear).

A variety of additional items for purchase are available on our FurryLove website: teething gel, stomachache drops, iron drops, TyleSoup,™ PorridgeQuit,™ Organix™ AppleSauce, and more!

*

On the third wail, the big bear's eyes lit up in blue. Operation mode. The bear's arms moved, and the entire bed rocked gently with them. "Bobby, Bobby, Bobby, Bobby," the bear murmured in a high and soft voice. "Bobby, Bobby," it repeated, high and melodious. "Don't be afraid. I'm here. You're not alone."

The baby stopped crying and stretched his arms up in front of him.

The big bear took the baby in its arms and raised him into the air.

The baby cooed.

The bear began to sing, "I bought me a cat and the cat pleased me. I fed my cat under yonder tree. Cat goes fiddle-i-fee."

The baby started to suck rhythmically on the bear's ear.

A plastic finger with a suckling nipple popped out from the bear's arm. The bear placed the finger gently on the baby's top lip, rubbing it back and forth. The baby licked the finger with his tiny tongue and then twisted his face; repulsed, he pushed the finger away. The apple sauce was a bit tart. The bear tried again to place its finger in, and this time the baby took the finger into his mouth and sucked on it ecstatically, an occasional drop or two leaking on the pink fur. From a crack in the bear's wrist, a biscuit emerged. The baby pounced on it, panting.

In the background, on the wall, a large and hypnotizing screen showed a photographed image of a forest in shades of black, white, and red. Once in a while, a small animal with large eyes passed by, making a squeaking sound. Cock-a-doodle-doo rooster. The branches rustled in the nonexistent wind. The bear sang in a sweet, feminine voice: "Little Igor, don't go through that door, the wolf will come and eat you ... rawr!"

The baby began to fuss.

*

First-time Use:
Open the fasteners behind the robot's left leg. See image A1.
Place batteries as instructed.
To turn on, unzip the back of BabyBot's head. The power button is located above the left ear. Slide the button from right to left. BabyBot's eyes will light up in blue.
The screen on BabyBot's belly should illuminate upon powering on. Enter your username and password immediately.
After entering your information, a VidCam™ Bubble will appear on all screens in use by your account. The VidCam™ Bubble transmits real-time footage from the face camera in BabyBot's nose. The VidCam™ Bubble cannot be removed.

VidCam™ Bubble control buttons:

1. Camera operation—top right corner, magnifying glass icon.
Functions: zoom in, zoom out, pan right, pan left, tilt up, tilt down.
Default mode: focus on the baby's face.
2. Audio control—centre right, musical note icon.
Functions: image only, baby image and sound, BabyBot

and baby image and sound. Default mode: image only, with distress sound alerts.
3. Video button—bottom right corner, parent and child icon. Functions: turn on two-way image and sound mode to enable direct communication with your baby. Upon operation, BabyBot will connect to your VidCam™ account and enable the baby to view your face on its belly screen. You and your baby will be able to see and hear each other. Default mode: off.
4. Data stream—Electronic ticker tape in a green strip at the bottom of Bubble.
Functions: ongoing monitoring of baby's body temperature, weight, pulse, and breathing.
Whenever any of these variables deviates from the normal zone for more than five seconds, an alert will go off.
5. Manual override—top left corner, hand icon.
Function: direct manual control of BabyBot
6. Activity modes—centre/bottom left. C P L letters
Three activity modes are available: care only; care and play; care, play, and learn.
Default mode: care, play, and learn.

Our FurryLove basic music and video package can be upgraded for only 24,999 RBC a month! Upgraded package includes children literature classics from *Mother Goose* to *Dr. Seuss* as well as a trilingual operation system bonus!

*

The mother sat in her office and glanced at the computer screen. The VidCam™ was streaming footage from the camera in the bear's forehead. She pressed the C button, opened the music library inside it, and changed the song, choosing "Itsy Bitsy Spider" from the play list.

The bear said: "I love you. Let's sing and play games. Pattycake, pattycake."

The screen blinked red. The mother's face froze under the menacing light.

She clicked the manual override button but nothing happened. She clicked the button again and again, but she couldn't get the damn thing to work. The bear was still singing repeatedly "Pattycake, pattycake," the screen was still blinking red, the baby was crying very loudly now, and none of the other buttons were working either. She clicked franticly on all of them. "Fuckity fuck" she murmured when a man, suited all in black entered her cube-like office.

"What's with the noise Calvin? It's killing my holo-meeting."

"I am so sorry Mr. Belmont. I am really trying to..."

"We do not TRY *here Susan. Take care of it. Now."*

Mr. Belmont slammed the door behind him. The walls shook. Then, amazingly, a green message appeared on the main screen of the mother's computer wall: "Virus: neutralized. Operation error: repaired." The tight muscles in her forehead and the corner of her mouth released.

The bear on the screen began to hum "The itsy bitsy spider climbed up the waterspout."

*

SmartBot™ by MultiBot™ is a smart algorithm enabling your BabyBot to study your baby and respond to his specific needs and wants.

FurryLove is programmed for triple usage through this algorithm. It detects and distinguishes different crying modes, categorizes necessary actions by speed and effectiveness, and tags each crying mode with cause and effect for future use.

1. **Crying due to need for movement**—the BabyBot will switch to movement mode. Movement operating options: rocking (Non-mechanical Rocking, Registered Patent 566/323), driving simulation, walking and cradling simulation.
2. **Crying due to wetness**—Our BabyBot Electronic Diaper is equipped with a monitor that detects the degree of waste absorbed. Default mode: 10% wetness. BabyBot will change the diaper within thirty seconds after waste is expelled.
3. **Crying due to hunger**—BabyBot will offer a bottle.

BabyBot operates according to a feeding program updated continually according to your child's weight and in compliance with dietary charts designed by the experts at Maternex.
4. Crying due to temperature discomfort—BabyBot creates, adjusts, and checks room temperature and product temperature at all times to match it to your baby's needs. Default mode: 24°C.
5. Crying due to gas—a separately sold soothing liquid can be mixed into the bottles following your doctor's orders. Your BabyBot is also equipped with BabyBot Optimal Burping Mechanism.
6. Crying due to need for suckling—BabyBot will offer a bottle nipple (located in BabyBot's left hand) and a pacifier.

If crying persists for over three minutes and all possibilities have been exhausted, visual and audio alerts will appear in the VidCam™ Bubble.

*

The mother pressed the visual button on the operation menu. Her face appeared on the large screen in the bear's belly. She smiled.

The baby noticed her and smiled back. He tried to grab her hair with his hand.

She cooed words of love at him. A few moments later the screen on the mother's desk blinked: 152 unread emails. She had to get back to work.

When the mother's face disappeared, blowing a kiss goodbye, the baby began to cry.

The bear cradled the baby, rocked the baby, offered him a bottle, a small bear, a pacifier, and after three minutes of crying reported to the mother.

The mother watched in silence for a moment. The baby's face twisted in pain. She wanted to stop the agony, and so contrary to the recommendations on the "getting to know your BabyBot" forum, she chose to appear on the screen again, speaking to the baby softly, "Bobby, Bobby," then hysterically, "My little Bobby,

Mommy's here, hush hush, settle down." Normally, a few moments of soothing and a pacifier were enough, but this time it didn't work. The baby kept crying. He cried as if his whole world were collapsing. As if the sun would never shine again. As if nothing had meaning anymore.

*

BabyBot FurryLove can also be used as a stroller or a car safety seat. Sold separately: sun/roof protection hood, anchoring dock for vehicle (required to lock BabyBot's arms and legs into safety seat mode).

This equipment has been tested and found to comply with the limits for a Class C robot, Class B digital device, pursuant to Part 15 of the FCC rules, Daneel Olivaw legislation. These limits are designed to provide reasonable protection against harmful interference in a residential installation.

*

She walked into the room and picked the baby up from his perch in the lap of the pink animal, and he settled down almost instantly. The bear's eyes shut down, turning black. It stood motionless.

She said, "My little Bobby, my little munchkin, how are you doing?"

The baby cooed. "Dahdahdah," he said, softly and rhythmically slapping on her arms. Pat pat pat, demanding something tangible to grab.

She pulled out her breast, and the baby latched on and nursed, crushing her hair with his fingers. She got into bed while the baby lay on top of her, pausing in his feeding from time to time to gag and call out with excitement. She caressed the fuzz of his hair, and he rubbed his wrist against the skin of her breast.

The suckling pauses grew longer and longer until finally, with his mouth still around her nipple, he fell asleep. Sleeping like a baby.

The mother glanced at the scene through the eyes of her robot doppelganger. The face of her beloved baby filled the screen: long lashes, a Botticelli angel in his sleep. After staring at him for a few moments, she felt the call. Her breasts were leaking. The mother pulled her pair of micro-pumps from the black plastic bag and attached them to her nipples. She connected the tube to the sanitized bottle and pressed the power button. Umtz, umtz, the milk poured from her in a monotone beat, spray by spray. The units were building up as her thoughts wandered to moment of reunion, the magical pieta, when she can take him in her arms again. Her shift would be over in exactly five hours.

The baby awoke with a sharp whine. Something had chased him in his sleep. He screamed before he opened his eyes. He reached out his hand to the empty space, fluttering the tips of his fingers to pull on something, anything tangible. He grabbed his mother's hair, and before he could begin to pull on it as hard as he could, he heard the soft voice speaking to him. "Little munchkin good morning. How are you? Why are you crying?" The baby writhed with pain, passing gas.

The mother took the baby in her arms, placed him at a forty-five degree angle over her shoulder, and patted his back. He burped but kept crying. The pain was terrible. It consumed him whole. He pulled on his mother's shirt, hoping for some comfort from her milk glands, the source of his joy. She complied immediately. He clung to her, weeping. A few minutes of continuous feeding later, he cried again, screaming to the seven heavens. The mother changed his diaper and then held him in her arms as she paced around the room, rocking him.

He kept crying, pulling on her hair, slapping and kicking her, his face reddening and then almost turning blue. She squeezed ten drops from a little purple vial onto his lips. He continued to cry; she gave him a bottle, a biscuit, a pacifier.

He screamed. She offered her breast, and he bit into it with anger. She tried to sing "Itsy Bitsy Spider," while she applied gel to his emerging right tooth; she shook the little pink bear before him. The baby continued to cry.

An hour went by, and the baby was still crying.

All this pain.

Then,

The mother laid the baby on the bed.

She stood before him motionlessly for a few seconds and then walked into the closet, sat down on the floor, closed her eyes, shed a tear, hit her head hard on the door, and pressed the button.

*

***Special offer coupon: 30% off MommyLove to celebrate our February 2052 launch!**

*** MommyLove—the Closest Thing to Mommy!**

(upon return of a used and operational FurryLove BabyBot. Valid only during February 2052. Single use only. Invalid in combination with other promotions)

Thanks to MommyLove, now you can leave your child with their favourite person in the whole wide world: you!

MommyLove, the newest generation BabyBot, provides your baby with the perfect mothering experience. Designed in collaboration with NASA Robotics, BabyBot MommyLove comes in one generic model available in six different sizes.

After an only three-hour scan performed at MultiBot headquarters in KioTokyo, a perfectly accurate Silkinetic™ moulding of your face and hands will be created, an enveloping suit replicating your physical appearance perfectly will be wrapped around one of the basic MommyLove BabyBot models. The process will be completed with a wig made of real hair culture from your own follicles, a built-in scent duplicating your body odour, and an audio recording of your voice.

This product is sold with a three years satisfaction guaranteed

MommyLove, why leave your loved one alone even for a minute, when Mommy can be with him always!

(Daddy version is also available)

Medea Chic

On the Necessity of Ethics as Part of the Critique of Motherhood

MIRI ROZMARIN

> *They say that we live a life free of danger at home while they face battle with the spear. How wrong they are. I would rather stand three times in the line of battle than once bear a child. But the same story does not apply to you and me. You have this city and your father's home, enjoyment of life, and the companionship of friends, but, alone and without a city, I am abused by my husband, carried off as plunder from a foreign land, I have no mother, no brother, no relative to offer me a safe haven from this disaster.* (Euripides 249-257)

EURIPIDES'S MEDEA is the archetype of the bad mother. From the start of the play, Medea openly makes known her hatred for the children and the fact that being a mother is something she would love to abandon. She shows no real attachment to the children or any interest in their being. She rebels against her role as a mother and regards critically her reality as a mother. Her account of her position as a mother is deprived of any idealization, and she performs what is considered the absolute negation of the role of mothers when she murders her children to avenge their father's betrayal of her. Contemporary readings of Medea focus on how her rebellion and rage designate her freedom, the latter associated with feminist struggles (Hadas 81; Reckford 336).

In this chapter, I offer suggestions toward creating a theoretical space in which a fundamentally new conception of good motherhood can appear. To this end, I present a metaphilosophical discussion about the relations between ethics and political critique in the context of the feminist discussions of bad mothers. As such, I do not discuss the women who are considered to be bad mothers or good mothers. I do not focus on how institutions shape and use these categories. My focus is on how the discussion of "bad mother" as a social category, an institution and a control mechanism reveals what I consider to be a challenge to the feminist critique of motherhood. I hope to show that the topic of "bad mothers" reveals a productive tension between the political critique and the ethical stance of motherhood. This tension has produced illuminating accounts of motherhood, but in some cases, ignoring this tension may lead to paradoxical conclusions. By pointing to this paradox, I stress the importance of further integration between the ethical and political in future feminist discussions of motherhood.

Western society presents a clear distinction between the good and the bad mother. Research refers to the contemporary model of good mothering in terms of "intensive mothering." Sharon Hays defines it as "child-centered, expert guided, emotionally absorbing, and labor intensive and financially expensive" (15). In this discourse, motherhood is associated with sacrificial and complicated techniques, all of which are centred on the child's needs and happiness. Intensive mothering demands that mothers be devoted to the every detail of their children's lives (Perälä-Littunen). Intensive methods of childrearing, according to Hays, require the total dedication of mothers in terms of time, emotional work, and complicated practices. Accordingly, the intensive mother should prioritize her child's needs over her own goals or wishes. As with the traditional image of the good mother, the present-day good mother is likewise required to devote a great deal of her time and energy to her child. Her emotional and practical work still remains largely unrecognized in terms of payment, social status, and other exchangeable resources. Moreover, mothering and work of care in general remains both culturally and politically devalued (Ridgeway and Correll; Folbre; Kittay).

Hays points to intensive motherhood as a dominant locus of ideological practices that shape a clear distinction between mothers who meet the intensive requirements and those who fail or refuse to accept the moral demands that are embedded in such practices. Through the intensive mothering lens, women who do not live up to the ideal of intensive mothering fear judgment and accusations of being bad mothers (Arendell; Christopher). They are more vulnerable to elicit feelings of anxiety, depression, and self-blame for failing to conform to the intensive mothering ideal. This ideal is especially abusive for those in intersectional positions who do not have the resources to cope with such high demands and, thus, are at risk of being negatively labeled (Phoenix and Woollett; Smart; Walls et.al.).

The critique of intensive mothering ideology is an important step in the feminist critique of motherhood. In order to illuminate what I find to be a tension between the political and the ethical stances of this rich discussion, I wish to go back to the theoretical heritage of the feminist critique of motherhood.

From its early stages, feminist critiques of motherhood have focused on two main projects: the denaturalization and de-idealization of motherhood. Across various analytical frameworks—from existentialists as Simone de Beauvoir, through materialists as Shulamith Firestone, to psychoanalysts as Dorothy Dinnerstein, Nancy Chodorow, and Jessica Benjamin—feminists have argued against attempts to explain motherhood in terms of some biological destiny. Each of these voices, among many others, has provided another aspect to the analysis of motherhood as a complex social institution.

Simone de Beauvoir was the first to present an extensive philosophical account of the contradictions between the subject position and motherhood. She argues that motherhood is an extreme manifestation of women's otherness. Motherhood in Western culture is being-for-another, determined by the needs and expressions of another. The mother is the ultimate other—the negation of whose subjectivity enables the existence of another as subject. As such, woman's maternal realization is her undoing as subject (Beauvoir 516).

In order to create a critical distance from this position of mother-as-other, Beauvoir chooses to depict motherhood from the viewpoint of the mother herself who aspires to become a subject but fails. Her text narrates the mother's experience and, thus, locates it as the first step toward being a subject whose consciousness tells the story of its own freedom and commitment.

De Beauvoir applies an image of a subject who is associated with the freedom to negate a given factuality of reality and who through his or her actions determines the meaning of his or her universe. For de Beauvoir, the mother's capacity to become a subject is contingent on motherhood being an embodiment of freedom. The mother may become free through her ability to negate any given value of her child's existence—establishing ad hoc who and what the child is for her. However, since the child, as a subject-coming-into-being, evades determination, maternal subjectivity depends on the mother's ability to be a subject in other areas of her life and to choose freely motherhood as a mode of existence for others. In this sense the child, and thus motherhood for de Beauvoir, is not a creative site for mothers and, hence, fails to be a site of subjectivity.

De Beauvoir views the relation between otherness and subjectivity as a dialectic relationship between two opposing states of consciousness. Therefore, if one takes upon oneself the situation of motherhood—the practical commitment and the consciousness of being for the other—one cannot be a subject as a mother but only choose moments of devotion in which one is another for one's child. The ability to live motherhood as a free subject, on de Beauvoir's account of existentialist ethics, means that the mother's responsibility is first and foremost to herself and to her freedom. Assuming responsibility for the child and for her or his wellbeing is only secondary.

Adrienne Rich's *Of Woman Born* presents a sharp distinction between motherhood as an institution and motherhood as an experience. As an institution, Rich argues, motherhood suppresses any attempt to live maternal relations and care as a creative subject. This order denies the unique quality of maternal relations and submits mothers to men's needs and interests. Good mothers as those who embody the patriarchal ideal of motherhood.

Jessica Benjamin's *The Bonds of Love* argues for the necessity of maternal subjectivity as an analytical category for understanding the intersubjective dynamic of the mother-child relationship. Benjamin describes the accepted role of mothers as limiting the subjective expression of mothers and stressed that maternal subjectivity is more fully lived if the mother can have a life outside her motherhood. Benjamin reveals how psychoanalysis has ignored the role of the mother's subjectivity in the child's development, thus contributing to the silencing of the maternal perspective in theory and practice.

In *Impossibility of Motherhood*, Patrice DiQuinzio argues that feminist accounts of motherhood are caught in a dilemma. On the one hand, these accounts resist what DiQuinzio calls "essential motherhood"—the ideology that defines both the value and essence of women individually and as a group in terms of motherhood. Thus, according to DiQuinzio, feminism turns to acknowledged accounts of individualism so as to reveal the oppressive nature of motherhood. On the other hand, feminists also argue against these very accounts of individualism that conceive of humans as isolated and independent rational beings. Feminists such as Sara Ruddick, Patricia Hill Collins, and Nancy Chodorow have argued that these accounts of subjectivity miss the unique meaning and values that appear in mother-child relationships, the acknowledgment of which is necessary for the undoing of a patriarchal order. DiQuinzio has argued that this dilemma renders motherhood impossible, consequently calling for paradoxical politics.

This critical heritage has yielded a wide range of empirical research, which locates the political and social forces that women are submitted to as mothers, and how their motherhood intersects with other aspects of social locations, such as race, sexuality, nationality, and class. Research has shown that women feel and are labelled bad mothers when they fail to perform the practices expected of a good mother. This includes a wide range of mothers, such as mothers who fail to cope with the normative standards of intensive mothering; mothers whose children do not meet standards expected of children in terms of weight, behaviour, academic aptitude, and so on (Bell et al.); mothers whose practices are abusive, primarily toward themselves, but which may harm their children's optimal development, as with smoking or drug use; and mothers who abuse their children. Focusing on the disciplinary and marginalizing effects of the labelling as "bad mother," many scholars put aside the ethical aspects of the different variations of mothering.

Gradually during the 2000s, more and more voices of mothers who narrate their experiences have been appearing in popular culture. In this flourishing contemporary popular genre of writing about motherhood, women write to share their complex experiences, feelings, and insights as mothers. Books—such as Ayelet Waldman's *Bad Mother*, Trisha Ashworth and Amy Nobile's *I Was Really a Good Mom Before I Had Kids*, Romi Lassally's *True Moms Confessions*, Jill Smokler's *Confessions of a Scary Mommy*, Esther Walker's *The Bad Mother*, and numerous others—celebrate what is sometimes presented as new cultural possibilities to go beyond the idealization of motherhood and to narrate the complexity of maternal experience. These personal narratives aim to empower mothers by breaking the grip of the perfect mother ideal and by articulating the silent secrets of motherhood that are shared by many. This kind of empowerment assumes that the articulation of mothers' perspectives enables women to take a critical distance from motherhood as an oppressive institution and thus act more freely in this aspect of their lives. It may be that the popularity of these public narratives of nonideal motherhood has also supported the growing interest of feminist research into nonideal voices of mothers.

Voicing the worlds of different mothers is an important project that serves to explore the ways in which emotions, relations, and social power intersect in one of the most intensive human positions. Looking at the bad mothers from a critical perspective that does not take for granted the ideological definitions of good and bad mother is crucial for confronting these ideological constructions. However, looking at the labels "bad mother" or "good mother" just as labels with no way to account for the ways "good" and "bad" are also ethical categories may yield a paradox. According to this paradox, bad mothers are freer and can more fully express their subjectivity. Good mothers, on the other hand, are victims, whose motherhood is not an expression of their subjectivity. Instead, it is a passive execution of social control. I do not believe that many scholars embrace this paradox explicitly. Nevertheless, it may be implied when the categories of "bad mother" and "good mother" are used with no reference to any moral meaning that they may have.

A good example of this kind of flight from any moral meaning of good and bad mothers in the name of critique can be found in Sarah LaChance Adams's *Mad Mothers, Bad Mothers, and What a "Good" Mother Would Do*. Adams begins with a story about a woman who drove her car into the Hudson River. Her four children were with her in the car. This act, which for Adams stands for a wide phenomenon of women who kill their children, reveals the structure of motherhood itself. As Adams writes:

> In both popular culture and scholarly work, maternal rage is frequently considered either a result of postpartum hormones, the product of a more pervasive pathology, or the consequence of living in a racist, heterosexist, and classist patriarchy that idealizes the nuclear family. These diagnoses shed necessary light on the hard facts that women confront, the situation they are responding to, and thus add to our understanding of their experiences. However, to begin the inquiry in this way invites us to diagnose maternal ambivalence. This assumes that maternal ambivalence is first and foremost an atypical problem to be overcome. (8)

Relating her research to the phenomenological tradition, Adams focuses on the lived experience of ambivalence as immanent to motherhood. She draws on Emmanuel Levinas, Maurice Merleau-Ponty, and Simone de Beauvoir to conceptualize maternal ambivalence as immanent to the human condition called motherhood. In that sense, Adams's discussion assumes that mothers who murder their children reveal the truth about motherhood. She argues that this intensive dependency and responsibility for the other lead to experiences such as rage, hate, and violent desires. Adams does not discuss narratives of mothers who do not share these experiences as dominant aspect of their maternal relationships, although she uses cultural examples to argue for ambivalence as an immanent aspect of motherhood. Thus, it seems reasonable to assume that in Adams's account, the mothers who do not express ambivalence are either in denial or totally submitted to the ideological image of the good mother, which prevents them from being aware of their internal ambivalence.

Adams stresses that her methodology aims to affirm ambivalence as a site of "resourcefulness, creativity, and agency" (9). With this move, she stresses that although her research is about maternal ethics, her starting point is only descriptive. She writes the following: "I see it [ambivalence] as primarily a phenomenon to be understood, one that can shed light on fundamental structures of our relationships with others. In considering this as a problem from the outset, too much has been decided beforehand. That is, we miss out on looking into its potentially positive, creative aspects" (8).

By assuming a nonjudgmental, "descriptive" point of view, and a philosophical construction of ambivalence as a necessary aspect of motherhood, Adams posits filicide as one tragic and extreme expression of maternal ambivalence, which demands society to take more responsibility in helping mothers for their children. However, mothers who do not share ambivalence as a dominant aspect of motherhood are not a source for understanding motherhood or for suggesting a productive notion of ethics of care.

Adams's account of maternal experience reveals what I take to be a paradoxical account of the good and the bad mother. The basic presupposition of this paradox is the noncontroversial statement that motherhood is an oppressive institution. Maternal bodies, behavior, and emotions are the object of normalizing disciplinary discourses. The ideal of a good mother submits women to this oppressive institution, and, thus, it is oppressive too (Hager 367). Following from this line of thinking, mothers who conform to the expectations of society lose, at least partially, their freedom and cannot establish their subjectivity as part of their motherhood. Their motherhood is controlled or manifests primarily normative ideology-governed practices. Since the good mother appears in this critical discourse as primarily a myth or an ideological representation, women who actually act in accordance with this myth are privileged because of the ways ideology sustains power structures, but they are also considered to be passive recipients of normative power. Bad mothers, on the other hand, gain their place as a good expression of what motherhood consists. Their behaviour or attitude is taken to express their agency, subjectivity, and freedom. To put it differently, all mothers are victims. But bad mothers resist and rebel. They can tell us more about motherhood.

Even if they do not mean it, they are politically important, whereas good mothers are not. Good mothers are victims of self-annihilating practices, and they have less potential to be the subjects of feminist transformations.

A paradox is thus established: although everyone agrees that motherhood is about caring for children, bad mothers, who in different ways do not present the best ways of caring, represent the true nature of motherhood as immanently violent (Motz 89) or violently ambivalent (Adams). Whereas mothers for whom rage, violence, and detachment are not dominant experiences are taken to be a lesser manifestation of motherhood. Are good mothers the new bad mothers? Do they have agency that is significant, ethically and politically? Or are they a herd captured in a web of techno-social discourses? Can good mothers and bad mothers even be spoken about as signifying something more than social category?

I do not believe that many scholars hold that paradoxical position. But I believe that it can be deduced from the general premises of the discussion. My point here is not to offer a generalization about all the research about motherhood, nor is it to criticize specific scholars. Instead, I believe that the paradox that I presented here in its general form stresses that further work should be done in thinking the relationship between the ethical and the political in the context of motherhood.

The notion that is at the heart of the gap between the political and the ethical is the concept of critique. The descriptive approach that looks at good and bad only as effects of social power assumes that the critique of motherhood can be carried with no normative or affirmative presuppositions concerning motherhood. This notion of political critique focuses on motherhood as a hegemonic power constructions. Its political analyses refrain from embracing any normative or moral presuppositions about what motherhood is about and are there any better and worst ways to live this human relation.

Thus, the bad mother appears in this approach as the negation of the oppressive and normative image of the good mother and as a label through which society devalues vulnerable groups of women. As such, the category includes many different groups of mothers, for instance, those who have no time to bake birthday cakes for their kids, alongside those who kill their kids, those who smoke around their kids, and those who emotionally abuse their kids. They are all labelled as bad mothers and suffer guilt and shame as a result of this labelling. The critical action focuses on the effects of labelling as control. The categories of good and bad lose in this approach any moral meaning, sustaining only political meaning—either going with the flow or against it.

One challenge that faces political critique of motherhood is to go beyond the "chooser-loser" paradigm of power, according to which there are only two basic positions in relation to hegemonic power constructions—either in submission or resistance to them. Those who resist choose; those who submit lose their autonomy and agency. As was argued in different context, this account of feminist subject fails to respond to the complexity of subjectivity power and norms (Grosz; Mahmud; Hutchings). This kind of discourse misses the multiple manifestations that individuals can take as part of their participation in normative practices and the wide range of transformative practices that are not strictly those of normative refusals. Thinking beyond "chooser-loser" approaches reveals new ways in which mothers can engage with normative power constructions by developing through practices a different sense of themselves, the meaning of their motherhood, and the goals of their commitments. This is true both for good and bad mothers.

In order to move beyond this paradigm, an affirmative stance of critique is needed that discusses the normative presuppositions that constitute feminism and how maternal practices and commitments may be part of this feminist political quest. The normative background of feminism should not be taken, first and foremost, as a tool for judging the other; rather, it is an analytical and political insistence on basic values, which enables feminism to argue that something is wrong with this reality and, on this basis, to engage in a social dialogue about what is wrong and what should be different.

Susan Babbitt argues in *Impossible Dreams* that oppressive normative orders undermine the ability of oppressed groups to act in ways that affirm their self-worth and value. She argues that oppressed groups lack a moral horizon that would attribute alternative moral value to actions that defy oppressive norms. Instead, these actions are doomed to be signified as crimes, personal failures, or lack of virtues and proper rationality. However, sometimes people act against the oppressive moral and normative order even though they lack the concepts to justify and articulate their sense of injustice and rebellion (100). According to Babbitt, these actions are led by a moral imagination that stresses what ought to be possible even though it is not yet justified. These imaginative creative experiences inspire actions that affirm "new interpretive positions" for individuals. Mavis Biss argues that moral imagination bridges the individual's moral beliefs with her or his moral social context. In situations of crucial gaps between the moral normative concepts, on the one hand, and the agent's insistence on self-worth and moral perspective, on the other, moral imagination also takes part in a dynamic of self-transformation that leads the individual from moral anxiety, perplexity, and dissonance to increasingly articulate her or his moral understating (951).

Thus, the moral affirmative stance is crucial to the feminist political critique. It requires discussing and posing normative presupposition as part of the critical action. I believe that in the case of motherhood, this intensive site of emotions, care, desire, and relationships can serve as a resource for moral imagination and inspire feminist struggles for equality and freedom.

In what follows I would like to briefly discuss Sara Ruddick's work as an example of how a political critique can integrate a moral vision about motherhood. I then outline a suggestion of a theoretical frame in which critique gains an affirmative and ethical aspect.

THE GOOD MOTHER'S COMEBACK

Notions of good and bad carry in the context of motherhood necessary moral values, unlike evaluations concerning other performances—let's say, being a bad swimmer or a good cook. This moral aspect of motherhood reflects that motherhood is a role involving other people's (the children's) wellbeing. Thus, being a bad mother is more like being a bad doctor; it is something that is morally problematic, since it can potentially harm other people.

Sara Ruddick's pioneering account of mothering integrates the ethical with the political. Ruddick argues that maternal practices immanently define success and failure in performing these practices. To perform maternal roles is to take upon oneself relations of care. Care practices assume constitutive goals that these practices aim to achieve. Failing to care properly (whatever that may mean in different contexts) is unethical, and since morality is intertwined with motherhood, failing or not wanting to care for one's child is a moral wrong. Ruddick argues that maternal practices aim to achieve three goals: preservation, development, and socialization. Ruddick's conceptualization of maternal practices suggests that there is an ethical core to maternal practices, although there are different practices that are considered as achieving the goals of mothering.

Even though preservation, nurturance, and socialization are constitutive goals whose achievement in nonviolent ways serves as the core of motherhood, concrete cultural variations are subjected to critique. In fact, in positing these three goals of motherhood, Ruddick opens the way for analyzing how ideological discourses, institutions, and policies produce concrete interpretations of mother's roles and practices and reframe maternal constitutive moral goals. In this respect, the moral aspect of Ruddick's account of maternal practices serves as an anchor for a critique against normative discourses and institutions.

One of the goals of integrating an ethical and political critique is to enable an analysis that differentiates between three kinds of bad mothers:

1. Mothers who fail to protect or actively hurt their children in conditions where they struggle for their own survival and lack almost any options of acting in defense of their children (Raz; Young).
2. Mothers who cause harm that they do not consider as harm because it is justified by their worldviews and cultural contexts. For example, mothers who hurt their children as part of educational norms or who circumcise their children as part of their religious convictions.
3. Mothers who fail to protect or deliberately hurt their children in situations where other courses of action are available to them.

The first kind of mothers reveals the vulnerability of mothers and calls for extending social responsibility for children's needs. The second kind of maternal violence is the most problematic for feminist critique because it calls for an ethical perspective that contradicts the mother's perspectives and her cultural contexts. In terms of Ruddick's three goals of maternal practices, these mothers are caught in a deadlock since they succeed in one maternal constitutive role—socializing their children to their social and cultural norms and values— while, at the same, time they risk their children's physical or emotional well-being. This kind of contradiction may put many mothers in a position in which it would be actually impossible to successfully meet both goals.

Here, Ruddick's moral assertion that the constitutive goals of maternal practices are moral goods leads to the conclusion that feminist critique should not lead to automatically embrace the inner cultural perspective that justifies violent or abusive practice. Instead, Ruddick's account focuses on the points of tension and contradictory practices that may lead to an account of mothering as a site of negotiation with contradicting moral codes. Her position stresses the practical freedom mothers have in either reproducing or challenging their culture.

As for the third kind of bad mothers, it is important for feminist critique to provide an ethical perspective that can explain the moral wrong in these actions. This perspective is inevitable if feminist critique seeks to point to the moral value of parenting and care, and employ parental relations as an imaginary sight for different social values. Ruddick creates such a theoretical option when she assumes that there are better and worst ways to meet the constitutive goals of mothering.

Thinking about motherhood as a resource for a new moral imaginary should not be used primarily as a tool for judging mothers' practices but for gradually developing a discourse about and for mothers—one that would enable women to transcend their different patriarchal locations and create cultural sites of freedom.

CONCLUSIONS

The feminist critique of motherhood has made a critical contribution. By denaturalizing and de-idealizing motherhood, it has helped to connect the experiences of individual women with political and social conditions that construct mother's role and practices. It has provided insights to challenge the power structures and discourses that construct the meaning of motherhood and the everyday lives of mothers, contributing to overcoming the divide of the private and the social. The analysis of concrete forms of social disempowerment and mechanism of control is crucial to prevent feminist discourse from becoming what Lois McNay calls "free-floating formulations of injurious social experience" (21).

Motherhood was and still is the foundation of patriarchy. It is the ultimate outside of the social, the axis of women's lives. Even today when women access the public sphere, the 'maternal' is the emotional outside that cannot be easily integrated with other aspects of their lives. I believe the next step that must be taken in the feminist critique of motherhood is the integration of the political and the ethical and to rethink the maternal as a possible resource for a new understanding of subjectivity. A normative horizon for the critique of motherhood should take into account what is at the heart of motherhood—the commitment to take care of one's children. This horizon should map how intersectional locations and ideological discourses shape this commitment and the conditions for its realization. It should analyze the efforts and challenges that are part of the lived experiences of mothers to help mothers meet this commitment as embodied creative subjects. It should allow for concrete practices of freedom to appear to help those who choose not to realize this commitment in their lives to do so. It should also help women to live this commitment as an aspect of their moral agency.

Of course, there are many thinkers who have suggested ethical accounts of the maternal, but these two stances of feminist engagements with motherhood are not fully integrated. There are feminist theoretical paths that look at motherhood as an affective relational practice that could challenge patriarchal society in its most basic logic. Prominent scholars—such as Julia Kristeva, Luce Irigaray, Kittay, Ruddick, Lisa Baraitser, and Alison Stone—aim to conceptualize such an ethics based on the critique of motherhood, as I do in my own work. As I see it, creating a theoretical space in which good motherhood can reappear is crucial for new feminist genealogies to inspire future feminist struggles.

WORKS CITED

Arendell, T. "Conceiving and Investigating Motherhood: The Decade's Scholarship." *Journal of Marriage and the Family*, vol. 62, no.1, 2000, pp. 192-1207.

Ashworth, Trisha, and Amy Nobile. *I Was Really a Good Mom Before I Had Kids: Reinventing Modern Motherhood*. Chronicle Books, 2007.

Babbitt, Susan. *Impossible Dreams: Rationality, Integrity, and Moral imagination*. Westview Press, 1996.

Bell, Kristen, et al. "Medicine, Morality and Mothering: Public Health Discourses on Fetal Alcohol Exposure, Smoking around Children and Childhood Over Nutrition." *Critical Public Health*, vol. 19, no. 2, 2009, pp. 155-170.

Benjamin, Jessica. *The Bonds of Love: Psychoanalysis, Feminism, and the Problem of Domination*. Pantheon Books, 1988.

Biss, Mavis. "Radical Moral Imagination: Courage, Hope, and Articulation." *Hypatia*, vol. 28, no. 4, 2013, pp. 937-654.

Chodorow, Nancy. *The Reproduction of Mothering: Psychoanalysis and the Sociology of Gender*. University of California Press, 1978.

Chodorow, Nancy. "Gender, Relations and Difference in Psychoanalytic Perspective." *Feminism and Psychoanalytic Theory*. Yale University Press, 1989.

Christopher, Karen. "Extensive Mothering: Employed mothers' constructions of the Good Mother." *Gender & Society*, vol. 26, no. 1, 2012, pp. 73-96.

De Beauvoir, Simone. *The Second Sex*. Translated and Edited by Howard Madison Parshley. Vintage Books, 1989.

Dinnerstein, Dorothy. *The Mermaid and the Minotaur: Sexual Arrangements and Human Malaise*. Harper & Row, 1976.

DiQuinzio, Patrice. *The Impossibility of Motherhood: Feminism, Individualism, and the Problem of Mothering*. 2nd ed. Routledge, 1999.

Euripides. *Medea*. Edited and Translated by David Kovacs. *Perseus Digital Library*, www.perseus.tufts.edu/hopper/text?doc=Perseus%3Atext%3A1999.01.0114. Accessed 31 Jan. 2017.

Folbre, Nancy. *Valuing Children*. Harvard University Press, 2008.

Grosz, Elizabeth. "Feminism, Materialism and Freedom." *New Materialisms: Ontology, Agency and Politics*, edited by D. Coole and S. Frost, Duke University Press, 2010, pp. 139-157.

Hadas, Moses. *Introduction to Classical Drama*. Bantam Matrix, 1966.

Hays, Sharon. *The Cultural Contradictions of Motherhood*. Yale University Press, 1996.

Hager, Tamar. "Maternal Autobiography as a Site of Feminist Negotiation and Resistance." *Qualitative Inquiry*, vol. 21, no. 4, 2015, pp. 366-375.

Hill Collins, Patricia. *Black Feminist Thought: Knowledge, Consciousness, and the Politics of Empowerment*. Routledge, 1990.

Kittay, Eva Feder. *Love's Labor: Essays on Women, Equality, and Dependency*. Routledge, 1999.

LaChance Adams, Sarah. *Mad Mothers, Bad Mothers & What a "Good" Mother Would Do: The Ethics of Ambivalence*. Columbia University Press, 2014.

Lassally, Romi. *True Moms Confessions: Real Moms Get Real*. Berkley Books, 2009.

Mahmood, Saba. *Politics of Piety: The Islamic Renewal and the Feminist Subject*. Princeton University Press, 2005.

Motz, Anna. *The Psychology of Female Violence: Crimes against the Body*. Routledge, 2001.

Perälä-Littunen, Satu. "Gender Equality or Primacy of the Mother? Ambivalent Descriptions of Good Parents." *Journal of Marriage and Family*, vol. 69, no. 2, 2007, pp. 341–51. Wiley, doi: 10.1111/j.1741-3737.2007.00369.x. Accessed 25 Jan. 2016.

Phoenix, Ann, and Anne Woollett. "Motherhood: Social Construction, Politics and Psychology." *Motherhood: Meanings, Practices and Ideologies*, edited by Ann Phoenix et al., Sage, 1991, pp.13-27.

Raz, Joseph. *The Morality of Freedom*. Oxford University Press, 1986.

Rich, Adrienne. *Of Woman Born: Motherhood as Experience and Institution*. W. W. Norton, 1986.

Ridgeway, Cecilia L., and Shelley J. Correll. "Motherhood as a

Status Characteristic." *Journal of Social Issues*, vol. 60, no. 4, 2004, pp. 683-700.

Reckford, Kenneth J. "Medea's First Exit." *Transactions and Proceedings of the American Philological Association*, vol. 99, 1968, pp. 329-359. *JSTOR*, doi: 10.2307/2935850. Accessed 25 Jan. 2017.

Ruddick, Sara. *Maternal Thinking: Toward a Politics of Peace*. Ballantine Books, 1989.

Smart, Carol. "Deconstructing Motherhood." *Good Enough Mothering? Feminist Perspectives on Lone Motherhood*, edited by Elizabeth Bortolaia Silva, Routledge, 1996, pp. 37–57.

Smokler, Jill. *Confessions of a Scary Mommy: An Honest and Irreverent Look at Motherhood—The Good, The Bad, and the Scary*. Gallery Books, 2012.

Waldman, Ayelet. *Bad Mother: A Chronicle of Maternal Crimes, Minor Calamities, and Occasional Moments of Grace*. Anchor Books, 2010.

Walker, Esther. *The Bad Mother*. The Friday Project, 2015.

Walls, Jill, et al. "Intensive Mothering Beliefs Among Full-Time Employed Mothers of Infants." *Journal of Family Issues*, vol. 37, no. 2, 2016, pp. 245–269.

Young, Iris Marion. *Intersecting Voices: Dilemmas of Gender, Political Philosophy, and Policy*. Princeton University Press, 1997.

About the Contributors

María Alonso Alonso is a teaching fellow at the University of Vigo, Spain. Her research interests centre on both Latin American and postcolonial literatures. She is the author of *Diasporic Marvellous Realism: History, Identity and Memory in Caribbean Fiction* (Brill, 2015) and a board member of *The Journal of Commonwealth Literature*.

Fernando Gabriel Pagnoni Berns (PhD candidate) is professor at Universidad de Buenos Aires, where he teaches American Horror Cinema and European Horror. He has published articles on Argentinian and international cinema in: *Imagofagia*, *Vita e Pensiero: Comunicazioni Sociali*, *Anagnórisis*, *Lindes* and *UpStage Journal*, as well as chapters in several books.

Rebecca Jaremko Bromwich is a mother of four who works as lawyer, legal academic, writer, artist, and activist. She has a PhD in law and legal studies from Carleton University, an LL.M. and LL.B. from Queen's University, a graduate certificate in women's, gender, and sexuality studies from the University of Cincinnati, and a BA (Hon.) in anthropology from the University of Calgary. She has published articles and texts on many áreas of law as they relate to mothers, gender, and equality, and she is author of *Looking for Ashley: Re-Reading What the Smith Case Reveals about Governance of Girls, Mothers, and Families in Canada* (Demeter Press, 2015). Rebecca has been practising law in Ontario, Canada, since 2003.

Alexandra Campbell is an associate professor of sociology at the University of New England. She has a PhD in criminology from the University of Cambridge, UK. Alexandra's work has focused on various forms of representation: from nationalism and racial identity to rape prevention literature and gender identities.

Nonavee Dale is a Canadian by birth whose home is now New Zealand. She is a visual artist and mother and works as a graphic design consultant. She is the illustrator of the Maori children's storybook *Ngā Tuna O Onewa* (*How the Eels Lost Their Wings*).

Pamela Downe is an associate professor of archaeology and anthropology at the University of Saskatchewan. As a medical anthropologist, her work focuses on HIV/AIDS, maternal health, motherhoods and fatherhoods, and the health repercussions of violence. Her areas of ethnographic expertise include western Canada, eastern Caribbean, and Central America.

Liat Elkayam lives in Tel-Aviv. She is a journalist and a columist for *Haaretz Magazine*. Her short stories have appeared in various international collections. She teaches at Sapir College. Elkayam received the 2015 Akademie der kunste literary fellowship. She is working on her first book (Kinneret Zmora Bitan Press).

Sophie Feintuch is a Master in Public Policy candidate at the Harvard Kennedy School. She has conducted research on incarcerated mothers and their children in Spain, Bolivia, and the United States. Feintuch holds a dual Erasmus Mundus Master's degree in Women's and Gender Studies from Central European University and the Universidad de Granada, and a Sociology Bachelor's from Vassar.

Susan Gair is associate professor at James Cook University and a social work scholar with more than two decades of teaching, research, writing, and practice. Her work has focused on advancing social justice, social policy and social work practice, particularly in regional Australia. She has contributed to informing national and international social work programs.

Tamar Hager is a senior lecturer in the Department of Education and Gender Studies at Tel Hai College, Israel. Motherhood, critical feminist methodology, art sociology and fictional and academic writing, multiculturalism and critical pedagogy are core issues of her academic research, writing, teaching, and social activism. She is the founder and the former co-director of the college's centre for Peace and Democracy, whose mandate is to academically and administratively develop and implement the multicultural vision of the college. She published in 2000 a book of short stories *A Perfectly Ordinary Life* (in Hebrew). In 2012, she published *Malice Aforethought* (in Hebrew), in which she attempts to reconstruct the elusive biographies of two English working-class mothers who killed their babies at the end of the nineteenth century.

Geraldine Hendrix-Sloan is a professor of criminal justice and criminal justice program coordinator at Minnesota State University Moorhead. Her research focuses on feminist perspectives of escort work and other sex work. She recently published and distributed a local resource guide for female ex-offenders, titled "Fargo-Moorhead Reentry Guide for Women."

Omri Herzog, associate professor, is the head of the cultural studies department at Sapir College, Israel. His main research interests are corporal politics, the interface between canonical and popular, the horror genre and Israeli culture. He is also an award-winning literary critic for *Haaretz* newspaper.

Michelle Hughes Miller is an associate professor of women's and gender studies at the University of South Florida. She earned her MA and PhD in sociology at the University of Nebraska-Lincoln while raising two wonderful children with her husband, Rob Benford. As a feminist criminologist, she researches motherhood within legal and policy constraints. In addition to publishing on criminalized and allegedly bad mothers, she is co-editor of *Addressing Violence Against Women on College Campuses* (Temple University Press, 2017) and *Alliances for Advancing Academic Women: Guidelines for Collaborating in STEM* (Sense Publishers, 2014). She is currently analyzing discourses of mothering in global economic and social campaigns, along with very much enjoying being a new grandma.

Kelsey Ioannoni is a PhD student in sociology at York University. With a BA in criminology and a master's degree in critical sociology, Kelsey is passionate about issues of social justice, body politics, and regulation. Her research includes fat studies, the regulatory politics of weight, and weight-based discrimination.

Juan Juvé has a Master's degree from the Universidad de Buenos Aires. He is a lecturer in sociology, horror cinema, and popular culture. He has published in *Lindes*, *Vita e Pensiero*, and in *Science Fiction and the Abolition of Man* and *Requiem for a Nation: Religion, Politics and Visual Cultures in Post-War Italy (1945-1975)*.

Marlee Keenan is a MA candidate in the Department of Sociology at Queen's University. Her research examines the continuation of colonial violence through the historic separation of Indigenous children from their families sanctioned by the state beginning with the residential school system and continuing today through contemporary Canadian child welfare policy.

Rela Mazali's hybrid-genre books and "essay tales" meld creative prose with research.An independent scholar and feminist anti-militarist from Israel, she co-founded "New Profile," with aim of demilitarizing its society and state, along with the disarmament project, "Gun Free Kitchen Tables." Her recent research includes "Speaking of Guns: Launching Gun Control Discourse and Disarming Security Guards in a Mlitarized Society" (*IFjP*, 2016).

M. Joan McDermott is an Emeritus Associate Professor of Criminology and Criminal Justice and former Director of Women's Studies at Southern Illinois University Carbondale. She is a feminist criminologist who has done research in areas such as the victimization of women and school violence and victimization.

Heather Munro is an Ottawa artist and illustrator specializing in pen and ink drawings that she creates with a ball point pen. In Toronto after graduating in art and art history at the University of Toronto and studio art at Sheridan College, Heather began doodling with her pen, creating creatures in her sketchbook.

Freddie Robins is an artist who challenges our perception of knitting as craft. Her work is internationally renowned, her practice crossing the boundaries of art, design and craft. She studied at the Royal College of Art, London, UK, where she is now a Senior Tutor and Reader in Textiles.

Miri Rozmarin, PhD, teaches at Bar-Ilan University, Israel, in the Gender Studies Program. Her research interests include feminist philosophy, critical theory and contemporary post-liberal ethics. Her book, *Creating Oneself* (2011), addresses the question of agency in a postmodern world. Her upcoming book, *Vulnerable Futures, Transformative Pasts*, considers the ethical significance of vulnerability as a basis for transformative non-matricidal lineages.

Patricia Vazquez has a Master's degree from the Universidad de Buenos Aires. She is a lecturer in horror cinema and popular culture. She has published articles in such journals as *Lindes* and chapters in *Racism & Gothic: Critical Essays*, and *Projecting the World: Classical Hollywood, the "Foreign," and Transnational Representations*.

Mandi Veenstra is a sociology graduate student at Queen's University, and a mother of three young children, with a passion for challenging social constructions and embedded dichotomies within Canadian social policy. Mandi's current research project examines manufactured ideologies of the "bad" mother within the Ontario child welfare system.

Keira V. Williams is assistant professor in the Honors College at Texas Tech University. She is the author of *Gendered Politics in the Modern South: The Susan Smith Case and the Rise of a New Sexism* (LSU Press, 2012), and she is working on a book about matriarchies in American popular culture.

Noa Arad Yairi, a sculptress, is living and working in Jerusalem. Arad Yairi studied graphic art and design. In 2007, she left her independent studio and now works full time as a sculptress. She participates in many group exhibitions in museums and galleries in Israel and abroad and has been teaching sculpture in the Emuna Art College since 2013.